KHAKI JACK

KHAKI JACK

JACK

THE ROYAL NAVAL DIVISION
IN THE FIRST WORLD WAR

E. C. COLEMAN

AMBERLEY

First published 2014

Amberley Publishing
The Hill, Stroud
Gloucestershire, GL5 4EP

www.amberley-books.com

British Library Cataloguing in Publication Data.
A catalogue record for this book is available from the British Library.

ISBN 978 1 4456 0469 5

Typeset in 10pt on 12pt Sabon.
Typesetting and Origination by Amberley Publishing.
Printed in the UK.

Contents

Major General Archibald Paris, the Royal Marine officer who led the Royal Naval Division in their early operations and was responsible for the continuation of its Royal Naval customs and traditions.

Introduction

In the peaceful cemetery at Nouvelles, on the outskirts of Mons in Belgium, there are nine British graves. Five of them are of soldiers who lost their lives in August 1914. The four remaining graves form a row of their own and all carry the same date of the deaths of their occupants – 11 November 1918. The sad symmetry of the date – the last day of the First World War – is counterbalanced by a further, coincidental, but nevertheless pleasing, symmetry. One of the men is an Englishman, one an Irishman, one a Scotsman, and one a Welshman. There, for many visitors, the symmetry ends, for two of the graves belong to soldiers who died while serving in well-established and well-known British regiments. The final two, on the other hand, clearly belong to able seamen with the proud distinction of an Admiralty-pattern fouled anchor carved upon their gravestones.

With the North Sea some considerable distance to the west, the finding of naval graves so far inland is puzzling until it is learned that many thousands of Royal Naval seamen and Royal Marines fought in the trenches of the Great War alongside soldiers from across the Empire. Such graves may be found around Antwerp, on the Gallipoli peninsula, and all along the Western Front. The seamen and marines, supported by Army battalions, fought at Anzac Cove, on the Somme, and at Passchendaele. They suffered giant siege mortars while delaying the enemy in Belgium, flies and the stench of widespread carnage on Turkish shores, and gas attacks while sheltering in flooded shell-holes on the Western Front.

At the armistice declared at 11 a.m., on 11 November 1918, the Royal Naval Division had suffered 46,794 casualties, of whom 10,797 lost their lives. At the same time, the Division earned many decorations for gallantry, including eight Victoria Crosses.

Yet why do gravestones bearing anchors and naval ranks or rates still surprise visitors to the battlefields? Possibly because naval historians cannot quite accept the Division as actually 'naval', while military historians have difficulty slotting them into the sort of 'Regimental' history that serves the record of the Army so well. The Germans, on the other hand, regarded the Royal Naval Division as 'one of the four most famous fighting Divisions of the British Army'.

There have been many occasions throughout the long history of the Royal Navy when its seamen have been called upon to fight against an enemy on land. Francis Drake led his men in ambushing a Spanish mule train crossing the Isthmus of Darien heavily laden with treasure gathered in Chile and Peru. Nelson lost the sight of his eye fighting ashore at Calvi in Corsica, and lost his arm leading a force of eighty marines, eighty pike-men, and a hundred seamen along the mole at Tenerife. During Victoria's reign the Naval Brigades made their mark in the Sudan, in India, China, and in southern Africa where their naval guns provided support for the British Army during the Boer War.

It would come, therefore, as no surprise to find British sailors tramping down sun-baked gullies, or wading through flooded trenches to reach the enemy during the First World War. What is surprising, however, is the degree to which they, fighting side-by-side with men of the Royal Marines and alongside old established Army regiments as an infantry division, made a considerable contribution to the Allied victory of arms over the enemies of the British Empire.

This is the story of those seamen, marines, and soldiers who combined together to make up that unique body of men – the Royal Naval Division.

CHAPTER I

In at the Deep End –
From Conception to Antwerp

Some years before the outbreak of war in 1914, it had been decided by the Committee of Imperial Defence that a land force must be available to the Admiralty to seize and hold ports and harbours for the use of the Royal Navy and for the landing and provisioning of a military expedition. This force, to be known as the 'Advanced Base Force', was brought into being as the threat of war with Germany was about to become a reality. Comprising a brigade of Royal Marines it was composed of one battalion from each of the Royal Marine Light Infantry Divisions at Portsmouth, Devonport, and Chatham, and one battalion from the Royal Marine Artillery Depot. Originally commanded by Major-General McCausland, they came under the leadership of Brigadier Sir George Aston KCB, a South African-born veteran of the Sudan and Boer wars. He took command as the German army crossed the Belgian frontier.

The Royal Navy was, by now, fully mobilised. The Fleet had gathered for a review at Spithead and the First Lord of the Admiralty, Winston Churchill, had, on 29 July 1914, ordered the assembled ships to their war stations in the North Sea.

Less than a week later, war was declared on 4 August and thousands of men came forward to take up arms and swell the ranks of the Royal Navy and the British Army. Naval reservists began to assemble at southern Naval Depots, where it quickly became clear that, in this first rush to volunteer, there were more men than could be accommodated. The Royal Naval Barracks at Portsmouth, already filled with men surplus to the Fleet's seagoing requirements, was forced to build a camp under canvas at nearby Browndown to take up the excess but, within a week, it was overcrowded. The same pattern was repeated at the other Depots. The only alternative, or so it seemed, was to send the men home until they could be called forward for training and deployment.

The First Lord, however, had other plans. Nearly 8,000 of the excess volunteers at the Naval Depots were men of the Royal Naval Volunteer Reserve (landsmen with some seamanship training), the Royal Naval Reserve (men of the merchant navy), and the Royal Fleet Reserve (men who had previously served in the Royal Navy). On 16 August, Churchill sent a minute to the Secretary to the Admiralty Board and to the First and Second Sea Lords. The reservists, he had decided, would be organised into two brigades along infantry lines. Each brigade would consist of four battalions, each battalion numbering 880 men. Sir George Aston's 'Advanced Base Force' was to lose its Royal Marine Artillery battalion and have instead a fourth battalion of Royal Marine Light Infantry supplied by the Deal Division. The two Naval Brigades and the Royal Marine Brigade were to combine under the title of the 'Royal Naval Division'. Churchill gave them one week to organise.

The Royal Marines had a long and distinguished history of warfare on land, and the First Lord's decision caused them little concern. The reservists, however, were a different matter. Certainly they had volunteered to fight, but at sea – not on land. With some it was a matter of pride, with others, disappointment. Many felt that, if they were to fight alongside the army, they should be allowed to return home and join their local regiments or 'Pals' battalions that were recruiting in their home towns. But, in the end, discipline and loyalty to the Navy and each other kept them together.

On 17 August, Churchill issued a second minute in which the War Office was asked for 700 tents and other items of camping equipment. The Royal Naval Division was to make its first camp on Walmer Downs, near Deal, on Wednesday 26 August, and the Board of Admiralty would carry out an inspection on Monday 31 August. The same minute noted the order of forty Maxim guns from the Vickers armament company, the organisation of horses and mules, and gave the authorisation for the supply of 12,000 khaki uniforms. A military band was ordered to join by Saturday 29 August; 'The quality is not important.'

Although a Divisional Artillery had been considered, nothing was done at this stage. There had even been thought of creating a Royal Naval Divisional Cavalry, light-heartedly referred to as the 'Royal Naval Hussars', but nothing came of the idea. Opposition to the whole concept came from quarters other than the reservist ratings. Captain Richmond, the Assistant Director of Operations at the Admiralty, wrote in his diary on 20 August, 'The whole thing is so wicked that Churchill ought to be hanged before he should be allowed to do such a thing.'

Despite such opposition the Naval Brigades started to assemble on Walmer Downs where the organisation into battalions began to take place. The senior officers had been selected from active members of the Royal Navy, the Royal Marines, the Royal Naval Volunteer Reserve, and, for their military experience, from the Brigade of Guards.

As the battalions were first being organised they were given numbers; the First Royal Naval Brigade had battalions numbered from 1 to 4 and the Second Royal Naval Brigade from 5 to 8. However, in keeping with their naval background, the battalions were given the names of famous British Admirals. The First RN Brigade, under the command of Commodore Wilfred Henderson ('Heavy weather Wilfred' Captain Richmond called him in his diary), had the Drake Battalion commanded by Cdr Victor Campbell (who had served as second-in-command to Captain Scott on his *Terra Nova* expedition), Cdr Fargus had the Hawke Battalion, Cdr Beadle the Benbow Battalion, and the Collingwood Battalion came under Lt-Col. Aymer Maxwell of the Coldstream Guards.

The Second RN Brigade was placed under the leadership of Commodore Oliver Backhouse. He had the Nelson Battalion commanded by Cdr C. D. Bridge; the Howe Battalion under Churchill's cousin, Cdr Viscount Curzon, the 4th Earl Howe, and the Hood Battalion commanded by Lt-Col. Arnold Quilter of the Grenadier Guards whose second-in-command was Viscount Bury, a Major in the Scots Guards. The Anson Battalion came under the command of Churchill's former stepfather George Cornwallis West, a Lt-Col. in the Scots Guards, and one of the few officers unpopular with all and sundry.

Admiral the Right Honourable Lord Charles Beresford became the Honorary Colonel of the Royal Marine Brigade while his old enemy, Admiral of the Fleet Lord Fisher, took on the same role with the First Royal Naval Brigade. The Second Royal Naval Brigade went to Admiral of the Fleet Sir Arthur Wilson VC who had earned his Victoria Cross fighting ashore.

Right from the very beginning, men of extraordinarily high social status and ability took commissions in the RNVR in order to serve with the Royal Naval Division. The Prime Minister's son, Arthur Asquith, and his nephew Bryan Melland were among the first. Allan Aitken, the brother of influential businessman and politician Sir Max Aitken, and the opposition Conservative Party leader Bonar Law's nephews, John and Christopher Robley, volunteered immediately. They were joined by the Cambridge classical scholar Arthur St Clair Tisdall along with Patrick Shaw Stewart, a Fellow of All Souls. Denis Brown, composer and music critic of *The Times* and *New Statesman*, joined early in September, as did the brilliant young poet, Rupert Brooke, who persuaded Churchill's private secretary, Edward Marsh to procure an RNVR commission for him.

A. V. W. Cotter had been the United States Deputy Consul General in Munich until the outbreak of war when, with hair-raising adventures, he cycled through Germany to escape in early August. Clyde Evans had navigated a Russian battleship to the East where he had witnessed the utter defeat of the Tsarist fleet by the Japanese at the Battle of Tsushima Straits. Lord Ribblesdale's son, the Honourable Charles Lister, left the service of the Foreign Office in Constantinople and became a Sub-Lt in the RND along with Allan Campbell, the son of the actress Mrs Patrick Campbell (whose husband had divorced Churchill's mother some months earlier). Lt L. W. Nelson had also served with Captain Scott, in his case as the expedition biologist. The youngest of the all was Midshipman the Honourable Vere Harmsworth, the younger son of newspaper magnate, Lord Rothermere. Harmsworth had already served in the Royal Navy, but had been invalided out after his hearing had been damaged by gunfire.

Some came from the Colonies and Dominions, and even foreigners took commissions in the RND to fight for the British cause. F. S. 'Clegg' Kelly, an exceptional musician, Oxford rowing blue and twice winner of the Diamond Sculls, came from Australia. Wallace Moir Annand left his desk in South Africa, and John Bigelow Dodge his home in the United States of America. New York-born Dodge came from a family which included business, diplomatic, and political leaders, a founder of the YMCA, and a twenty-one-year-old who was the youngest Brigadier General in the Union Army. He was also distantly related to Winston Churchill. Bernard Freyberg, a powerfully built man from New Zealand, had served with that country's Field Artillery Volunteers and, with a territorial battalion, sought out a Major Richardson who had served with him in his artillery battery. Richardson had the right contacts all the way up to Churchill, and Freyberg was granted a commission in the RND. Churchill's dispensing of naval commissions in such a way was not at all unusual. Many friends, favourites, and men who chimed with the First Lord's instincts were given instant commissions. The heir to the pottery fortune and Member of Parliament, the Right Honourable Josiah Wedgwood, was made a Lt Cdr and given command in the Royal Naval Air Service Armoured Car Squadrons. The Austrian-born Baron de Forest, also an MP, was given the same rank and command, while The Honourable Geoffrey Howard MP was made a Lt RNVR before marring the daughter of a Field Marshal and transferring to the Royal Marines.

The War Office had also experienced an early overmanning problem. The Durham Light Infantry, for example, had been increased to thirty-seven battalions in the first few days of the war. Consequently, the Admiralty was badgered to take surplus men from the DLI, the Northumberland Fusiliers, and the King's Own Yorkshire Light Infantry into the RND. Their Lordships, at first reluctant, eventually agreed, and the Naval Brigades received drafts of huge, superbly fit men from mining backgrounds, who spoke in accents that caused bewilderment among their officers and instructors.

With this new influx of men, it was decided that the RND bad outgrown its camp on Walmer Downs and so, on 9 September, the Second Royal Naval Brigade moved to a new camp at Lord Northbourne's nearby park at Betteshanger.

It was soon discovered, both at Walmer Downs and at Betteshanger, that the new battalions had enough on their hands in training men in infantry tactics without undertaking the basic training required for raw recruits. In response to this problem, a Divisional Depot was set up by mid-September in the fragile bulkheads of the Crystal Palace. Built on Sydenham Hill in the London borough of Penge, the remarkable glass structure was officially known as HMS *Victory VI,* and HMS *Victory II.* The former title referred to the training and administration staff, while the second covered the recruits under training. Nevertheless, the place was known to all as HMS *Crystal Palace.* The depot was commanded by Commodore Sir Richard Williams Bulkeley RNR who had previously commanded the Mersey Division of the RNVR. Its senior officers were made up of officers considered to be too old for active service. The young officers passing through the Depot nicknamed them 'Sea Captains' and held them in a high degree of awe.

The new men who entered the Divisional Depot were fitted out in Royal Naval uniforms with their 'cap tallies' lettered in gold wire, 'ROYAL NAVAL DIVISION'. After slinging their hammocks in the huge 'Canada' building they would 'go ashore' into Sydenham and Penge to have their photographs taken with their caps worn at a rakish angle and striking nautical poses. The following song was often heard in the public houses around the Crystal Palace:

'The Crystal Palace Army'

I thought when them Germans turned nasty,
I'd join up to give 'em 'What for'.
Though I reckuned they must have got plenty,
when they started to bellow for more.
I gazed at the ads on the 'oardings,
and thought I'd look proper in blue,
so I makes up me mind for the shillin',
and I honoured the Palace crew.

So there we were, a merry crew,
The Crystal Palace Army;
Butchers, bakers,
Pattern-makers,
Grocers, tailors,
Dressed as sailors,
Good 'ole Palace Army.
They took me and fed me and washed me,
and cut off me bootiful 'air,

and dressed me in funny-shaped trousers,
the same as the sailor chaps wear;
They taught me to handle a rifle,
And 'ow to do 'shoulder' and 'slope',
While the sergeant 'e sez quite politely,
That 'e reckunds us 'England's last 'ope'.

So there we were, a merry crew,
Winston Churchill's Army.
'Yde Park talkers,
Swell shop walkers,
Cooks and waiters,
Wearing gaiters,
Good 'ole Palace Army.

The irrepressible Ivan Heald, a reporter and humorist at the *Daily Express*, signed on as an Ordinary Seaman and had difficulty in getting used to naval ways. Put on guard-duty, he wrote:

> I should have been a real success as a sentry if it had not been for the saluting business. It happened that the gorgeously uniformed man to whom I presented arms was neither an admiral nor a field-marshal, but only the doorkeeper at the local picture palace, and my chief petty officer could not decide whether I was to be hanged at the yardarm or shot at dawn. Eventually, I was put to clean the steps at the Crystal Palace. Thank God it wasn't the windows.

Heald was soon commissioned as a Sub-Lt.

There were many variations among the uniforms worn during the early days of the Naval Brigades. Although most of the ratings wore the dark blue naval uniform, some were seen in a khaki version while others had navy-blue bell-bottomed trousers with khaki jerseys. The majority of the newly recruited officers wore army-style khaki service dress, but with fawn-coloured rings around their jacket cuffs in the manner of Royal Naval officers seen in blue uniform. Freyberg even turned wearing a double-breasted jacket in a khaki copy of a naval officer's uniform into a fashion. Soon, all attached to the Royal Naval Brigades were known by the sobriquet 'Khaki Jack.'

Equipment of every kind proved difficult to obtain. Outdated rifles had to be shared during practice on the range, and many had never seen an entrenching tool. The War Office claimed that it had enough problems supplying the Army and could find little to spare for the Navy.

Basic training at the Crystal Palace was to last for five weeks and consisted of instruction in 'cleanliness, care of feet, discipline, orders, and such regulations as immediately affect the men of the Royal Naval Division Depot.' They underwent physical training, squad drill, bayonet fighting, musketry instruction, and 'elementary night training'. Parade drill was to be carried out on the Palace's gravel terraces – the grass plots not being 'suitable'. Above all else, however, was 'Development of the Service spirit.'

While the Naval Brigades were sorting out their teething troubles as they were taught to be soldiers, the Royal Marine Brigade – consisting of the 9th (Portsmouth) Battalion, the 10th (Plymouth) Battalion, the 11th (Chatham) Battalion, and the 12th (Deal) Battalion – had been getting closer to the enemy.

It was of extreme importance to the British war effort that the Channel ports should not fall into enemy hands. The German master plan of attack – the Schlieffen Plan – included an advance to the west of Paris in order to bring about the encirclement of the French capital. This westward march would bring the German forces to well within striking distance of the Channel ports of Ostend, Zeebrugge, Dunkirk, and Calais. Although the Schlieffen Plan had been modified, and the swing to the west of Paris had been omitted, it was with some concern that report of German patrols active in the vicinity of Ostend reached the Admiralty. On 23 August, the British Army on the European mainland – the British Expeditionary Force – had begun a major delaying action against the enemy at Mons, and the direction of the German assault could be changed at any moment. Patrols spotted near Ostend might indicate an advance to the west and the vital ports. However, if the ports were defended, and enough of the enemy troops could be drawn away from the southward advance, the British and French armies might blunt the German attack at the French border. Churchill decided to send the Royal Marine Brigade to Ostend.

On 25 August, General Sir George Aston received the following from the First Lord:

> The objective of this movement is to create a diversion, favourable to the Belgians, who are advancing from Antwerp, and to threaten the western flank of the German southward advance. It should therefore be ostentatious. You should not push inland from Ostend without further orders, but some enterprise may be permitted to the patrols. ... The objective in view would be fully obtained if a considerable force of the enemy were attracted to the coast.

The next day 3,000 Royal Marines embarked for Belgium. They were transported by eight of the Channel Fleet battleships and escorted by a light cruiser, six destroyers and three monitors. Held up by bad weather, they were finally disembarked on 28 August. The fleet that had brought them over was to remain off Ostend to give the Marines gunfire support should it be required, although, as was soon discovered, the terrain was unsuitable for such support.

There being no immediate sign of the enemy, the Marines were put to work on the defences of Ostend. Trenches were dug around the perimeter of the town, and between the railway at Marrakerke, near Bruges; and the coast. The German army, however, appeared to be making no effort to launch an attack against Ostend.

On 31 August, a large contingent of Belgian soldiers arrived in the town and began to take over the trenches from the Marines. That night, because there was an urgent requirement for the fleet standing off Ostend to be elsewhere, the Marine Brigade re-embarked and returned to England. The Admiralty report on the operation said of the Marines 'The promptitude with which the Brigade was embarked, landed and re-embarked was highly creditable'. They were not, however, to have long to rest on their laurels.

The Belgian army was retreating slowly towards Antwerp in the face of a German force under the command of General von Beseler. In the south, at the battle of the Marne, the British and French armies counterattacked the main German advance and caused the enemy to fall back beyond the River Aisne along a 180-mile front. At this point, it seemed that the combatants were evenly balanced and little would be gained by continued frontal attacks. Behind the German lines, troops began to move to their right – in the direction of the coast. If this movement was allowed to continue unmatched, the Germans would achieve two major aims. Firstly, they would link up with von Beseler's army in Belgium and secondly, they would reach the French coast as far south as possible, raising the danger of the major Channel ports being trapped behind enemy lines. In an attempt to prevent the Germans from achieving these aims, the Allies had to delay von Beseler for as long as possible in Belgium, to stop his left flank from joining the right of the southern German army, and not allow their own left flank to be turned by the westward flanking movements of the enemy. The 'race to the sea' was on.

On 12 September, 200 Marines from the Royal Marine Brigade – fifty men from each of the battalions – were sent to Dunkirk. A Royal Naval Air Service base had been set up there under the command of Cdr Samson whose task was to launch attacks against all German air bases within range. The Marines were to help defend the base by manning the armoured cars of the RNAS. Armed with unexpected mobility, and determined not to be tied down to the air base, the Marines used the cars to roam far and wide seeking out the enemy. Eventually they moved near to Hazebrouck and made contact with detachments of enemy cavalry and cycle troops. The Germans, believing that they could outwit what had become known in England as the 'Dunkirk Circus', dug trenches across roads to bring the cars to a halt. The RNAS, however, quite used to improvisation, on a suggestion by Churchill, began to carry thick boards to bridge these obstructions. At some stage it was suggested that caterpillar tracks might be fitted to the cars to enable then to clear such obstacles, a thought that lodged in the mind of, among others, the First Lord, who before long, had advanced the idea to a devastating result.

The French, increasingly concerned for the safety of the Channel ports, requested that the British make a large show of force at either Calais or Dunkirk. In response, it was decided that, once again, the Royal Marine Brigade should be used for the task, this time reinforced by the Oxfordshire Hussars – a distinguished Yeomanry regiment – and a detachment of the Royal Engineers. General Sir George Aston took command of the force and landed at Dunkirk on 21 September. Shortly after the Brigade's arrival, the French sent an urgent message requesting assistance in withdrawing their troops from Lille. The Plymouth Battalion left for the retreating front line immediately.

After a few days in France, General Aston, the Royal Naval Division's first Divisional Commander, fell ill and was invalided home. His replacement was Colonel Archibald Paris of the Royal Marine Artillery. Col Paris was a fifty-three-year-old, tough but popular, veteran of the war in South Africa where he had three times earned mentions in dispatches. He had served with Naval Intelligence and as an instructor on the staff of the Naval College. On 27 September, the new Divisional Commander moved the Brigade headquarters inland to Cassel.

In addition to the armoured cars of the RNAS, some other form of transport had to be found for the Marines. Some cars had been made available, but the most novel form of transport to come across the Channel was the London motor omnibus whose drivers had been enlisted as Royal Marines at Chatham. But, as the Marines rode around north-west France in their London buses giving great encouragement to the local population, the plight of the Belgian Army was becoming desperate as it fell back on to Antwerp.

In Britain, quite apart from treaty obligations to defend Belgium, there were also, it was felt, sound moral reasons. Both Britain and Germany had guaranteed Belgian neutrality in 1839 and in 1871, and stories coming from the invaded country caused an enormous shock to the British public. Although many of the tales of alleged atrocities to reach the ears of the British people were greatly exaggerated, many thousands of civilians had been shot, some as hostages, at Dinant, St Trond, Tirlemont, Tongres and Louvain. Town after town had suffered from wholesale pillaging.

Lord Kitchener was equally concerned that the fall of Antwerp, which now seemed inevitable, should be delayed for as long as possible. Already the race to the sea had reached Lens, and the German army was closing in on the vital Channel ports. If the two enemy armies were to link up before the Allies had reached the coast, the risk to the ports was increased greatly.

The French had offered a force of 15,000 troops for the defence of Belgium, and an attack on von Beseler's flank if the British would also agree to send troops. Churchill suggested to Kitchener that the Royal Marine Brigade should be sent to help in the defence of Antwerp. The Minister of War agreed. He would send, in addition, the 7th and 3rd Cavalry Divisions.

The First Lord set off by train to visit Cdr Samson and the 'Dunkirk Circus' (whom the Germans were now calling 'Motor Bandits') when, with less than 20 miles of his journey completed, he was recalled by Kitchener. Churchill was requested to go instead to Antwerp to see the situation there at first hand. He arrived in the besieged city with his secretary, Admiral Hood, on 2 October.

Antwerp was defended by an outer line of thirteen large forts to the north, east, and south of the city. Westwards, across the River Scheldt, another six forts completed the circle of outer defences. The Scheldt itself formed a western water barrier linking up with the River Nethe to the south and the Albert Canal to the east and north – the whole length of connected waterways forming a barrier within the ring of outer forts. Still further in, a series of eight forts guarded the city's south and south-east, each fort connected to its neighbour by trenches. These forts were numbered from the most easterly, Fort Number 1, covering the Albert Canal, to Fort Number 7, close by the eastern bank of the Scheldt. A further five inner forts protected the west and north of the city. Each of the forts had a moat protecting its front and sides. Behind the inner forts, only the medieval walls of the city remained as a defence. Should, however, the situation become desperate, sluices could be opened which would flood some 70 square miles north-west of the city. 15 square miles to the south of the Nethe had already been inundated.

Part of the main plan for the defence of Antwerp, had included the possibility that transports bearing supplies and reinforcements would pass up the Scheldt from the North Sea. This lifeline, however, was cut by the Dutch who refused permission for any ships to pass through their territory.

As Churchill entered the city, wearing the uniform of an Elder of Trinity House, German troops broke through the outer line of forts and the Belgian army fell back onto the line of the Nethe. Massive Austrian 'Skoda' siege howitzers, fresh from destroying the Belgian and French defences at Namure, began to rain destruction on to Antwerp while 60,000 German troops of the 3rd Reserve Corps, the 4th 'Ersatz' Division, a Marine Division and three Landwehr Brigades attacked the trenches along the Nethe.

On the morning of 3 October, Kitchener ordered Col Paris to take the Royal Marine Brigade to Antwerp as the British Foreign Secretary, Sir Edward Grey, sent the following message to the Belgian Prime Minister:

> We feel that the importance of Antwerp being held till the course of the main battle in France is determined justifies a further effort. We are trying to send you help from the main army, and, if this were possible, would add reinforcements from here. Meanwhile a brigade of Marines will reach you tomorrow to sustain the defence. We urge you to make one further struggle to hold out. Even a few days may make the difference. We hope Government will find it possible to remain and the field army to continue operations.

The Marines travelled by train through Ghent and, in the early hours of the morning of the 4th, arrived at the small town of Edegem, 4 miles south of Antwerp. By nine o'clock they had moved into the trenches along the Nethe and relieved the exhausted soldiers of the Belgian 21st Regiment. They had been positioned so that they opposed the enemy where the ring of outer forts had been breached at Lier. The trenches were in poor condition having been hastily dug when it appeared that the outer forts could not be held. They offered little protection against a concentrated bombardment. Other local forces and further detachments of British forces were immediately placed under Col Paris's command giving him a force consisting of the four battalions of the Royal Marine Brigade, the Belgian 7th Infantry Regiment and 1st Caribineers, a small machine gun section from the RNAS, and a detachment of the Royal Engineers.

The Chatham, Plymouth and Deal Battalions manned the front line trenches in company with the Belgian 7th Regiment with the Portsmouth Battalion and the 1st Caribineers forming a general reserve.

When all his forces were in position, Col Paris and his battalion commanders met Churchill who led them on a tour of Antwerp's defences. The situation was as precarious as possible with the Belgians utterly exhausted from the long, protracted, fighting across their homeland. The promised French troops had failed to materialise, and the British 3rd and 7th Cavalry were still preparing in England.

On completion of the tour, the First Lord met the Belgian Prime Minister, the Comte de Broqueville, and informed him that he had decided to send for the Naval Brigades of the Royal Naval Division. Churchill had already sent a message to the Admiralty, Kitchener, and to the Foreign Secretary:

> Send at once both Naval Brigades, minus recruits, via Dunkirk, into Antwerp, without tents or much impedimenta, but with five days rations and 2,000,000, rounds of ammunition.

Captain Richmond wrote in his diary:

> The First Lord is sending his army there; I don't mind his tuppenny untrained rabble
> going, but I do strongly object to 2,000 invaluable Marines being sent to be locked
> up in the fortress and become prisoners of war if the place is taken.

The 'tuppenny untrained rabble' were fast asleep under canvas after a hard day's
training when they were woken at 5 a.m. and told they had to be ready to leave
by 9 a.m. Many had been given anti-typhoid inoculation the day before, and it
was with great difficulty that they roused themselves to pack their kit. For a long
time the majority were convinced that the whole disturbance was merely a poorly
timed exercise.

At nine o'clock, the battalions began their march to Dover; the 1st Brigade
from Walmer Downs and the 2nd from Betteshanger. Still desperately short of
equipment and training, the men had 120 rounds of ammunition per man, mainly
stuffed into pockets, as few had ammunition pouches or haversacks. Bayonets and
scabbards were pushed down canvas gaiters for lack of belts, and water bottles
had to be carried by hand. The Reverend Canon H. Clapham Foster, Chaplain to
the 2nd Naval Brigade, recorded the preparations and departure –

> The news that we were to leave immediately for France spread very quickly round the
> camp, and among the men there was a scene of boundless enthusiasm; loud cheers were
> raised as they hastily dressed and got their kits together. There was no time to lose.
> Breakfast was at seven a.m., and at eight we were told the transport would be ready to
> convey our baggage to Dover. The Second Royal Naval Brigade started on the march
> to the pier at about nine a.m., amid scenes of great enthusiasm, two brass bands and a-
> drum-and-fife band accompanying them. The men selected some curious words for their
> own special 'marching songs,' and these are, as a rule, set to familiar melodies...

> There's a man selling beer over there;
> There's a man selling beer over there:
> Over there, over there, over there, over there –
> There's a man selling beer over there.

Another favourite ditty with men on the march was a song with a somewhat
unsavoury refrain:

> Wash me in the water
> Where you wash your dirty daughter,
> And I shall be whiter than the white-wash on the wall.

Singing such ditties as these, we marched from Betteshanger to Dover. We were accorded a magnificent reception in the streets by crowds of people who cheered lustily and waved flags and handkerchiefs as we made our way to the pier.

The Naval Brigades arrived at the port at midday and, after a snatched meal, began the task of loading the cross-Channel ferries with their baggage and equipment. Far too much baggage had been brought; the ratings had packed full kit bags and the officers had brought along large uniform trunks. Those not employed in the loading of the transports were kept waiting in a street full of public houses – an inconvenience that kept the officers and senior ratings busy prising the thirsty men away from the tempting beer.

The loading went on until the early evening before the transports left port to a background of probing searchlights. The ferries were so overcrowded that many of the men were unable to sit or lie down until the ship reached Dunkirk at noon on the following day, 5 October.

There had been no food available on the transports, and so, by the time Dunkirk had been reached, the Naval Brigades were hungry as well as weary. But the ferries had to be unloaded before any thought could be given to sustenance. Eventually, with all the equipment and baggage unloaded, the battalions were mustered in huge warehouses by the docks to await orders. Gradually the 'buzz' began to get around. This was not to be, as many still thought, a large exercise, but the real thing. The mood changed from boredom and irritation to eager anticipation – excitement built up in the air. The men began to write letters home while Sub-Lt Asquith and other officers searched the town for medical supplies for their men – none had been brought from England.

By 9 p.m., the battalions began to board trains for Antwerp with the Drake, Hawke, Benbow, and Collingwood battalions of the 1st Naval Brigade being the first to depart. By 11.30, the 2nd Brigade had left with its Nelson, Howe, Hood, and Anson battalions.

There was a risk that the enemy might attack the trains. If this was the case, the battalions had been instructed, true to naval tradition, to disembark 'Port' or 'Starboard'. The men had also been told to remain awake in view of the threatened attack, an order that was ignored by almost the entire force as they headed eastwards for Antwerp.

The 1st Naval Brigade arrived at Antwerp in the early hours of the morning dressed in greatcoats, bell-bottomed trousers tucked into knee-high gaiters and wearing sailor's caps and collars. As they prepared to march to a southern suburb of the city called Wilryk, crowds of Belgians pressed jugs of beer and coffee onto the appreciative men. Flags were waved and kisses exchanged with enthusiastic ladies. They had not marched far, however, when, having left the cheering throng behind, they began to hear the low rumble of heavy artillery ahead of them.

On the battalion's arrival at Wilryk, just behind forts 7 and 6, it was hoped that they would find accommodation and rest after the long journey, but their hopes were short lived. Ordered to press on further east, they arrived at another suburb, Vieux Dieu, slightly in front of forts 5 and 4. Breakfast was made and distributed to a background of loud explosions amid the thunder of heavy guns.

Whilst the seamen rested, the senior officers were called together to meet Churchill who had come to explain the situation. The line of the Nethe had to be held, he told them, until reinforcements could arrive. The 7th and 3rd Cavalry Divisions were preparing to embark for Ostend, and the French Marine Fusiliers were approaching towards Ghent. Once these two new forces could link up, they would strike at von Beseler's western flank.

Breakfast over, the Brigade left Vieux Dieu and moved forward into old trenches between the Nethe and the inner line of forts. They were to wait in reserve.

In the meantime, the Royal Marine Brigade had seen considerable action in the front line. The Belgians had attacked during the night and had had some initial success, but massed counter-attacks by the Germans had retaken the lost ground. This was followed by a violent enemy bombardment on the lines held by the Marines. Col Paris, now promoted Major-General with the arrival of the Naval Brigades, decided to fall back to an intermediate line between the Nethe and the inner forts. The retirement had become a necessity. The Belgian soldiers in particular were desperately tired, and their lives would have been wasted in foolhardy counter-attacks. Nevertheless, delaying tactics were all-important – an enemy breakthrough could not be allowed to happen.

When Paris heard that the 1st Naval Brigade had arrived, he ordered its commander, Commodore Henderson, to bring his battalions up to the trenches on the left of the Marines.

To get to their new place in the line, the Brigade had to re-enter Vieux Dieu. As they did so, they met the incoming 2nd Naval Brigade under the command of Commodore Backhouse. The new arrivals had been met at the station by civic officials and the town guard. Once again crowds had cheered the sailors and given them coffee, beer, and kisses. More crowds had lined the town's streets as they had marched eastwards, their very presence spreading infectious enthusiasm among the beleaguered people.

The 6,000 men of the naval brigades took up most of the space in the town square as they halted while the brigade and battalion commanders reviewed the situation. All around, chaos reigned. Dispatch riders on urgent business roared through on motorcycles, swerving around clattering horse-drawn guns headed for the front. Staff officers seemed everywhere, issuing orders while transport wagons pressed their way through. In the midst of it all, the face of Antwerp's anguish began to show. Refugees shuffled through the milling square carrying their meagre belongings, and shepherding bemused children. An even deeper impression was made on the waiting seamen by the haggard faces of the war-weary troops of the Belgian Field Army as they made their way from the front-line trenches.

Following a short rest, the Brigades marched out of the square, the 2nd Brigade to the gardens of a large chateau, and the 1st into the trenches, the Drake and Benbow Battalions to the right of the Chatham Battalion, and the Hawke and Collingwood to support trenches behind the remainder of the Marines.

During the day, General Sir Henry Rawlinson had arrived in Antwerp. He had been sent by Kitchener to take command of all the British troops, particularly the still-preparing cavalry divisions. However, apart from a few detachments and units of the Royal Engineers and the RNAS, there were only the 8,000 men of the Royal Naval Division available to him, along with the remnants of the Belgian 2nd Division and the Belgian troops manning the forts. Directly opposing them were the 4th Ersatz Division, the highly trained Marinekorps, the 5th and 6th Reserve Divisions, and the 26th Infantry Brigade.

The man who appeared to have taken charge of the entire situation, however, was Winston Churchill. He drove by car along the front lines, held councils of war, encouraged failing politicians, and issued orders. Colonel John Seely, sent by the British Commander-in-Chief, Sir John French, to assess the events at Antwerp wrote:

> From the moment I arrived, it was apparent that the whole business was in Winston's hand. He dominated the whole place - the king, ministers, soldiers, sailors. So great was his influence that I am convinced that with 20,000 British troops he could have held Antwerp against almost any onslaught.

Such was Churchill's enthusiasm for the events around him that he offered to resign from his office as First Lord if he could be given command of the troops defending Antwerp. Kitchener refused and ordered Churchill home.

As he departed, news arrived that the expected British reinforcements, the Army's 7th Division, would arrive at Zeebrugge on the following day, but would not be able to concentrate before 8 October – and then only at Ostend. The news from the French was even worse. They had decided that their Marine Fusiliers, now at Ghent, would not be sent to Antwerp.

The exhausted Belgians now wanted to continue their withdrawal but, after urgent discussions had taken place, they agreed to leave their Field Army's 2nd Division in the front alongside the British troops. Nevertheless, General Paris decided to withdraw to the line of inner forts as the Belgian troops on the right of the Benbow Battalion had already been withdrawn.

The forts were manned by specially trained fortress troops under the command of the Belgian Lt-Gen. Deguise. The connecting trenches were rudimentary and offered no protection against artillery bombardment – neither were there any communication trenches to link them with reserve trenches. This meant that any attempt to support the front line by the reserves, or any withdrawal of the front line, would have to be done over open ground. Despite these disadvantages, they were capable of being held against infantry attack. There was an open field of fire in front for at least 500 yards, and the front was thickly laced with barbed wire. By holding up the infantry on this line until heavy artillery could be brought forward, the enemy could be delayed several, vital, hours.

General Paris ordered up the 2nd Naval Brigade from their chateau garden and put them in the trenches between forts 5 to 8. The 1st Naval Brigade entered the trenches between forts 2 to 5. The Marine Brigade was placed in reserve to rest. They had not been there for long when the Chatham Battalion was ordered forward to relieve the Belgians manning the trenches between fort number 8 and the river Scheldt – the right flank of the defence line.

The Germans, apparently realising the difficulty of an infantry attack, contented themselves with desultory shell-fire during the night. Most of the shells passed over the manned trenches destroying buildings behind the inner line, while giving the men of the RND a chance to become used to the sound of bombardment.

Before dawn had broken, a large explosion was heard from the fort on the left of the Anson Battalion trenches. As the debris settled, Belgian fortress troops could be seen fleeing from their position. A patrol of the Ansons, sent to investigate the cause of the panic, found that two of the fort's guns had burst, killing and wounding a number of the defenders. Other guns, however, were still in working order and had ammunition remaining. Naval gunners from the battalion entered the fort to keep them operational.

The following day, 7 October, saw no attempt by the enemy to advance against the trenches, so the opportunity was taken to supply the sailors with food while those who had entrenching tools dug shrapnel shelters to the rear of their trenches under the direction of the Royal Engineers. The rations were brought up to the line – and, for a while, actually in front of the line – by the London omnibuses, some still carrying destination placards offering journeys to 'Edgeware Road' and 'Golders Green'. Behind them, the sky glowed red with the deliberate burning of the huge oil tanks on the banks of the Scheldt, and a series of dull thuds announced the blowing up of the boiler and engine rooms of merchant ships at the docks.

In the early hours of the next morning, a German patrol was seen moving in front of Cdr Campbell's Drake Battalion. Immediately rifle-fire broke out along the battalion's trenches. The firing spread along the whole line held by the Naval Brigades, and was only stopped with some difficulty. The inexperience of the men was beginning to show. The only clear result from the erratic fusillades was one dead cow.

This incident had just been brought to an end when the first shells from the newly advanced Austrian howitzers began to fall on the inner line trenches. The 2nd Naval Brigade suffered a few injured men, but the 1st, which seemed to be getting the worst of the bombardment, had four dead in their trenches, one of whom was Lt-Col. Aymer Maxwell of the Coldstream Guard, the Commanding Officer of the Collingwood Battalion. An extract from the diary of an unnamed petty officer, written during the shelling, was published in a national magazine. He wrote –

Later. – We seem to be in a pickle. Our baggage party have just got here. Report the town in flames and all our gear lost. Shells coming in like one o'clock. Man on my side got a bit in his leg, but says he can shoot just as well on one leg. Belgian artilleryman reports that he and two others are all that are left of our covering fort. We seem to have nothing to do but wait for the end. These trenches would be all right against savages, but against their huge artillery, like so much dust. These shells come with a whizz like an express train and then – crash! The spirits of our troops are top hole. Not one the slightest bit excited. Just smoking or yarning and dodging shells; but it's just rotten not coming alongside them. Here she comes – dip, crash! Saved again. Another non-stop for Antwerp. When they shorten the range for us – well, cheer oh! Officer just given us the bird for laughing.

The shelling had proved the final straw for the Belgian fortress troops, who abandoned their posts and retreated into the city. The forts were then manned by men from the Naval Brigades. At the same time, information arrived that five German infantry battalions had moved eastwards, crossed the Scheldt west of Termonde (Dendermonde), and were advancing northwards in a obvious attempt to outflank the British and Belgians in Antwerp. If they reached the Dutch border to the north, the only evacuation route would be sealed off. The soldiers of the Belgian Field Army, led by their king, Albert I, were still holding their ground, but the time was clearly coming when they would begin to fall back under the mounting pressure. By seven o'clock on the morning of the 8th, General Paris had decided that he must make preparations for the withdrawal of the Royal Naval Division. He telephoned General Rawlings at his headquarters in Bruges and informed him of the situation and of his plans.

It was now imperative that there should be an escape route available to the

Division when the time to retire came. The Brigades would have to march through the suburbs of Antwerp and cross the Scheldt. A pontoon bridge, assembled from a series of boats, had been already secured and, should the bridge be destroyed, boats had been commandeered to get the sailors across. The most important thing remaining was to secure rail transport once Antwerp had been left behind.

Despite preparations being made to cover the retirement of the Division, it was still of vital importance that the enemy should be held back for as long as possible. As the position stood, it was still possible to hold the line for several hours and possibly days, but much depended on the fight left in the Belgian Army. General Paris moved his headquarters closer to that of General Deguise in order to watch the situation closely. As the day progressed, more and more Belgian troops left their frontline positions. With every withdrawal of their allies, the situation of the Royal Naval Division became increasingly precarious. The artillery support they had enjoyed since their arrival, meagre though it had been, had now gone, and the Belgians were beginning to fall back all along the line.

The 7th Division had entrained from Zeebrugge to Bruges but, shortly after their arrival, had been forced to withdraw towards Ostend. During the withdrawal, they came across Belgian soldiers who had been relieved at Antwerp by the Royal Naval Division. The official history of the South Staffordshire Regiment recorded that –

> Haggard in looks, broken in spirit by the terrific bombardment of the Germans, these men presented a pitiable sight, and plainly showed the trials and hardships they had endured.

By the late afternoon of the same day, General Paris had decided that if the Division was to be saved, it must be withdrawn. The Scheldt had to be crossed, preferably while the pontoon bridges were still intact. At five o'clock, he telephoned the First Lord and told him of his decision. Churchill agreed.

Within the hour, the order for retirement had gone out from the Divisional headquarters. The 1st Brigade would leave via the city's Malines Gate to the city pontoon bridge and then, having crossed the river, march on to the divisional rendezvous at Zwyndrecht, some 14 miles from the inner line. The 2nd Brigade and the Marine Brigade would take a shorter route and cross the Scheldt by the Burcht pontoon bridge, to the south-west of the city, and then on to the rendezvous. The rear of the withdrawal would be brought up by the Royal Marines of the Portsmouth Battalion. The operation was to begin immediately the order was received.

Staff officers took the messages to the Brigade headquarters by hand. The 2nd and Marine Brigades received their orders and began to respond promptly. The officer delivering the orders to the 1st Brigade, however, was Sir John French's Staff officer, Col Seely, who, despite having spent two years as Secretary of State for War, mistakenly gave the message to Cdr Campbell of the Drake Battalion under the impression that he was Commodore Henderson. Campbell, believing that the rest of the 1st Brigade was already withdrawing, ordered his battalion out of the trenches and began the march to the Scheldt.

It was not until after 7 p.m. that Col Ollivant, the staff officer who had delivered General Paris's order to the Marine Brigade, came across the 1st Naval Brigade still in their trenches.

Seeking out the Brigade Cdr, he gave him the orders before leaving for the Divisional Headquarters. However, one vital point had still not been clearly made to Commodore Henderson – that the order must be acted upon immediately upon receipt. The Benbow, Collingwood, and Hawk Battalions did not begin the withdrawal until 10 p.m.

The 2nd Brigade and the three Marine battalions reached the River Scheldt without incident, although everyone was desperately tired having had little sleep for the past few days. As they crossed over the pontoon bridges, the horrors of the dying city began to crowd in around them. Huge stores of petrol had been fired by the retreating Belgians, and the flaming fuel poured on to the river spreading on the surface in sheets of searing fire. Loud detonations crashed through the evening air as black smoke blotted out the light of the setting sun, and eight-inch shells from the siege howitzers fell among the burning tanks and buildings. Sub-Lt Rupert Brooke of the Anson Battalion later wrote of 'houses wrecked by shells, dead horses, demolished railway stations, engines that had been taken up with their lines and signals, and all twisted round and pulled out, as a bad child spoils a toy'.

There was, inevitably, a human side of the tragedy. As the battalions reached the other side of the Scheldt, they encountered a teeming mass of refugees fleeing from the destruction and the advancing enemy. The roads were packed with families dragging or carrying pitiful remnants of their homes, children bewildered by the events around them clung to their mother's skirts and the aged, eyes blinded by tears, shuffled away from the flames and explosions. The sight prompted an outraged Brooke to write:

> The central purpose of my life, the aim and end of it, now that God wants it of me, is to get good at beating Germans.

It took the battalions six hours to reach the rendezvous at Zwyndrecht. It was 11.30 p.m. and the weary men sank to the ground to rest. In addition to their normal equipment they had also carried many trench stores, including boxes of ammunition, along the entire route. But their time for rest was short indeed. General Paris had been assured by his staff that all three brigades were present and, consequently, he gave the order to start immediately for Beveren – a two-hour march – where they would find trains to take them to Ostend.

But events were determined to try the Royal Naval Division to the full. As the battalions reached the railway station, it was learned that yet another mistake had been made and that there were no trains to be had. Their destination now had to be the small town of St Gillaes-Waes – over 5 miles to the east.

No time could be taken to rest the division. The route to St Gillaes-Waes had no main road, and what roads did exist were packed with refugees.

As the brigades made their weary way through the darkened country lanes, they had to be repeatedly encouraged and cajoled by their officers and senior ratings. Men, stumbling on, exhausted by lack of sleep, helped each other to avoid the temptation, despite the bitter cold, to lie down and sleep. The cohesion that had marked the withdrawal so far, began to collapse as groups of men made their own way to St Gillaes-Waes.

Under such conditions, it was quite remarkable, that, by 9 a.m., more than seven hours after they had left Beveren, the last of the battalions were onboard the trains heading for Ostend. Not one man had been lost.

To their rear, the remaining three battalions of the 1st Naval Brigades had not moved from the front lines until ten o'clock the previous night. The Hawke Battalion reached the Scheldt first and found the pontoon bridge at Burcht intact. The Benbow and Collingwood, taking the correct route to the city bridge, found the pontoons destroyed and had to cross by boat. They were followed by the rearguard Portsmouth Battalion led by Col Luard.

The battalions found the march to the Zwyndrecht rendezvous reasonably easy as most of the refuges had fled the city and delays were few. Upon reaching the suburb, however, they were held up for two hours while Commodore Henderson tried to get information on the whereabouts of the remainder of the Division. Learning that there were trains available at St Gillaes-Waes, the 1st Brigade began its march across country. In doing so it caught up with the main body of refugees. The minor roads and country lanes were packed with shuffling refugees, and the battalions began to become separated. At one stage the Hawke Battalion lined up two deep across a turnip field and opened fire on, what they believed to be, a party of mounted enemy soldiers. The fire was promptly returned and, for few moments, the air above a Belgian field was thick with flying bullets until Cdr Beadle ordered a cease-fire. The horsemen turned out to be Belgian cavalry. By a miracle no one had been hit on either side.

From 11.30 p.m., small parties of men began to arrive at the railway station.

Stragglers continued to turn up and were still arriving in the late afternoon. As each appeared, they were put on the trains to wait for the rest of the widely separated seamen and marines.

Whilst Commodore Henderson waited for his dispersed battalions to reassemble, he received shattering news. The German 1st Bavarian Brigade had crossed the railway line between him and Ostend and had cut the line at Moerbeke, the next but one station, 12 miles from St Gillaes-Waes. As he gave the order for the men to leave the trains, he weighed up his options. He could try to fight his way through but, with his entire force exhausted through lack of sleep and a long march, even if he were to succeed, the loss of life would be enormous. He could stay where he was and risk capture by the enemy, but that would have been unthinkable. There remained one further option, almost as distasteful as the first two, but one which would save lives and yet not let his men fall into the hands of the enemy. Just 4 miles away, within easy marching distance, lay the Dutch border at De Klinge. Holland was a neutral country and any forces belonging to the combatants who crossed her border would be interred for the duration of the war.

Henderson called together his battalion commanders and told them of his decision – the three battalions of the 1st Naval Brigade would march into Holland.

As the men were paraded for their final, sad, march to internment, small groups drifted away from the main body, determined to attempt to escape. Lt Charles West, the son of a Woking clergyman, had been invalided out of the Royal Navy in 1905, but had rejoined at the outbreak of the war. In company with Chief Petty Officer Stewart, and Leading Seaman Shelton, he headed off across country and escaped through Holland disguised as a workman, the three becoming the only men from the Hawke Battalion to escape. According to a favourite story of Winston Churchill, two Benbow Battalion officers also demonstrated their share of initiative rather than be interned. When ordered to cross the border by a superior officer, Sub-Lt Charles Modin replied 'That means we shall be interned; no use for the rest of the war!' The superior officer responded by demanding 'You will obey orders.'

'I will be damned if I do,' answered Modin who then, raising his voice, shouted, 'Come on any men who will follow me!' A large group of men mustered around the young officer, and he marched them off to Selzaete (Zelzate), where the railway line to Ostend remained intact, and eventually saw his companions safely returned to England. Modin transferred to the Royal Marines, then to the Royal Flying Corps, and ended his Service career during the Second World War as an Air Commodore in the Royal Air Force.

Lt Gordon Grant did things differently. He crossed the border in obedience to his orders only to announce, 'And now military discipline is at an end, come on, lads!' At this, forty men followed him in recrossing the border from where he led them, to the railhead and a safe return home.

For their disobedience of orders, both Modin and Grant were awarded the Distinguished Service Cross on the recommendation of General Paris.

The Portsmouth Battalion, bringing up the rear, received information from Belgian sources that the train to take them to Ostend would have to be met at Kemseke, the next station down the line from St Gillaes-Waes. As they made their way to the new destination, they came across 600 stragglers from the 1st Naval Brigade being led by Lt Grossman of the Collingwood Battalion. The seamen and marines now pressed on together and arrived at Kemseke a little after eight o'clock that evening. The train for which they had been hoping was waiting for them and, shortly afterwards, with most of its exhausted passengers fast asleep, it was on its way to Ostend.

But the long night was not over. As the train reached Moerbeke, it was derailed by the enemy who had just taken the small town. The Royal Marine officers jumped from the train and rallied their men around them. Major French and Lt Gowney led a party of Marines forward and began to engage the enemy with small arms fire. Under this cover, the Battalion Cdr, Col Luard, took the remainder of the Marines and some of the naval ratings forward along the railway line. The bulk of the seamen remained on the train – fast asleep. Lt Grossman forced those around him to wake up and, sending some through the train to rouse the rest, he took a small party with him to support the Marines.

The sleepy seamen stumbled from the train and made their way along the track. They had, however, left the train on the wrong side. Instead of going forward they were going back towards Kemseke. They were all captured by the advancing Germans.

The small party providing the covering fire, now reduced due to casualties including Grossman, had to leave the wounded in order to make its getaway and join Col Lourd's party who had found a way through the enemy line. They all managed to escape, arriving at Selzaete the following day. Major French earned the Distinguished Service Order for his work that night, and the wounded Lt Gowney, the DSC.

The prisoners were marched south the following day (9 October) and, that night, having spent the day without food and desperately tired, they lay down where they were and attempted to sleep. One of the seamen, however, decided to attempt to escape and ran off. The Germans opened fire randomly, killing five of the seamen. One of the guards raised his rifle and was about to fire when he was jumped on by Lt Cdr Oswald Hanson of the Benbow Battalion. Hanson, a Cambridge-educated London solicitor before the war, wrestled the guard to the ground before being arrested. He was executed by firing squad the following day.

Seven officers and fifty-three men of the Royal Naval Division had lost their lives in the defence of Antwerp, and three officers and 135 men had been wounded. They had, however, achieved the task they had been set. The pursuing Germans had been slowed down even after the surrender of Antwerp on 10 October. The retreating forces had been given time to open the sluices of the River Yser and flood vast areas of land between Dixmund and the channel ports. At Ypres, the left flank of the British Expeditionary Force had been secured despite vicious fighting in which even cooks and batmen had been involved. The line was carried north to the Belgian coast by the French and Belgians. Ostend and Zeebrugge had been lost to the enemy, but Dunkirk, Calais, and Boulogne had been saved. The battle lines had been drawn, and vast, extended, armies began to dig their trenches. The mobile war was over, the static war was about to begin.

The Royal Naval Division had left Ostend on 10–11 October, and returned to Walmer and Betteshanger to find a furore in process about their involvement in the defence of Antwerp. Most of the rage was directed at the First Lord, Winston Churchill. A letter to the *Times* fumed,

> When rumours first got about in this neighbourhood that these raw levies were going to the front, it was scoffed at as incredible. The opinions of many naval and military officers were unanimous that to send the Brigades in their present condition to any fighting line was nothing less than 'deliberate murder'. Individual officers, non-commissioned officers, and men of the force itself laughed at the base suggestion of being employed as a fighting unit. When, shortly after their departure, it was reported on undeniable evidence that these Naval Volunteers and recruits had actually been sent to Antwerp, the general feeling throughout this district was one of intense anger and consternation.

The *Morning Post* wrote:

> The attempt to relieve Antwerp by a small force of Marines and Naval Volunteers was a costly blunder for which Mr W. Churchill must be held responsible.

and the *Daily Mail* protested over the sacrifice 'of a considerable number of gallant young Englishmen'. Support for the First Lord came from the *Daily News*, *The Star*, and the *Observer*. The Prime Minister, whose son and nephew had been involved, wrote to the King:

> The failure of French co-operation made it impossible to despatch General Rawlinson's divisions as a relieving force; and as the Belgian army had become tired and dispirited, and the German bombardment of the town was being steadily

pressed, no useful object would have been served by a continued defence of the entrenchments by our unsupported Naval Division.

After a talk with his son, the Prime Minister wrote in his diary:

Marines, of course, are splendid troops and can go anywhere and do anything but Winston ought never to have sent the two Naval Brigades.

The Official History of the war gave a more charitable interpretation, reminding everyone that the Naval Brigades

Without any training in field fortifications, they entrenched themselves; without training in musketry, they used their rifles to good effect: without any supply service or regimental transport, they lived on such food as could be procured locally from time to time.

Churchill, true to character, remained unshaken in his conviction that he was right. In his message to the Royal Naval Division on its return, he said:

The First Lord welcomes the Royal Naval Division home, on its return from active service. Officers and men of all ranks and ratings have acquitted themselves admirably, and have thoroughly justified the confidence placed in them. The loss of a portion of the 1st Brigade, through a mistake, in no way reflects upon the quality or character of the Division.

'The Brigade of Royal Marines, throughout the operations, sustained fully – by their firmness, discipline, and courage – the traditions of the Corps. It is not necessary to say more than this. The Naval Brigades bore themselves admirably under the artillery fire of the enemy, and it is to be regretted that no opportunities of closer contact with his infantry were afforded them.

The 936 officers and men who had been captured by the Germans survived on scraps offered by their captors, and raw turnips found in a nearby field before their arrival at a prisoner of war camp at Termonde. From there they were sent to a prisoner of war camp at Doberitz – to the west of Berlin. There they saw out the war under the rigorous conditions and depravations normally associated with such places.

Those who, under the leadership of Commodore Henderson, had crossed the border into Holland, found circumstances considerably more relaxed than their shipmates in Germany. The Dutch were reluctant captors who only consideration was to stay out of the war. Whilst utterly rigid in their insistence on neutrality, the 1,479 officers and men in their hands were well treated throughout. The internees were sent to an internment camp at Groningen where they lived a relatively comfortable life in wooden huts collectively named HMS *Timbertown*. The men were paraded and inspected as if at a normal naval shore establishment, while the Commodore's wife organised a supply of 'comfort' from home. They launched a successful camp magazine entitled with stunning originality *The Camp Magazine*, and founded opera and dramatic societies, a camp orchestra, and a football league. They recycled paper to raise funds, and arranged a provision of bread for the men at Doberitz.

Although there was an unwritten agreement meant to prevent escapes, several officers did break out and make their way back to Britain. When this happened, the men were not referred to as 'escapees' but, in order to continue the application of Dutch neutrality, where known as 'refugees'. On their return to the Crystal Palace depot, the 'refugees' were given a congratulatory dinner at which they were encouraged to talk about their experiences. One of the escapees was the youngest officer in the Division – Midshipman the Honourable Vere Harmsworth. Another was Sub-Lt Sydney Flowitt who, on being appointed to the Nelson Battalion, wrote to his former fellow inmates saying –

> We all must, and I know do feel it an unsurpassed honour to be attached to such a Division. I am sorry to say that hundreds of our Antwerp comrades will not share the glories of our return. They have forfeited their lives in the great cause of Freedom, but with what magnificent bravery they gave their lives, will never be told.

Ordinary Seaman A. P. Herbert – with a First in Law from Oxford.

Sub-Lt A. P. Herbert wearing his khaki uniform ('which I resented').

CHAPTER II

From Dorset to the Dardanelles

On its return from Antwerp, the Royal Naval Division faced two major problems. Was it going to survive the attacks of its critics, and, if it did survive, where would it be based?

The first question was not long in being answered. The Divisional Depot at Crystal Palace was authorised by the Admiralty to begin recruiting men to replace the battalions now in Holland and Germany. Officers were to be recruited for the Division from selected civilians between the ages of twenty-five and thirty-five, and from ratings already serving on the 'lower deck' of the Division who had demonstrated their suitability as candidates for a commission on active service at Antwerp. Leading Seaman Robert Shelton, one of only three Hawke Battalion men to escape being interred, received promotion in this manner.

The tented camps at Walmer Down and Betteshanger grew less and less habitable as the winter approached, and the Division was dispersed until a more permanent base was found. The site eventually chosen was on high ground just outside Blandford in Dorset.

Until the new camp was ready, the Royal Marine battalions were sent to Deal, Tavistock, Gravesend, and Browndown, near Gosport. Brigadier-General Charles Trotman of the Royal Marine Light Infantry was appointed as their new Brigade Cdr.

The 2nd Naval Brigade battalions were spread around the major naval shore bases. The Nelson Battalion went into barracks at Portsmouth, the Howe to Portland, the Hood to Plymouth and the Anson to Chatham. Drake, the surviving battalion of the 1st Naval Brigade, went north to do coastal defence duties at Alnwick in Northumberland. They too had a new Brigade Cdr, Brigadier-General David Mercer.

During this period, several of the regular army officers and some of the naval officers left the Division to serve elsewhere. Three new Battalion Commanders were appointed. Lt-Col. Moorhouse of the regular army took over the Anson Battalion; Lt-Col. Everleigh RMLI, the Nelson; and Cdr Collins RNVR, who had been a company commander with the Hood, took command of the Howe.

The newly-established 'Royal Naval Divisional Engineers' had been introduced in mid-September and were based at Ringwould, near Dover. They were commanded by Major Carey of the Royal Engineers and were composed of two Field Companies and one Signal Company. All the recruits were members of one of the three Institutes of Engineers; the Mechanical, the Electrical, and the Civil. The extraordinary high standard of the Divisional Engineers was reflected in the quality of the work they would eventually achieve in often very trying circumstances. In due course, as many as 90 per cent obtained commissions in the Division.

The new base at Blandford on the long, rolling Dorset downs was beginning to take shape. Working parties from the battalions and the Depot set to work building the lines of huts. Sappers from the Divisional Engineers began to build 'Hospital Lane' from the camp to the town itself.

The Division's medical services underwent reorganisation. A medical unit was set up under the command of the Irish rugby international, Captain Francis Casement of the Royal Army Medical Corps, and manned mainly by men of the St John's Ambulance Brigade recruited as Royal Marines. The medical services for the Division when in action were provided by three Field Ambulances commanded by Fleet Surgeon Arthur Gaskell.

A Divisional Train was formed at Crystal Palace to look after supply, transport, and ordnance, the Ordnance Company being led by Lt. Col. Henry William Ward, 6th Viscount Bangor, of the Royal Artillery. As the RND was not to have its own cavalry, a Cyclist Company, commanded by Major A. H. French DSO RMLI, was being raised and trained at Forton Barracks, Gosport. There was still no Divisional Artillery.

By late November, the lines of huts at Blandford were ready to be occupied and, on the 27 November, the Nelson Battalion arrived from Portsmouth to take up residence. The other battalions of the 2nd Brigade, and the Drake of the 1st, quickly followed.

The Division lost no time in getting down to seven weeks of field training. The battalions marched backwards and forwards over the downs day and night. As winter set in, so did the rain, but the marching and training continued despite the whole area being churned into a sea of mud. The seamen launched attacks against the ancient Badbury Rings, and defended nearby Pimpern and several other, small local villages. Trenches were to be assaulted in four lines:

The first two lines carrying rifles and bayonets, the third line carrying dummy bombs, hand grenades and shovels. The fourth line carrying sandbags.

This was followed by instruction in

> rapidity of loading, aiming and firing at heads and shoulders on open ground and from constructed trenches.

Despite all this military-style activity, the RND was determined to hold on to its naval traditions. The White Ensign still fluttered on the 'Quarterdeck' (which had to be saluted when stepping on to it), and bugle calls were the same as those that ordered a ship at sea. Officers and men requested and were granted, 'leave to grow' beards and, when night leave was permitted, they 'went ashore' into Blandford. A 'run ashore' into the small town was often enlivened by a clash with the Military Police, whose zealous attempts to return all the seamen to the camp by eight o'clock at night irked even more than the mud and rain. Officers lived in the 'Wardroom' while ratings 'slung hammocks' on 'mess decks'. An afternoon away from drill was a 'make and mend', and rumours came in the form of 'buzzes' (from the noise emanating from a ship's signal office when Morse code was being used). Nevertheless, after the error made by the Army staff officer, Col. Seely, during the operations around Antwerp, some recognition for the fact that they would be working alongside the Army was made. The Officer of the Day, for example, was referred to as the 'Orderly Officer', who was assisted by the by the 'Orderly Sergeant' rather than by the Duty Petty Officer. The senior Chief Petty Officers of battalions and companies were known as 'Sergeant Majors'.

Two days before Christmas, most of the Division was granted six days leave. One of those who remained behind was Rupert Brooke, by now transferred to the Hood Battalion. In a letter to Violet Asquith, the Prime Minister's daughter, he wrote,

> Never say we're not an hilarious nation. Christmas day in the Naval Division is a revelation. The Battalion CPO, a very fat man, who has been drunk since dawn, is conducting the band in an Irish jig in the middle of the parade-round. He can't beat time, but he dances very convincingly. He's slightly like Pelessier. Half my stokers are dancing half-naked in their huts. They spent the night on cheap gin. The surrounding woods are full of lost and sleeping stokers. I expect most of them froze overnight... I've discovered that this is the site of a Roman camp.

> And drowsy drunken seamen
> Straying belated home,
> Meet with a Latin challenge,
> From sentinels of Rome.

In dreams they doff their khaki,
Put greaves and breastplate on:
In dreams each Leading Stoker,
Turns a Centurion.

In the meantime, the three new battalions were being assembled at the Crystal Palace. Once again, many of the men came from the north-east of England where the reputation of the RND was spread by the families of the miners who had joined in the earliest days. Another, completely contrasting, walk of life was represented when one of the Companies of the Hawke Battalion was made up of volunteer public schoolboys.

Among the new men of the Benbow Battalion was Ordinary Seaman A.P. Herbert, formerly of Winchester and New College, Oxford, who arrived bearing a distinguished 'First' in Jurisprudence. Upon being discovered on the 'lower deck' by officers with whom he had studied at university, Herbert reluctantly accepted a commission as a Sub-Lt in the Anson Battalion – but only after marrying the Commanding Officer's daughter.

The new Hawke Battalion was commanded by Lt-Col. Leslie Wilson DSO, MP, of the Royal Marines, who had once served as a government whip. Col J. Oldfield – another Royal Marine officer – commanded the Benbow Battalion, and Cdr Y. C. M. Spearman, the Collingwood.

Second in command of the Collingwood Battalion was the newly promoted Lt-Com. West – one of the escapers from Belgium. The second in command of the Hawke Battalion had an even more illustrious history. Cdr George Ramsey Fairfax had served with the sea going navy and with the Yeomanry in South Africa. In 1903 he had decided that the machine gun was to play an important part in future warfare and, consequently, financed, entirely out of his own pocket, a machine gun detachment, which he led fighting in Somaliland. Between 1903 and 1904 he had been busy exploring the Blue Nile, but not so busy that he could not find time to be a founder of the Divorce Law Reform Union. From the time the war had started to his joining the RND, he had been the Executive Officer in an armed merchantman. The Hawke's Adjutant was Douglas Jerrold, a descendant of the founder of the magazine, *Punch*, and destined to become the Division's first biographer. One of the Hawke's Company Commanders was Sub-Lt the Honourable Vere Harmsworth, the youngest officer of them all. He was to become known for his absolute loyalty to his men, writing later that his 'whole being is bound up with my men. Nothing else seems to matter.' Clearly, the bright light of individuality that had gleamed through the early battalions was amply reflected in the new.

The War Office, however, was keeping a wary eye on the Division and was soon testing the waters with heavy hints that all land forces should come under their total command. Churchill, on the other hand, went straight to the Minister for War himself – Lord Kitchener on Christmas Eve. He had heard a rumour that naval personnel serving ashore with the Army were to be offered the option of transferring to the Army. The First Lord, seeing such an action on a par with poaching, furiously penned a note to the Minister:

> I cannot for the life of me understand why the various naval units now serving with the Army in France cannot be treated in the same way as naval detachments have always been treated by the Army in Egypt, South Africa, and many other campaigns. On returning to the Admiralty today I have been shown numbers of precedents where small and large detachments of sailors, under the Naval Discipline Act, serving in their own units and under their own officers in charge of guns, in charge of armoured trains, or as infantry, have served all over the world side by side with their military comrades, receiving their orders from the military commander. I cannot understand why the precedents of the past should be thrown over entirely now and the choice put to every sailor of either becoming a soldier or being sent home.

His assault worked, and the idea was, at least for the time being, quietly dropped.

By the end of January 1915, most of the Royal Naval Division had assembled at Blandford. Only the three battalions at Crystal Palace and one Field Company of the Divisional Engineers were missing. In order to provide more of a balance between the brigades, the Nelson Battalion had been transferred to the 1st Brigade under Brigadier-General Mercer.

'Buzzes' were rife as to the Division's future employment – garrisoning St Helena or serving in East Africa were the most persistent. Then orders for overseas duty came through. On 28 January, the Plymouth and Chatham battalions of the Marine Brigade, along with the Brigade Staff, were to sail for an unknown destination, departing from Plymouth on 6 February.

By early February, despite lack of official guidance from the Admiralty, changes in the Divisional uniforms began to suggest an active role was shortly foreseen for the whole Division. Some of the ratings were still wearing navy-blue bell-bottom trousers, and jumpers with sailor's collars, but the dark blue of the Antwerp trenches was about to be completely replaced by khaki. This, however, was still the *Royal Naval* Division and the links with the fleet were to be preserved. Officers kept their buff-coloured rings on their sleeves and wore a bronze version of the naval officer's cap badge. As a concession to the military, with whom they could be expected to be co-operating closely in the field, the insignia of army rank was worn on their shoulder straps. Chief Petty Officers wore a metal version of their naval cap badge, and Petty Officers and junior ratings who had previously worn the bell-bottomed 'square-rig' uniform were issued with army-designed jackets, trousers, and puttees. They retained, however, a khaki version of the naval rating's cap complete with a black 'cap tally' bearing the name of the man's battalion in gold-wire letters. In the first weeks of February, the rumours concerning service abroad were given a boost by the issue of tropical service helmets. Sub-Lt Rupert Brooke complained that his was too small, but upon being ordered to get a haircut, found the problem satisfactorily resolved.

Just in case the Division was not finding enough activities to keep it busy, the First Lord of the Admiralty informed General Paris at his headquarters at Stud House, near Blandford, that he would like to inspect the Division on 17 February. On the appointed day, the battalions mustered at a place known as 'Three Mile Point' on the downs, in an unrelenting deluge. After half an hour, General Paris decided that the weather had made the whole review quite impossible and dismissed the parade. He had reckoned without the First Lord. Churchill turned up and demanded that the Division be prepared for his inspection. The rain continued unabated as Churchill inspected the battalions and watched them wheel and march over the low hills. At the end of the review, he announced that he was well satisfied with the Division and that, in a week's time, on 25 February, the RND was to be singularly honoured – they would be reviewed by His Majesty, King George V.

The following day, Churchill issued orders that the battalions at Blandford were to follow the Plymouth and Chatham Battalions. The destination was still supposed to be a secret, but rumour and speculation had, with unerring accuracy, pinpointed Turkey.

'Figure me celebrating the first Holy Mass in St Sophia since 1453,' wrote Rupert Brooke to his friend, Dudley Ward, with complete disregard for security. Churchill was elated by the scheme (which in the main was his own), and imagined marching the RND into Constantinople. 'That will make them sit up – the swine who snarled at the Naval Division!' he gleefully exclaimed to Violet Asquith at an Admiralty dinner. Not everyone had such a heroic view of things however. The Chief of the Admiralty War Staff, Vice Admiral Henry Oliver, retorted to Captain Richmond, 'It's about time that the Naval Division earned its keep and should go out en masse for the business. They are pretty rotten, but ought to be good enough for the inferior Turkish troops now at Gallipoli; and a bit of work would finish off their training properly and make them fit for service on the continent later.'

On the 25 February, the RND was paraded to meet its sovereign. The weather, so appalling at their last inspection, was now at its best – a perfect Dorset spring day. The First Lord, determined that everything should be perfect on this royal day, closely inspected the battalions before the king, waiting in his car, was allowed to start his review. When Churchill was satisfied, the Royal Standard was broken at the masthead and the king carried out his inspection. A march past followed with each of the Battalion Cdrs at the head of their men. Lt-Col. Quilter's Hood Battalion marched behind their newly acquired silver band – a gift from the people of Dundee, the First Lord's parliamentary constituency.

From the moment the royal visitor departed, the Division busied itself with preparing to leave. Personal kits were brought to completion and packed, equipment was furbished, and ammunition and rations distributed. Unfortunately, the Division had been issued with Lee-Metford rifles that had been obsolete for almost twenty years. Designed to fire black powder bullets, the 1895 introduction of cordite bullets saw the Lee-Metford rifle barrels rapidly wear out. The Army had been issued with the Lee-Enfield rifles, which had been developed to accept the new bullets, but none were available for the Royal Naval Division.

By the evening of 28 February, the RND was ready to leave Blandford, leaving the camp in the hands of the Collingwood Battalion and the Third Field Company of the Divisional Engineers, who were still completing their training.

As the light faded over the scenes they had come to know so well, the battalions marched through Dorset lanes to board trains at Shillingston. By the next morning they were at Avonmouth and soon the sailors were lining the rails of the troopships to catch their last glimpse of England. Although still supposed to be a secret, everyone knew that they were heading for the Eastern Mediterranean, and Turkey.

When the war in Western Europe had broken out at the beginning of August 1914, Turkey had remained neutral. The Ottoman Empire stretched from the Turkish border with Bulgaria in the west to Baghdad and Basra in the east. To the south, the Ottomans' rule held down the Eastern Mediterranean and the eastern side of the Red Sea. Damascus, Jerusalem, Akaba, Medina, and Mecca were all under Turkish rule, and had been since the days of the Crusades. But the foundations of the Ottoman Empire were showing signs of stress. Until the last quarter of the nineteenth century, the empire had stretched as far west as the Serbian borders with Bosnia. But, in 1878, after almost 500 years of Turkish rule, Serbia achieved its independence. In the Balkan war of 1912–1913 the empire lost Albania; the Serbs took Novibazar and Macedonia; the Greeks took back their northern territories, including Salonika; and the Bulgarians advanced southwards to the Aegean. By late 1914, Arabs under Turkish domination were beginning to grow restless and, in October, the Prince of Asir led a revolt supported by the Independent Emir.

At home, the Turks had gone through a stage of political turmoil. Its new rulers, remembering the Balkan war, kept a wary eye on Greece and Romania whose support leaned towards the Allied Powers. To the north and north-east, the Turks were surrounded by another old enemy, Russia, who was already engaged in conflict with Germany.

The Germans had made several overtures to the Turkish Government, but it was the *Goeben* and *Breslau* incident that finally took Turkey to war on the side of the Central Powers.

Long before the war in Europe had begun, the Turkish Government had decided that it needed modern warships to operate with its ageing fleet. The money was raised by public subscription, with villages competing to out do each other in the amounts raised and a medal being awarded for large contributions. The order for the ships was given to Great Britain, and the whole of Turkey followed the building with keen interest. However, with the outbreak of war, the Royal Navy had taken over all ships being built for foreign navies. Acute disappointment and dismay was felt throughout Turkey as the *Reshadieh* and the *Sultan Osman*, for which they had waited so long, were taken from them and renamed HMS *Erin* and HMS *Agincourt* (the latter regardless of any French sensibilities).

On the 3 August 1914, the German battle cruiser, *Goeben*, bombarded the French Algerian port of Phillippeville. At the same time, the German light cruiser, *Breslau,* opened fire on Bone, further along the coast to the east. Having done considerable destruction, the two ships joined forces and headed eastwards through the Mediterranean Sea. By skill and good fortune they managed to avoid the British fleet searching for them and, on 10 August, dropped anchor off Constantinople. The Germans, aware of the Turkish feeling towards Britain over the commandeered warship, offered to sell both the *Goeben* and the *Breslau* to the Turks. The Turkish Government accepted the offer and, as Turkey joined the Central Powers on 28 October, the ten 11-inch guns of the *Goeben* began to bombard the Russian Black Sea port of Odessa.

As early as 31 August, Churchill had strongly advocated an attack on the Gallipoli Peninsula – a tongue of land with the Aegean to the west and the Dardanelles Straits running down its eastern shore. This early plan came to nought as the Greeks, who were to have provided the military strength, had not entered the war. On 25 November, Churchill raised the subject again, but Kitchener would not make troops available. By the end of 1914, both the British Government and the military were divided into 'Westerners', who maintained that the war should only be prosecuted in France, and 'Easterners' who believed that pressure exerted in the Middle East would break the stalemate of the trenches.

During the first days of January 1915, such indecision began to be overtaken by events. Bulgaria's joining the Central Powers, with the subsequent threat to Serbia, appeared imminent, and the Grand Duke Nicholas – the Russian Commander-in-Chief appealed to Britain for a 'demonstration, either naval or military' against Turkey to take pressure off Russian forces in the Caucasus.

On 3 January, the First Lord sent a signal to Vice-Admiral Carden, commanding a squadron of British ships off the Dardanelles. 'Do you think that it is a practicable operation to force the Dardanelles by the use of ships alone?' Carden replied, with some caution, 'I do not think that the Dardanelles can be rushed, but they might be forced by extended operations with a large number of ships.'

The Dardanelles Straits run in a north-easterly direction from the Aegean to the sea of Marmora – a distance of about 41 miles. Never more than 5 miles wide, the straits begin to narrow to about 2 miles wide, 11 miles from the southern, Aegean, entrance. At the Narrows, a point between Chanak on the Asian side and Kilid Bahr on the European, the straits are no more than ¾ mile wide. The southern entrance to the Dardanelles was protected by forts at Kum Kale on the Asian side and at Sedd-el-Bahr on the tip of the Gallipoli Peninsula. As the straits began to narrow, major gun batteries at Messudieh and Dardenos formed the intermediate defence. At the Narrows, the passage was defended by eleven, searchlight supported, forts containing eighty-eight guns among which were included six 14-inch guns manufactured by the German company, Krupps. Easily concealed mobile howitzers moved up and down each side of the straits in-between the forts. Finally, ten lines of contact mines were moored between the Dardanos fort and the Narrows.

The idea of forcing the Dardanelles had taken a firm hold on Churchill's mind. He allowed nothing to get in the way of his conviction that a naval assault could force the passage, destroy the *Goeben* and *Breslau*, and, with Constantinople under the guns of the fleet, take Turkey out of the war. His First Sea Lord, Admiral of the Fleet Lord Fisher, opposed the plan preferring a scheme of his own for an attack in the Baltic or on the Belgian port of Zeebrugge. The prime minister had been asked to arbitrate, and had come down on the side of Churchill and the Dardanelles. Although not prepared to help out with any troops, Kitchener supported the plan. On 28 January, the War Council gave their approval to the naval assault on the straits.

Carden made his first attack on 19 February. His force consisted of one battle-cruiser, *Inflexible*; sixteen battleships, of which four were French under the command of Rear-Admiral Guepratte; and a large collection of smaller vessels including cruisers, destroyers, and minesweeping trawlers.

The attack probed the entrance forts, with only the *Inflexible* and five battleships being employed. The bombardment continued all day with the range coming down to 5,000 yards by late afternoon before the ships pulled back as evening set in. The next day, gales swept the area, preventing a continuation of the assault. The enemy, however, remained in no doubt that an attack upon the straits was imminent.

Four days later, the Plymouth and Chatham battalions of the Royal Marine Brigade arrived at Mudros harbour on the island of Lemnos, to the south of the Gallipoli Peninsula. Lt-Col. Godfrey Matthews (accorded the courtesy title of 'Pasha' after having served in Egypt) of the Plymouth Battalion, and Lt-Col. Cunliffe Parsons of the Chatham, were briefed on the situation, and made their plans accordingly.

On 25 February, the large ships once again shelled the forts at the entrance to the straits, with the bombardment continuing until all the enemy guns were silenced. The next day, naval demolition teams were landed at Sedd-el-Bahr to complete the destruction of the fort and the local gun emplacements. Royal Marines were landed at the same time to provide covering parties. There was very little opposition to the landing, and, when the recall was given, twenty guns had been destroyed. One Marine had been killed and one wounded.

The landings were repeated on 27 February, 1 March, and 2 March. In all, more than fifty guns were destroyed and it seemed that the defences at the entrance to the Dardanelles had been subdued.

Admiral Carden, feeling well pleased with the way that things appeared to be going, decided to advance his attack further up the straits to begin the reduction of the Dardenos and Messudieh forts. As he understood the situation, the only problem he had were the mobile howitzers operating on either side of the straits. With his ships vulnerable to such weapons, he decided that a force of Royal Marines should be landed at Sedd-el-Bahr on the Gallipoli side, and at Kum Kale on the Asian shore. They could deal with the howitzers and provide cover for spotting parties who would control the fire of the ship's guns. The four companies of the Plymouth Battalion were chosen for the task, two companies for each landing.

On the morning of 4 March, the two groups headed for their respective beaches, towed in open boats. Col Matthews had elected to go in with the Kum Kale landings.

The companies approaching Sedd-el-Bahr met little opposition as their boats grounded on the beach, but as they began to move inland, heavy machine guns and small-arms fire opened up, forcing them to stop their advance. The Marines returned the fire, but with little effect against the well-entrenched Turks. After several attempts to move forward, attempts which only succeeded in increasing their casualties, it was decided to withdraw. But even the withdrawal would produce many more casualties unless they were assisted. Upon hearing this, Carden sent the old battleship, *Majestic*, to close in and shell the Turkish fort and trenches. Under this covering fire, the Marines withdrew. Nineteen-year-old

Lt Lamplough noted – 'We had quite a nice little scrap and then they sent a lot of shrapnel over, but they did not get us. A sniper killed one man in the picket boat ... I quite enjoyed the day although we were lucky to get out as we did, three dead and one wounded.'

At Kum Kale, the landings met the same small opposition at first, but once they had pressed on and passed the fort, they came up against large numbers of the enemy, once again securely entrenched. Lt-Col. Matthews led a party forward to find out the strength of the Turks. It quickly became obvious to him that the enemy had learnt his lesson well from the earlier landings, and were now determined to repel any further attacks. As he and his party withdrew to rejoin the main body, they came under concentrated rifle-fire. Doubling across the bullet-swept ground, twenty-two men were killed and a further twenty-two wounded. A general withdrawal was then ordered, which was safely accomplished.

The next day Carden returned to the desultory shelling of the entrance forts while the newly arrived super-dreadnought HMS *Queen Elizabeth* fired her 15-inch shells from the Aegean over the Gallipoli Peninsula at the Narrows forts. Nevertheless, it was clear to all that the tempo of the naval attack was winding down.

On board the transports of the Royal Naval Division, there was an atmosphere of excitement and adventure. Many had seen their first ever foreign lands, and few had known the warmth of a Mediterranean sun. They had called into Malta on 8 March, and by 11 March were sailing into busy Mudros harbour, by now alive with ships of every shape and size. The *Queen Elizabeth* was in port, along with many of Carden's battleships. The French battleships *Henri IV*, *Suffren* and *Charlemagne* lay at anchor surrounded by cruisers, depot ships, destroyers and submarines - all less than 50 miles from the Dardanelles.

The battalions went ashore to march and exercise in order to become acclimatised to the Aegean spring. Each day, the training continued while the great warships slipped their moorings and sailed from Mudros. After just a week on the island the RND sailed at 6 p.m. on 18 March and headed for Gallipoli.

Vice-Admiral Carden had been found medically unfit on 16 March and his place had been taken by his deputy, Vice-Admiral de Robeck, a popular and energetic commander. De Robeck had already agreed to a plan proposed by Carden to make an assault on the Dardanelles and, on the morning of 18 March, he ordered the attack to begin.

Four of the largest British warships, *Queen Elizabeth*, *Agamemnon*, *Lord Nelson*, and *Inflexible*, sailed 6 miles up the Dardanelles. Aiming their guns further up the straits, the ships opened fire on the Narrows forts. On the flanks of this first wave, *Prince George* and *Triumph* poured shells into the intermediate defences of the Dardenos and Messudieh forts. By noon, the return fire from these forts had stopped and de Robeck ordered Guepratte's French squadron forward. The *Gualios, Charlemagne, Bouvet,* and *Suffren* passed through the British line and opened fire on the Narrows forts from 8,000 yards. By early afternoon, the fire from the forts guarding the narrows had all but quietened. De Robeck now ordered the French to withdraw while the British battleships *Vengeance, Irresistible, Albion,* and *Ocean* came up to open fire on the Narrows forts from 10,000 yards. As the French withdrew, the *Bouvet* struck a mine and, within a few minutes, had turned over and sunk with the loss of 640 men.

Undeterred, de Robeck next sent in his minesweeping trawlers to clear a path through the known minefields. But few were even able to get their sweep-gear out. The slow vessels, designed for trawling in the North Sea, made easy targets for the mobile howitzers on either shore and, within minutes, the sheer weight of gunfire forced them to retire. As they did so, *Inflexible,* approaching the area where the *Bouvet* had gone down, also hit a mine and had to limp out of the straits. Shortly afterwards, *Irresistible* was mined and began to drift towards the Asian shore.

With such losses, it seemed to de Robeck that the attack had failed and, at 5 p.m., he ordered the withdrawal of his ships from the straits. It was not gunfire that had halted the attack, but mines – the existence of which the Allies were completely unaware.

A few days earlier, a small Turkish steamer, the *Nousret,* had laid a line of twenty mines near the Asian shore, about 2 miles from the nearest, most southerly, point of the main minefield further up the straits. The mines had been missed by the sweepers who had expected mines only in the centre of the waterway. As the attacking force withdrew, the *Nousret*'s mines claimed another victim. The battleship *Ocean,* while going to the aid of the *Irresistible,* struck one. By the following day both ships had foundered.

At 5.30 the following morning, the transports of the Royal Naval Division arrived off the western coast of Gallipoli. The ships moved slowly down the coast until, off Tekke Burnu – the south-western corner of the peninsula – they met up with the cruiser HMS *Dublin.* The sailors of the RND mustered on the upper decks of their transports wearing their full kit, and with bayonets fixed to their rifles. As the light lifted, they could see Turkish soldiers moving about on the peninsula and it seemed to those looking out to sea as if they were about to face an invasion – but it was not to be. The RND's role been simply to make a threatening gesture on the western coast which – it was hoped – would attract Turkish forces away from the straits where, by now, the naval attack should have succeeded, and the warships been beyond the Narrows. Now, however, having merely waved their bayonets in a threatening manner, there was nothing left to do but return to Mudros.

As the transports sailed through the warships crowded around the entrance to the Dardanelles, many of the passengers saw for the first time the Straits that had held the world's imagination for so many centuries. To the east lay the celebrated city of Troy, and the open Trojan plains swept down to the Hellespont, as the Dardanelles had then been known. The hero, Leander, had swum and drowned in the waters of the straits, Lord Byron had swum across them beyond the Narrows. To the west and south of the peninsula, lay the incomparable 'wine-dark' waters of the Aegean. Again, far to the west, could be seen the purple mountains of Samothrace, gentle peaks that glowed coral-pink in the early dawn light. It was a place for living and breathing – not for death and decay.

After a few days of military manoeuvring on Lemnos, the RND and its transports were ordered to Port Said. It had been decided that the only way to secure the passage through the Dardanelles was to land a large military force on Gallipoli. To be known as the 'Middle East Expeditionary Force', it had as its commander General Sir Ian Hamilton, a brave and elegant leader who enjoyed writing poetry. The only information he had when he left England on 13 March, was a vague set of instructions from Kitchener, a pre-war report on the Dardanelles defences, an out-of-date map of the area, and the handbook of the Turkish Army dated 1912. His force was to consist of the British 29th Division – all regular soldiers from fine regiments; the Australian and New Zealand Army Corps (ANZAC); the French 'Corps Expeditionnaire de l'Orient' under General d'Amade, made up of French territorial and Senegalese troops; and the Royal Naval Division minus the three battalions still training at Blandford. Hamilton noted in his diary that he considered the RND to consist of 'an excellent type of officer and man, under a solid commander – Paris'.

The main reason for the RND's move to Port Said was that the ships had been stored in a haphazard manner and required to be re-stowed before any landing could be undertaken. The situation was not helped by the, often strange, collection of stores and equipment with which the Division had managed to surround itself. Machine guns of ancient and modern patterns, Rolls Royce armoured cars, pack ponies, motor cycles, and the nearest thing the Division had to artillery, one 6-inch howitzer, two twelve-pounder guns, and three 4.7-inch guns mounted on pontoons and designed for use on large rivers – a geographical feature that was singularly lacking on the peninsula.

The Division camped on the sands outside Port Said while the ships were being re-stored and leave was allowed to visit the town. Strict instructions were given to the sailors not to go into the Arab quarter, but few of the men had come this far without the urge to delve into the mysterious Orient – and such instructions were frequently forgotten in the heat and confusion of a 'run ashore'.

On 1 April, General Paris received orders that he was to send a detachment from the Division to guard a section of the Suez Canal. Apart from the threat of a Turkish attack on the waterway itself, rumour had it that the local Senussi tribesmen could not be trusted and their recent activities were giving cause for concern. Half of each of the Nelson, Drake, Anson, and Howe battalions combined to make a composite force under the 2nd RN Brigade commander, Brigadier-General Mercer. They left by train that evening.

The remainder of the Division were inspected by General Sir Ian Hamilton on 3 April. He wrote in his diary, 'The RND marched past very well indeed.' Praise indeed for a body of men who, to a man, considered parade drill to be one of life's irritants. While with the Division, the Commander-in-Chief carried out a promise that he had made to Violet Asquith. He offered Sub-Lt Rupert Brooke a place on his staff. The young poet declined the offer and the General wrote in his diary, 'Young Brooke replied – as a prex chevalier would naturally reply – he realised the privileges that he was foregoing, but he felt bound to do the landing shoulder-to-shoulder with his comrades.'

By 5 April, the 29th Division transports were arriving at Alexandria and, much to their disgust, the Anson Battalion, believing that they would miss the landings, were sent to assist the 29th in restoring their ships.

The remainder of the RND, their equipment now stowed correctly, sailed for Mudros on 8 and 9 April. They arrived in the early morning of 16 April and were promptly redirected to Trebuki Bay on the Greek Island of Skyros, there to await their orders for the landings.

It was intended to use any time remaining to get as much practice as possible at landing on beaches and moving over country. Consequently, day after day, the battalions landed, marched inland, and staged mock attacks on hill and ridges, planting Union Flags on the crest of each hill as they were 'taken'.

There was little time to relax, but the whole Division turned out to cheer their favourite when Sub-Lt Asquith challenged the newly-promoted Lt Cdr Freyberg to a swimming race back to the ships. Freyberg won the race by a narrow margin, but the loser had no reason to feel humbled, the victor had been a national champion.

Not everyone, however, felt in the peak of condition. During a lunch break between exercises Sub-Lt Rupert Brooke, who had felt unwell for several days, turned to Lt Gamage and said, 'What a lovely spot to be buried in.' They were sitting in an olive grove that formed part of a lonely valley sloping gently down to the sea. Shortly afterwards, Brooke, unable to stand, was taken to a French hospital ship in Trebuki Bay. The next day, this most English of the New Georgian poets died of acute septicaemia. It was 23 April – St George's Day. Only a few days before, on Easter Sunday, Dean Inge had read one of Brooke's poems from the pulpit of St Paul's Cathedral. The poem had been reported in *The Times* and had been taken to the heart of Brooke's fellow countrymen.

If I should die, think only this of me:
That there's some corner of a foreign field
that is for ever England. There shall he
in that rich earth a richer dust concealed;
A dust whom England bore, shaped, made aware,
Gave, once, her flowers to love, her ways to roam,
A body of England's, breathing English air,
Washed by the rivers, blest by suns of home.

And think, this heart, all evil shed away,
A pulse in the Eternal mind, no less
Gives somewhere back the thoughts by England given.
Her sights and sounds; dreams happy as her day;
And laughter, learnt of friends; and gentleness,
In hearts at peace, under an English heaven.

His grave was dug by men of his own platoon and his body carried by Freyberg and Sub-Lts Dodge, Asquith, Browne, Lister, and Kelly. They buried him on a spring day in his olive grove, beneath the Skyros mountains, the air fragrant with thyme and sage. As the firing party, commanded by Lt Shaw-Stewart, fired their salute, the sound of the volleys rang through the ancient hills. A remarkable collection of young men paid their final tribute to the most remarkable of them all.

When he heard of Brooke's death, Sir Ian Hamilton wrote in his diary, 'Death grins at my elbow. I cannot get him out of my thoughts. He is fed up with the old and the sick – only the flower of the flock will serve him now, for God has started a celestial spring cleaning, and our star is to be scrubbed bright with the blood of our bravest and our best.' Churchill's obituary of Brooke appeared in *The Times* on 26 April, 'Rupert Brooke is dead.' Aubrey Herbert, Member of Parliament for the Southern division of Somerset, and liaison officer serving with the Army wrote –

He who sang of dawn and evening,
English glades and light of Greece,
Changed his dreaming into sleeping,
left his sword to rest in peace.
Left his visions of the springtime,

Holy Grail and Golden Fleece,
Took the leave that has no ending,
Till the waves of Lemnos cease.

But the war does not stop because a light flickers, fades, and dies, no matter how brightly it may have once shone. The day after Brooke's burial, the American Sub-Lt Dodge left for Mudros with 300 ratings from the Hood and Howe battalions to take up beach duties with the landing forces. Lt-Col. Moorhouse's Anson Battalion, on completion of restoring the 29th Division's transports, learned to their delight that they were to land alongside the army. The Plymouth Battalion of the Royal Marine Brigade was also given the honour of being among the first to land on the peninsula.

As the remainder of the Royal Naval Division sailed on the evening of 24 April, cheering ring out across the waters of Trebuki Bay – cheering that found an echo in Mudros harbour where the 29th Division, with the Plymouth and Anson battalions in company, was slipping out to sea and turning towards Gallipoli.

CHAPTER III

Feint and Fortitude – The Gallipoli Landings

On the eve of the landings, General Sir Ian Hamilton's Expeditionary Force numbered over 75,000 men. The largest proportion was made up of 30,000 men of the Australian and New Zealand Army Corps (ANZAC) under their British General, Sir William Birdwood. The 29th Division, commanded by General Hunter-Weston (known to his troops as 'Hunter-Bunter'), had 18,000 men, and General d'Amade's French and French Colonial troops also numbered 18,000. Finally, there were the 10,000 seamen and marines of General Paris's Royal Naval Division.

The Commander-in-Chief's plan of attack was to land the 29th Division, with detachments of the RND, on the toe of the peninsula, with the ANZAC troops landing at Gaba Tepe, about 12 miles up the western coast. The RND were to make a distracting show of strength in the Gulf of Xeros off Bulair on the narrow neck of the peninsula, as the French made an equally important feint by landing on the Asiatic coast at Kum Kale. Once the 29th Division had secured a foothold, the RND and the French would withdraw and join the forces on Gallipoli.

General Birdwood's ANZACs were to advance across country to take the high ground at Sari Bair, with its dominating positions Chanuk Bair and Koja Chemen Tepe, and to Mal Tepe, a further high point overlooking the Dardanelles.

There were five different places for Hunter-Weston's forces to make their landings. 'V' beach, at Sedd-el-Bahr, and 'W' beach, a mile westward of Cape Helles, were the targets for the main force. To the westward of 'W' beach, around Tekke Burnu, and less than a mile up the western coast, a subsidiary landing was to take place at 'X' beach to attack the right flank of the Turkish front line as it came under pressure from the south. Two remaining landings were to take place behind the Turkish lines in order to strike at the enemy as he retreated from the frontal attack. The first was 'S' beach, on the northern sands of Morto Bay, 1 ½ miles up the eastern coast from Cape Helles. The second was at 'Y' beach,

3 miles north of 'X' beach. Once the main landings had been secured, the chief objective was to be a prominent hill, Achi Baba. Over 700 feet high, and six miles from Cape Helles, the hill dominated the low ground at the southern end of the peninsula.

Most of the troops would land on the peninsula from open ship's boats towed by naval cutters and pinnaces. Many of the crews for these boats were made up from detachments of the Hood and Howe battalions. The 'Y' beach troops, including the Plymouth Battalion, were to be put ashore by trawlers.

On 'V' beach, a bold new initiative was to be put to the test. An old collier, the *River Clyde*, had exits cut in to her side. The ship, filled with troops, was to be run aground, bows first, onto the beach. Naval parties, assisted by a steam hopper, would then connect a line of lighters from the ship to the shore, ramps would be lowered, the exits opened, and the troops would emerge to race along the lighters to the shore. This scheme was the brainchild of Cdr Unwin, who had been given the command of the ship during the attack.

On 25 April, as the dawning sun began to light the Trojan Plain, soldiers and seamen began to take their place in the invasion craft. Engines rattled into life, and towing lines tautened. Soon, bow waves etched their herring-bone patterns on an amethyst sea as the boats headed for the hostile shore.

Off Gaba Tepe, things were already beginning to go wrong. The landing boats, tied in 'tows' of three behind a steam pinnace, with the rear boat of each tow under the command of young midshipmen, had left the ships at 3.30 a.m. in the pitch black of a moonless sky, and approached the coast in a line-a-breast formation. Their orders were to 'keep station' on the boat immediately to their port side. Unfortunately, Cdr Charles Dix, in charge of the pinnaces and their tows, was on the most northerly pinnace and found that the boats on his starboard side were closing with him, forcing him northward. In the darkness, the officer in charge of the third pinnace from the south had chosen a wrong landing site, almost 2 miles north of the intended landing, and began to nudge the pinnaces to the north further and further to port. Consequently, all the accompanying steamers, keeping station as instructed, followed his lead and, when the boats were cast off from the pinnaces, the troops found themselves facing the black wall of a cliff-lined cove named Ari Burnu. Just at that moment, one of the pinnace funnels flared with 3 feet of flame and sparks. If the Turks were not previously aware of the approach of the boats, they could not fail to see the bright blaze, which roared skywards for what seemed an eternity. The first voice to be heard in the silence that followed was that of Cdr Dix – 'Tell the Colonel that the damn fools have taken us a mile too far north.'

The young midshipmen in charge of the boats looked like schoolboys, and attracted the scorn of the ANZACs who considered them to be little more than children. But when sustained bursts of machine gun fire suddenly erupted from the cliffs above them, the soldiers crouched down in the boats as the midshipmen sat upright, and even stood, to urge the rowing seamen on towards the beach. Major Drake-Brockman, who was to become a senior Australian judge, recorded that, as the boat grounded on the beach, the tiny red-haired boy who sat in the stern of his boat, pulled out a pistol, clambered over the backs of the soldiers, and jumped ashore shouting in a high-pitched voice, 'Come on, my lads! Come on, my lads!' He reached the base of the cliffs before realising that, in his urge to get at the enemy, he had to get his boat back to his ship.

The beach at this spot led directly to a maze of gullies surrounded by high ground, and every inch was covered by Turkish machine guns. As Birdwood's soldiers began to advance against the enemy, the name 'Anzac Cove' began to etch its name into military history.

On 'S' beach, the men of the 2nd Battalion of the South Wales Borderers landed with little opposition. The light casualties made an immediate advance possible, and they closed quickly, with the Turks guarding the northern slopes of Morto Bay. After a short, sharp engagement, the enemy withdrew, leaving the Borders in possession of three lines of trenches. Their first objective attained, they then prepared to attack the Turkish flank as the enemy withdrew in the face of the assault from the south.

As the 2nd Battalion of the Royal Fusiliers headed for 'X' beach, HMS *Implacable* fired shell after shell over their heads and on to the cliffs that dominated the beach. The naval gunners had done their work well, and the Turks overlooking the beach were driven back. Once the cliffs had been scaled, the fusiliers came under frontal fire, but held their ground until reinforced by the Inniskillings and the Border Regiment. Despite this, the Turks increased the pressure causing the last reserves to be brought forward – 'C' and 'D' companies of the Anson Battalion under the command of the Dutch internment 'refugee', the newly promoted Lt Cdr Grant.

'W' beach was a 250-yard breach in the tall cliffs between, to the west, Tekke Burnu, and Cape Helles to the east. Never more than 40 yards in depth, the beach had a wide gully down its centre. The surrounding cliffs and the gully sides were all heavily entrenched and packed with Turkish soldiers. Barbed wire had been strung across the beach and beneath the water at the edge of the sea.

Against these defences, towed in open boats and rowed ashore for the last few yards, came the 1st Battalion of the Lancashire Fusiliers and 'B' Company of the Anson Battalion. Landing with the Ansons was their commanding officer, Lt-Col. Moorhouse.

Even as the boats approached the beach, they came under a storm of fire but, with great courage, the fusiliers leapt from the boats and immediately engaged the Turks. By good fortune, the boats on the left of the landings had drifted from the others and discharged their soldiers onto a small ledge beneath the cliffs of Tekke Burnu. Also advancing immediately, they opened a flanking fire on the Turks which enabled the frontal attack to be pressed even more firmly. By 9.30, all the trenches along the sides of the gully had been taken, and the beach – to be later given the name 'Lancashire Landing' – was in the hands of the invaders.

While the soldiers were consolidating their newly won positions, the sailors from the Anson Battalion returned to the beach to help with the landing of the 4th Worcestershire and the 1st Essex battalions. For the remainder of the day, the Ansons, later assisted by men from their own 'A' company, cleared the beach of barbed wire, landed stores, and buried the dead. In the latter task, they were assisted by the Reverend H. C. Foster, the 2nd Naval Brigade's Anglican Chaplain – the first clergyman of his denomination to land on Gallipoli. As at 'X' beach, the Ansons, with a small detachment from the Hood and Howe battalions, were the only reserves available for the expected Turkish counter-attack.

At 'Y' beach, the landings were commanded by Lt-Col. Matthews of the RM Plymouth Battalion. The trawlers had discharged the marines and soldiers beneath tall cliffs stretching along that part of the coast but, luckily, no opposition appeared. Even the clifftops were achieved without casualties but, just as they prepared to advance, their left flank came under fire from about 1,000 yards. A defensive flank was formed from two companies of marines, and the remainder advanced 500 yards to the edge of Gully Ravine, a deep, wide, dried-up watercourse that ran almost parallel to the coast for more than 2 miles.

Spreading out on a wide front, the 1st Battalion of the King's Own Scottish Borderers under the command of Lt-Col. Archibald Koe, two companies of marines, and one company of the 2nd South Wales Borderers entered the gully. A few isolated Turkish units defending the ravine opened fire, but were quickly subdued and prisoners were taken. The advance came to a halt on the crest of a low ridge almost 300 yards beyond Gully Ravine. From this position, looking across the peninsula, they could see small groups of the enemy making their way southwards towards the action at Cape Helles. To their left, on the lower slopes of Achi Baba, the small village of Krithia lay in full view.

Matthews sent a report of his position to General Hunter-Weston. For two hours he waited for a reply. None came. Perhaps fortunately, Matthews was unaware that General Hamilton, cruising around the Cape Helles area in HMS *Queen Elizabeth*, had seen the success of his landing and had signalled Hunter-Weston saying, 'Would you like to get more men ashore at 'Y' Beach. Trawlers are available.' The signal was ignored for several hours before Hunter-Weston replied rejecting the idea of reinforcements. The 29th Division's commander believed that the show of force in the eastern Aegean was part of a plan to cajole and bribe

Bulgaria to enter the war on the Allies' side. With that achieved, two key events were likely to follow – the Greeks and Romanians would also join the Allies, and a large Allied force could be landed at the Bulgarian port of Dedeagatch (later, the Greek port of Alexandroupolis) ready for an invasion of Turkey. Hunter-Weston had opposed the whole idea of a landing on Gallipoli. He had written to his wife before the landings saying, 'The chances of success being so small and the consequences of defeat being so disastrous, I expressed that view to the C-in-C, but he decided otherwise.' Hunter-Weston had a point to prove.

Unwilling to face an unsupported counter-attack against the ridge, Matthews then ordered his troops to reduce the extended line and to fall back to the eastern edge of Gully Ravine. Repeatedly, messages were sent to Hunter-Weston informing the General of the situation, but none received a reply. By 3 p.m., the new position was secure, and the troops prepared to support any advance from the south. But, by early evening, there was still no sign of either a hoped-for advance, or of any reinforcements to further secure the advantageous position behind the right flank of the enemy's front lines. Then, with the fading light, came the first signs of the expected opposition. Facing machine gun and small-arms fire, Matthews decided to pull back his right flank to the clifftops, ready to face any assault from the south.

'V' beach, at Cape Helles, had been the easiest to defend against an enemy landing. About 350 yards wide and curving round in a natural amphitheatre, the slopes to the rear of the beach were riddled with deep and extensive trenches and protected by wire. On the invaders' right as they landed sat the squat, ruined, Sedd-el-Bahr fort, its walls and towers shattered by the marines of the Plymouth Battalion during their landings nearly two months earlier. To the left a cliff rose steeply while in the centre the well-protected ground sloped more gently to the same height as the cliffs. Machine guns were placed on the cliff top, on the crest of the rising round, and in the small village between the rising ground and the fort. In the centre, two pom-pom guns, capable of firing belt-fed 1-pound bullets at the rate of 100 per minute, looked over the beach. Wherever a landing was made on 'V' beach, it would come under intense close-range small-arms fire. The sole shelter the attackers would be able to find was a sandbank, no more than a few feet high at its highest point, that stretched along parts of the beach.

On the morning of 25 April 1915, six lines of open boats and the steamer *River Clyde* headed straight for the enemy, alert and waiting at 'V' beach.

The left of the attacking force was made up of six pinnaces, each towing four cutters. Each cutter contained twenty-five men, a total in all of 600 soldiers and sailors. The majority of the troops in the towed cutters were from three companies of the 1st Battalion of the Dublin Fusiliers, the remainder being the Anson Battalion's 4th Platoon under the command of Lt Denholm.

Many of the boat's crews were men detached from the Hood and Howe Battalions.

To the right of the open boats steamed the *River Clyde*, carrying the remaining company of the 1st Dublin Fusiliers; the 1st Battalion of the Royal Munster Fusiliers; the 2nd Battalion of the Hampshire Regiment; 'A' Company of the Anson Battalion, led by Lt-Com. Smallwood; and the Anson's 13th Platoon under Sub-Lt Tisdall.

Lt Cdr Josiah Wedgwood, a Boer War veteran and Member of Parliament for Stoke-on-Trent, was in command of the Royal Naval Division's armoured cars. He had eighteen Bradford-manufactured Scott motorcycles loaded on the forecastle of the *River Clyde* ready to be deployed with their sidecar mounted Maxim machine guns once the landing had been secured. There he was joined, at his own request, by Sub-Lt the Honourable Arthur Coke. Coke, the second son of the 3rd Earl of Leicester, was in command of a small machine gun detachment and had pleaded with Wedgwood to be allowed to mount his Maxim machine guns at the bows and on the bridge of the ship. With his guns in position, Coke told Wedgwood, 'This is to be my seat in the stalls, and many a man now in England would give £1000 for it.'

The towed boats and the old collier arrived at the beach at almost the same moment, the *River Clyde* grounding on the sand as the cutters cast off from the pinnaces. As the Dublins and the Ansons began to jump from the boats and splash through the shallow water, a devastating fire broke out from the fort and the defending trenches. Within seconds, scores of men were cut down and several boats were full of the dead who had not even got their feet wet. The edge of the beach was whipped to a pink foam by the hail of bullets and, barely minutes after the first cutter had cast off its tow, more than 400 men had been killed, were drowning as their heavy equipment dragged them beneath the surface, or were dying on the blood-soaked sands. Others, in small groups, charged across the beach and, against all odds, entered the ruined Sedd-el-Bahr fort only to be cut down at the muzzles of the defending guns.

The *River Clyde*, which should have been landing its troops at the same time as the cutters reached the shore, had found difficulty in securing the bridge of lighters between the ship's side and the beach. The running tide, although not strong, was making the task more difficult as the pontoons attempted to drift apart. The ship's captain, Cdr Unwin, Midshipman Drewry, and several seamen, jumped into the water and swam from light to lighter securing the pontoon ropes. When, eventually, Unwin was satisfied that the lighters were ready, he shouted for the troops to begin their dash for the shore. At this, the Dublins, the Munsters, Hampshires and the Ansons left the shelter of the ship's side and ran down the ramps in a race against death. Groups of men, encouraging each other onwards, tore along the pontoons only to be immediately reduced to a tiny number of survivors huddling for shelter beneath the precarious protection of the sandbank. Behind them, the dead and wounded piled up on the lighters or toppled over the sides to sink beneath the water. Unwin and his sailors ignored the fearful conditions and concentrated on keeping wounded men afloat or dragging them off the bullet-swept pontoons. On several occasions, the ropes holding the pontoons were cut by machine gun fire and Unwin, Drewry, and Able Seaman Williams held them together until they could be re-secured.

Among the earliest of the men trying to get ashore was the American Sub-Lt Dodge of the Hood Battalion, who had been appointed Assistant Naval Landing Officer for 'V' beach. As he sprinted along the pontoons, crouched over and jumping over the bodies of fallen soldiers, he was hit in the arm by a bullet. He kept running and gained the beach, throwing himself behind the cover of the sandbank. Seconds later he was joined by Lt Cdr Smallwood, also wounded in the dash for shore.

Waiting his turn to run along the pontoon bridge was Sub-Lt Arthur St Clair Tisdall of the Anson Battalion. Tisdall, the son of a missionary, was a rugby-playing classical scholar who could speak fluent Latin and Persian as a child. Now, as he stood ready to disembark, he could hear desperate cries for help coming from the wounded men on the beach. Looking down, Tisdall saw a small boat drifting by the pontoons. He jumped into the water and swam to the boat and, using it as a shield, attempted to push it towards the shore. It was, however, too much for one man to manage, and he made little headway. Seeing this, Leading Seaman Malia jumped into the sea and joined Tisdall. Together, they began to push the craft inshore, ducking their heads as bullets repeatedly struck the boat, sending splinters flying through the air. Around them the water, by now red with blood, foamed as it was lashed by a deluge of Turkish firing. Upon reaching the beach, they crawled up the sand to rescue the wounded, dragging them back to the boat and rolling them over the gunwales to lie in the flimsy protection of the boat's bottom. When they had collected as many as they could manage, the two men swam back to the ship, pushing the boat ahead of them. Back alongside the *River Clyde*, the wounded were taken from the boat and into the protection of the ship as Tisdall and Malia struck out once again for the beach. Soon they had returned with more casualties. As the wounded were being unloaded, Chief Petty Officer Perring took the place of Malia. On his return, Tisdall completed two more rescues, assisted by Leading Seaman Curtis and Leading Seaman Parkinson, before the senior officers present called a halt to the landings. There was little to be gained from the continuing carnage. The forays from the *River Clyde* were stopped and the remaining troops held within the safety of the ship's hull. Ashore, men pressed against the sandbank would have to remain where they were until darkness allowed them to be reinforced, the only firepower keeping the enemy from falling on them being Sub-Lt Coke's machine guns firing from the ship's forecastle.

So ended a day of both carnage and courage at 'W' and 'V' beaches. At Lancashire Landing, six Victoria Crosses had been earned. So widespread had the courage been seen, that the decorations were awarded by ballot. At 'V' beach, Cdr Unwin, Sub-Lt Tisdall, Midshipman Drewry, and Able Seaman Williams were all awarded the Victoria Cross, Tisdall and Williams posthumously. Leading Seamen Malia, Curtis, and Parkinson were awarded the Conspicuous Gallantry Medal in company with CPO Perring who was also promoted to commissioned rank. Sub-Lt Coke, with his machine guns from the Division's armoured cars, had not paid £1,000 for his 'seat in the stalls' – he paid, instead, with his life.

More than 30 miles to the north of the Cape Helles landings, the early morning light of 25 April had revealed a sight that caused a shock to the Turkish troops guarding the Bulair lines. Off the western coast of the narrow neck of the peninsula, in the Gulf of Xeros, a large fleet of ships had appeared overnight. It was the Royal Naval Division with their transports in an attempt to lure Turkish troops away from the Cape Helles area. Accompanying the troopships was the battleship HMS *Canopus* carrying General Paris and his staff, the cruisers *Dartmouth* and *Doris*, and the destroyers *Kennet* and *Jed*.

The eleven transports and the *Canopus* remained well out to sea, out of range of any guns that the Turks might bring to bear, while the two cruisers closed with the shore and began a bombardment of the defences. As the morning progressed, and the enemy refused to reply to the shelling, General Paris sent two of his staff officers, Antwerp veterans, Cols Ollivant and Richardson, across to the *Kennet*. Taking the destroyer close inshore, they scanned the beaches for signs of the Turkish army. As they did so, they heard the rushing sound of a small artillery shell as it passed astern and exploded in the sea some way off. No more shells followed, and they reported back to Paris that, apart from the single incident, there seemed to be little sign of life on the shore. Such news was disconcerting. To succeed, the feint had to draw as many of the enemy troops as possible away from the southern end of the peninsula and, so far, there appeared to be almost no enemy activity in the area. A seaplane was launched from the *Doris* and flown along the Bulair lines. It returned with the news that the trenches were empty. The defences appeared to be deserted.

The truth of the situation, however, was somewhat different. When the fleet had first been sighted off the coast there had been few troops in the region but, before long, excited messages began to arrive at the Turkish headquarters and rapidly came to the attention of the Turkish army's Commander-in-Chief, the German general, Liman von Sanders. Suddenly convinced that the Allied attack would fall upon northern Gallipoli, he dashed northwards and set up his command headquarters on a high point of the Bulair lines. Even before his arrival, orders had been issued, and one division was marching up from the south, soon to be followed by another. Two further divisions, stationed at the town of Gallipoli on the Dardanelles coast, were put on alert.

Unaware of this activity, General Paris remained concerned at the apparent lack of an enemy along the shore facing his ships. He felt that the feint had to become more aggressive before the Turks would be duped into believing that the landings were about to take place off Bulair. So, with the setting sun lighting up the mountain peaks of Samothrace behind them, the RND transports moved in closer to the beach. As the last light began to fade, onlookers from the shore saw the ship's boats being swung out and lowered to the water. Filled with men wearing full kit and sun helmets, and carrying rifles, the boats began to pull for the shore as darkness settled over the Gulf of Xeros. But, within a few hundred yards of the shore, the order was given to return to the ships. The Turks had not attempted a defence.

As the mock invasion returned, another, more spectacular, demonstration was being put in to operation. 'A' Company of the Hood Battalion, on board the transport *Grantully Castle,* had been ordered to make a landing on the coast. Once ashore, they were to fire machine guns, rifles, and flares in a manner that would lead the Turks into believing that a full-scale landing was being carried out. One outcome, however, seemed certain. It was felt that, with the effort already put in to the feint, the Turks would have begun to mass troops along the Bulair lines and the low hills behind the beaches. The chances of the Hood's 'A' Company surviving the inevitable heavy retaliation that could be expected were slim indeed.

It was this, almost certainty of annihilation that prompted the New Zealander, Lt Cdr Freyberg, to propose a modification to the plans for 'A' Company. Having twice been the New Zealand 100 yards swimming champion, he suggested that the Hood men should approach the shore in their boats but, some way off, he would go over the side, swim ashore, and let off a series of flares along the beach. As the flares were ignited, his men could open up with their weapons to tempt the enemy. If the original plan could be expected to work, there was no reason why his modified one would not. After a short discussion among the senior officers, Freyberg's scheme carried the day.

Whilst his men took their places in the boats, Freyberg prepared himself for the task ahead. Stripped down to a pair of shorts, he was first covered from head to toe in lampblack to reduce the chances of being spotted by the Turks. Next, his body was smeared all over with a thick layer of grease as a protection against the cold – there was a strong possibility of a frost that night. In a waterproof canvas bag, Freyberg placed three oil flares, five calcium lights, a signalling lantern, and a small revolver. A knife was attached to his belt and, on his wrist, he wore a luminous compass. Thus equipped, he took his place in one of the cutters and, towed by the *Dartmouth*'s steam pinnace, Hood's 'A' Company headed towards the darkened shore.

3 miles from the beach, the pinnace cast off, the oars were shipped, and boats rowed closer in. The darkness made it impossible to see where the coastline lay and so, after some time on the oars, a guess was made and it was decided that the boats should not get any nearer to the land. Freyberg had no way of knowing that he was actually still 2 miles from the shore as he slipped over the side of his cutter and began to swim. It was forty minutes past midnight.

After swimming hard for one and a half hours in the bitterly cold water, Freyberg touched bottom and crawled up the beach. He listened for any sounds of the enemy, but nothing could be heard. Taking one of the flares from his waterproof bag, he stuck it into the sand and lit it. Running along the beach to escape the bright light of the flare, he returned to the water as machine gun fire opened up from the cutters. Moments later, the warships began to shell the area.

To a background of heavy detonations and the chatter of small arms, Freyberg swam 300 yards along the coast. Leaving the water once again, he lit another flare and, this time, decided to stay close-by to watch if any Turks appeared on the scene. None came, so he decided to take a look further inland. He knew that trenches had been spotted behind the beach at that point and, crawling up a long slope, he began his search. Shivering from the cold, Freyberg came upon the apparent trenches. They were, he quickly recognised, just dummies, consisting of no more than a couple of feet of earth thrown up in front of shallow ditches.

Returning to the beach, Freyberg lit the last of his flares. All the firing from the cutters had stopped and, looking out to sea, he could see nothing in the intense blackness. His options were limited. He could remain where he was and wait until dawn when he would be able to see the ships, but that might mean the risk of capture or being shot by the Turks as he swam through the water. Alternatively, he could re-enter the water immediately and strike out into the dark, hoping to come across one of his boats. Freyberg took to the water and began to swim.

He was still swimming towards the ships as the sun rose above the Gallipoli hills when he was sighted by a cutter commanded by Lt Nelson, the polar biologist. The exhausted, frozen man was hauled inboard and taken back to the *Grantully Castle*. Freyberg had been away for more than nine hours, earning a well-deserved Distinguished Service Order in the process.

At the toe of the peninsula, the Cape Helles landings had not passed the night without incident. As darkness fell over 'V' beach, the troops had left the *River*

Clyde and made their way across the bridge of lighters to join the survivors of the day's bloody assault. In the shelter of the darkness, they took up positions and prepared themselves for a dawn advance against a well-entrenched enemy just a few yards ahead of them.

During the same night, the trenches held above 'W' beach had been subjected to a succession of attacks by the Turks. The fighting had often been so heavy that beach parties from the Anson Battalion had been rushed up the gully and into the trenches to help drive the enemy back with the bayonet. There were no reserves and no support. Behind the trenches were just the dead, the wounded, doctors, and chaplains. But, despite the ferocity of the attacks, by the morning, the trenches were still in British hands.

Up the western coast at 'Y' beach, Lt-Col. Matthews' force came under several heavy attacks during the night. Private William Parnham, serving as Matthews' orderly, recorded that the Turks made 'continuous savage attacks, each of which ended in hand-to-hand fighting in our own position, wrestling, kicking and punching.' By 5.30 a.m., almost half of Matthews' men were dead or wounded. Then, with the dawning sun brightening the Asian skies behind them, Turkish troops charged in strength at the left of Matthews' line. Striking at the junction of the Marines and the King's Own Scottish Borderers, the attackers broke through and, again, savage hand-to-hand fighting broke out. A desperate counter-attack forced the Turks back at the point of the bayonet, and the line was reformed. The enemy's charge had been their final attempt to dislodge the invaders, and they began to draw back leaving only artillery fire to harass the soldiers and Marines.

Matthews took stock of his situation. His casualties were high, but probably no higher than could have been expected. The enemy had withdrawn having failed to remove him, and the remainder of his force were steady, though short of water and ammunition. Nevertheless, the position could not be held for much longer without reinforcements. His troops were far too tired to withstand much more of the enemy attacks. Matthews signalled his summing up of the situation to the warships now covering his landing. In his message, he pointed out that, without reinforcements and supplies, he would be forced to withdraw. Having sent the signal, Matthews set about inspecting the left flank of his position. He was completely unaware that General Hamilton had suggested to Hunter-Weston that the six battalions of French infantry now proceeding to Cape Helles should be landed in support at 'Y' Beach. Just as with Hamilton's earlier suggestions for reinforcements, Hunter Weston ignored his superior once again and sent the French to 'W' Beach.

After about half an hour spent in checking his marines' conditions and giving them as much encouragement as he could muster, Matthews' attention was drawn urgently to the centre and right of his line. To his utter shock and consternation, Matthews saw his men, apparently of their own accord, withdrawing to the beach – indeed, some were already in boats being taken back to the ships. It turned out that his signal had been misread (perhaps deliberately, if Hunter-Weston was involved) as an urgent request for withdrawal, a request that had been acted upon promptly while he was inspecting his left flank. It was too late to restore the position and, with no news, no orders, and no reserves, Matthews had no other choice but to oversee the final departure from 'Y' beach with himself as the last man to leave.

'Y' Beach had probably been the most successful of all the landings, and Hamilton had been right to include it in his overall plan. If his suggestions for reinforcements, and Matthews' requests to be supported, had been acted upon, 'Y' Beach could have been the key to success at Gallipoli. But Hamilton was too much of a gentleman to demand obedience, and Hunter-Weston needed to prove his point.

At 1 a.m. on the morning of 26 April, as Freyberg was swimming towards the beach, General Paris was ordered to send the Drake Battalion down to Cape Helles to provide reinforcements for the landings. They came ashore on 'W' Beach at 8.30 and Cdr Campbell took them up the gully to take their places in the line with the 87th Brigade. The Ansons, who, in-between manning the trenches, had spent the night organising the beach to prepare for further landings were sent to assist at 'V' Beach. There, the British had pushed the Turks back and were in possession of Sedd-el-Bahr fort and the adjoining village. The Ansons were to assist the five French battalions who, after their demonstration at Kum Kale, were about to land on 'V' beach to take their place on the right of the line as it advanced up the peninsula. Among those working towards this aim was Sub-Lt Dodge who, despite being wounded as he dashed ashore from the *River Clyde*, had insisted on remaining at his post as Assistant Naval Landing Officer. His determination and activities that day and night had earned him the Distinguished Service Cross (which the *New York Times* report elevated to a Distinguished Service Order), but his injuries meant that he had to be invalided home.

To the north, the fighting at the newly named 'Anzac Cove' had been raging all night, and General Birdwood's casualties had been severe. At one stage, he had signalled Sir Ian Hamilton requesting permission to re-embark his force, but Hamilton had replied that they must 'dig yourself right in and stick it out'. But, no matter how brave or stubborn, no troops could stand their ground indefinitely against repeated and determined attacks. Hamilton decided to reinforce the Anzacs landing with four battalions of the Royal Naval Division. The Chatham and Portsmouth battalions were landed on 28 April. The next day, the Deal Battalion landed accompanied by the Nelsons from the 1st Naval Brigade.

Birdwood was singularly unimpressed with his reinforcements and wrote in his diary:

> I have been given some so-called Marines and Naval Battalions who are, so far as I can see, nearly useless. They are special children of Winston Churchill, immature boys with no proper training, and I am quite afraid of them giving me away some day.

Whatever his opinion of the RND, Birdwood had no choice but to put them straight in to the front line while his own, shattered, Anzacs could be reorganised.

Meanwhile, on 27 April, the Cape Helles troops began their advance up the peninsula. The Turks had retreated to their second line of defence on the southern slopes of Achi Baba, about 4 ½ miles from their front line at the Cape. Their line stretched the three miles across the peninsula from a point about ½ mile north of Col Matthews' 'Y' Beach to where a large ravine, Kereves Dere, broke the shore of the Dardanelles straits. The small village of Krithia, once under the gaze of the 'Y' beach troops, lay less than a mile behind the new front. This second line had been chosen with deliberate care. Anyone advancing from the Cape would first have to pass over open, flat country where every movement could be seen from the heights of Achi Baba. After two miles of this level plain, the land began to rise into the lower foothills at the base of the hill. These undulations were dominated by three major gullies. The largest, Gully Ravine, ran down the western coast and entered the sea between 'X' and 'Y' beaches. In the centre, Krithia Nullah and, to the east, Achi Baba Nullah, opened out on to the southern plain. During the winter months, these gullies provided watercourses that drained the Achi Baba slopes.

The advance on 27 April had been unopposed as the Allies marched across the open ground. By the evening, they had reached the start of the low hills and nullahs and a halt was called. Their line ran from where Gully Ravine met the sea on their left, to where the South Wales Borderers had held 'S' Beach on the north of Morto Bay. The left of the line was held by the 87th Brigade and included the Drake Battalion of the RND. The 88th Brigade had the centre, and the five French battalions, the right. The reserve was formed of the 86th Brigade.

At eight o'clock the following morning, the whole line moved forward to attack the enemy. In the beginning, where the ground remained level, there was little opposition but, as they reached the Achi Baba foothills, trench after trench was encountered – each having to be taken. As the advancing forces reached a trench, they would often find it deserted, only to find it swept by fire by another, manned, trench. Equally often, they would find themselves subjected to determined counter-attacks. On the left, the 87th Brigade advanced on either side of Gully Ravine for about a mile but, in the centre, the 88th Brigade made little progress up the Krithia and Achi Baba nullahs. The French, faced with the slope up the Kereves Dere, made no progress at all.

The Drake Battalion and the South Wales Borderers advanced through the remainder of the 87th Brigade and tried to carry the assault further along the tops of Gully Ravine, but the slow progress in the centre forced them to a halt. Then came orders to dig in. While no further advance could be made, the line had to be held against counter-attacks. As they were digging in, two companies of the Drake Battalion under the command of Cdr Campbell were detached and sent back to the cliffs above 'W' Beach where General Hunter-Weston had his headquarters. From there they were sent to the right of the line. The French battalions had fallen back before a determined counter-attack, and some had even retreated as far as Sedd-el-Bahr.

By nightfall, the only advance had been on the left of the line, which now curved back dramatically on the right. Casualties had been high and Hunter-Weston decided to bring up his slender reserves. The next day, having disembarked the four battalions at Anzac Cove, the RND transports brought the Hood and Howe battalions round Tekke Burnu to 'W' Beach. Once ashore, they were assigned to the role of Corps reserve while the Drake Battalion – after being under heavy fire all night, leading to the loss of their adjutant, Major Godfrey Barker, among others – joined the Plymouth Battalion and took over beach duties. All the RND battalions were camped among the ruined Turkish trenches above 'W' Beach under the command of Commodore Oliver Backhouse of the 2nd Naval Brigade.

At Anzac Cove, the Chatham, Portsmouth, and Deal battalions had relieved the exhausted Anzac troops in the trenches on the right of Deep Gully. The Nelson Battalion was in reserve. The high ground on the left of the gully, The Sphinx, Walker's Ridge, and Russell Top had been taken by the Anzacs, but the centre of the line was dominated by Pope's Hill, much of which was held by the Turks who poured down a continuous fire into the exposed trenches of the invaders.

The section of front now in the hands of the Royal Marine and Naval battalions had been attacked twice before in a most determined manner, but had been held with great loss by the Anzacs. The Turkish commander on the Anzac front, Mustapha Kemmal, intended to attack with all the force that he could muster and, on 30 April, the brunt of his assault fell upon the Marines. The battle raged for most of the day. Parties of Turkish soldiers broke through the line and had to be driven out by the bayonet. Many men died in the close-quarter fighting, but nowhere along the Marines' lines did the enemy achieve a breakthrough in strength.

HMS *Crystal Palace*. New entrants arriving at the Crystal Palace

New entrants forming up at the Crystal Palace. (CMcC)

Commodore, staff officers and officers under training at Crystal Palace.

New entrants arriving at Crystal Palace. (CMcC)

The ratings' Writing Room at
Crystal Palace.

The hammocks the men slept in, as on board ship, at the Crystal Palace. (CMcC)

Marching off parade ('Divisions') at the Crystal Palace.

Ratings undergoing physical training at Crystal Palace. (CMcC)

The Anson Battalion marching past at Divisions. (CMcC)

A cheery Able Seaman of the Royal Naval
Division.

Able Seaman James of the Benbow
Battalion wearing the khaki field dress
and equipment issued after Antwerp.

Members of the Drake Battalion outside their hut at Blandford. The wide range of uniform
variation can clearly be seen.

Ratings outside a Blandford hut ine arly 1915. The mixture of clothing suggests a period of uniform change.

Ratings relaxing inside one of the Blandford huts. The lack of cap badges suggests that they had yet to be allocated to a battalion.

Able Seaman Clark raising men for the RND at a rally on London's Tower Hill.

The band of the Hood Battalion in 1917. In the centre of the front row is former Commander Bernard Freyberg VC (here dressed in the uniform of an Armyd Lt-Col). On Freyberg's left is Lt Cdr Arthur Asquith.

Recruiting march through London.

Raising men for the RND. The possible candidate is invited to look in the mirror and see himself as 'the man we want', London.

Above and left: RND recruiting posters. (CMcC)

One of the Naval Brigade platoons marching towards Dover for embarkation to Antwerp. The role of the Royal Marine in the centre of the front rank is to demonstrate the skill of marching with a rifle (note that the officer in charge is out of step).

Above: The Royal Marine Battalions land in France 1914. (CMcC)

Below: Royal Marines in Ostend, 1914. (CMcC)

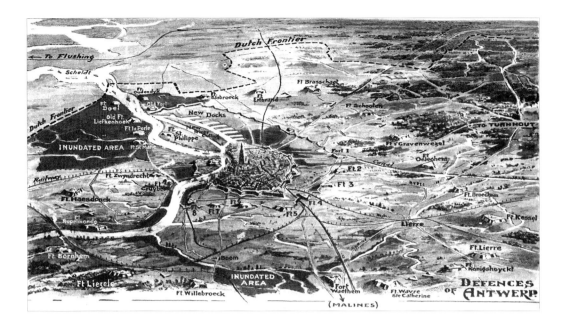

A contemporary sketch of the Antwerp defences.

A British transport vessel arriving at Antwerp bearing RND battalions. (CMcC)

RND armoured cars and transports manned by men of the Royal Marines. They have been joined byd members of the Belgian Army.

RND Seamen building anti-shrapnel roofs over their trenches in front of Antwerp.

Royal Marines transferring their stores at Ostend prior to leaving for Antwerp.

Seamen from the Naval Brigades manning the front line trench in front of Antwerp.

Seamen and Royal Marines of the RND with an armoured car.

Royal Naval Division armoured cars in Antwerp. (CMcC)

Bluejackets in Belgium handing out bully beef. (CMcC)

Preparing food for the RND at Antwerp. (CMcC)

Above: Supplies of bully beef being distributed in the RND trenches.

Below: Men of the RND carrying ammunition into the trenches. (CMcC)

Above: Naval armoured train with guns in action in Belgium. (CMcC)

Below: Royal Marines in an improvised shelter at Atwerp. (CMcC)

Seamen making their way to the trenches in defence of Antwerp. (CMcC)

RND officers and
seamen at Antwerp.
(CMcC)

Left: Commander Y. C. M. Spearman –
Commanding Officer of the Collingwood Battalion.

Below: The widely acclaimed poet Sub-Lt Rupert
Brooke.

During the night, after three days and nights of fighting without supplies of food or water, a small trench in the forward part of the line sheltering the remnants of two platoons of the Portsmouth Battalion – under the command of Lts Empson and Alcock – became isolated and subjected to repeated attacks by the Turks. The defenders hung on grimly and repelled each attack, but their ammunition was being rapidly depleted, and their water was already gone. Shouting across the 400-yard gap to the nearest trench, they called for supplies. Parties tried several times to reach them, but every time they were shot down as they tried to cover the open ground. To make matters worse, dawn was breaking, the light making things even easier for the Turkish riflemen. Soon Lt Empson lay among the dead.

As another party of men were being assembled to try and reach the beleaguered trench, a volunteer was sought from among the stretcher-bearers. Someone was needed to render first-aid to the wounded men in addition to taking supplies. Lance-Corporal Parker stepped forward. He had been already noted as a brave and efficient marine over the previous three days when he had been in charge of the Portsmouth Battalion stretcher-bearers. Now he crouched with the rest of the party ready for the dash to the isolated trench. When the word came, and they broke into a run, they had not gone more than a few yards before one of the party was hit. Parker, ignoring the intense rifle fire, organised a stretcher team from two men and had them carry the wounded man back. Gathering the remainder, he led them in a desperate sprint to the trench. By the time he jumped in to its precarious protection, he was the only one left alive – the rest had been cut down by the hail of Turkish bullets. Parker tended to the wounded but, because no ammunition had got through, it was quite clear that the trench would have to be evacuated. When the time came to leave, Parker helped to get the wounded clear of the trench. As he was doing so, he was hit and seriously injured. Hauling himself painfully to his feet, he continued to attend to the other casualties until they were all being assisted back across the bullet-swept gap. When there was nothing remaining to be done, he hobbled back to join the other Marines. For his outstanding courage and leadership on that occasion, Lance-Corporal Parker was awarded the first Royal Marine Victoria Cross of the war. For his leadership in holding the trench for four days and three nights, Lt Alan Alcock was awarded the Distinguished Service Cross.

The next day, the RND detachments attached to the Anzacs were relieved and went into reserve for an attack on the Turkish-held Pope's Hill. Timed to begin at 8 p.m. on 1 May, the broad assault was intended to take the heights at the end of Deep Gully. The New Zealand Otago Battalion was to advance up the left arm of the gully, as Pope's Hill in the centre and Monash Valley on the right would be attacked by three Australian battalions. In support at the rear were the three

Marine battalions – Deal, Portsmouth and Chatham – and in reserve were two companies of seamen from the Nelson Battalion.

As darkness fell across the peninsula, the troops began to move forward and engaged the enemy entrenched along the tops of the steep slopes. The advance very rapidly degenerated into a series of disorganised skirmishes along the whole front. Instead of linking up with each other, the battalions pressed on, losing touch on the flanks. Nevertheless, some progress was being made. In many places, the tops of the hills had been reached and the Turks had been ejected from the trenches that overlooked the gully. At midnight, the Turks lit a huge bonfire on the top of Pope's Hill, its flames giving light to a scene of utter confusion. Hundreds of men stumbled around the battlefront either leaderless or without anyone to whom they could give orders. The attack had broken down and lost its impetus. At this point, Col Monash – the officer commanding the Australian troops – ordered up the two Nelson companies. They were to move forward in support of the 15th Australian Battalion engaging the enemy on the right-hand slopes of Pope's Hill. When the Nelsons reached the fighting, they found an advance in progress which was promptly joined by their forward platoons. The seamen became quickly disorganised, and much time was lost in getting them regrouped in order to operate efficiently as a cohesive unit in the field. With this finally achieved, they were ordered to move to their left across the lower slopes of the hill and to join up with the Otago Battalion. No one, however, knew where the New Zealanders were and, after wandering over the battlefield for some time, the Nelsons were finally ordered to return to a position behind the 13th Australian Battalion where they were told to dig in.

With the arrival of dawn, the true situation of the attacking forces was made clear. The Turks still held most of the high ground. Repeated attacks had failed to move them, trenches that had been gained in the first advance had been lost to counter-attacks, bodies of fallen men lay everywhere, and the wounded who could move were crawling through the scrub trying to reach assistance. The fighting, however, still continued, and the Portsmouth and Chatham battalions were ordered up Monash Valley. As they did so, the line held by the 16th Australian Battalion was breached and the Chatham Marines were thrown forward to plug the gap. This was done with such determination that they overshot and captured two of the Turkish front-line trenches. Unfortunately, they were forced to withdraw in the face of fierce fire on their flanks.

In the centre of the front, the Nelson companies, after spending all night in the middle of the fighting, were ordered to attack the enemy threatening the flank of the 13th Australian Battalion. Time and time again they charged against devastating machine gun fire, but to no avail. Eventually, despairingly tired, they began to fall back but were rallied once more by their officers who again led them into the trenches alongside the 13th Battalion. There they stayed, fending off repeated attacks until 5.30 p.m. when a general withdrawal was ordered.

By that time, the RND had lost many brave men. The Chatham Battalion had lost almost 300 officers and men. The two Nelson companies had lost one company commander, five platoon commanders, and nearly 200 ratings.

For several days after the battle, bodies of Marines killed in the Chatham Battalion's advance lay on the slope they had held for a short time. One night, a Marine climbed the hill again and rolled the bodies of his fallen comrades down into Monash Valley where they were buried. Afterwards the slope was always known as 'Dead Man's Ridge'.

The Marine battalions were back in the front line the day after the attack and were given the vital posts of Courtney's, Quinn's, and Pope's where they were repeatedly in contact with the enemy. Their relief came some days later when their trenches were taken over by the Australian Light Horse Brigade.

The Marines sailed for Cape Helles on 12 May and were followed the next day by the Nelson Battalion. The seamen had been guarding the left flank of Anzac Cove since the battles of 1 and 2 May. The much criticised seamen and Marines had demonstrated their worth – and had left behind their fallen to prove it.

Chief Petty Officer
George Prowse VC.

Sub-Lt Edwin Dyett.
Shot at dawn on 5
January 1917.

CHAPTER IV

Death, Disaster – and Departure

By 30 April 1915, the line held by the British and French forces on the toe of Gallipoli stretched across the peninsula with the left further advanced than the right. Just 2 miles ahead of them poppies bloomed on the crest of their goal – Achi Baba.

With the halt of the initial advance on 28 April, the Turks under their German commanders had been strengthening their defences and building up their reserves. General Liman von Sanders had ordered three extra infantry divisions to join him, two from Constantinople, a third from the Asiatic side of the Dardanelles. He had decided to launch a large counter-attack. Preceded by a short, but heavy, artillery bombardment, the infantry were to advance in strength, driving the invaders back into the sea. His Divisional Commanders were told that there could be no holding back or digging in; the attack had to be carried through. Von Sanders was taken at his word. His subordinate Colonel von Sodensten informed the Turkish regimental commanders:

> Let it be clearly understood that those who remain stationary at the moment of attack, or who try to escape, will be shot. For this purpose machine guns will be placed behind the troops to oblige such people to advance and at the same time to fire on the enemy's reserves.

In addition, the first wave of attacking infantry would not be issued with ammunition. They would have to rely upon the bayonet.

The bombardment broke out along the line at 10.30 on the evening of 30 April. Immediately it did, so the 2nd Royal Naval Brigade, under Commodore Oliver Backhouse, were told to move from their camp above 'W' Beach and take up reserve positions behind the thinly held front line. The Drake Battalion of the 1st RN Brigade and the Plymouth Battalion of the RM Brigade remained behind to guard the beach.

Moving up behind the front line, the Hood and Howe Battalions entered the Achi Baba Nullah and occupied support trenches behind the heavily engaged 86th Brigade. Backhouse set up his headquarters in this position. Marked by an army biscuit tin painted black with the words 'Backhouse Post' in white, it became the best-known reference point for the RND for the remainder of their time on the peninsula.

As the Howe and Hood battalions took their places in the support trenches, Lt-Col. Moorhouse's Ansons were facing the grim business of a determined Turkish assault against the right of the line where they had been sent in support of the French. As they approached the French line, it soon became clear that the French Senegalese troops were collapsing before the attack. The bombardment had unnerved the colonial troops with its ferocity, and the resolution of the attacking infantry had caused many of them to flee. The sailors advanced straight into the front line alongside the remaining French troops and, with each supporting the other, brought the Turkish onslaught to a bloody halt. So started almost two weeks of continuous attack and counter-attack in which both sides tested the other's determination and endurance.

By the following morning the Turks had been repulsed all along the line. The Ansons withdrew to support trenches behind the now rallied French on the right, while the Hood and Howe battalions moved up into the front line to relieve units of the weary 86th Brigade.

Although he had little in reserve, General Hunter-Weston ordered a counter-attack at 10 a.m. on the morning of 1 May. At his signal, the whole front line rose from their shallow trenches and began their walk towards the enemy.

The Hood and Howe battalions advanced steadily up the Achi Baba Nullah. But, before they had gone 200 yards they came under machine gun and rifle fire from well-entrenched positions along the sides and bottom of the wide gully. With their casualties mounting, the seamen pressed on, moving forward in short rushes. Suddenly, red and green flares arced into the skies from the Turkish trenches as ranging signal for their artillery. The naval battalions had advanced no more than 400 yards before they were forced to dig holes as shelter from the increasing ferocity of the heavy field guns.

From some distance behind the line, it appeared to a senior army officer as if the naval battalions merely needed reinforcements to get them on the move again. Accordingly he ordered the 2nd Battalion of the Hampshire Regiment to advance in support.

The men of the RND watched in astonished amazement as the proud body of professional soldiers moved up the nullah as if they were on parade. They made an impression on the naval battalions that was never to be forgotten, and provided them with an object lesson in discipline and determination in the face of the most severe opposition. But even the most steadfast and gallant cannot endure indefinitely against an accurate, close-range, artillery bombardment. As the Hampshires had advanced, the shelling had increased and Lt-Col. Quilter of the Hood Battalion, his casualties increasing by the minute, decided to withdraw. The Howe and 2nd Hampshires had no option but to follow. While the withdrawal to the original front-line trenches was proceeding, the RND 3rd Field Ambulance saved many lives by bringing out as many of the wounded as they could. Among the wounded was one of Rupert Brooke's pall-bearers, Sub-Lt the Honourable Charles Lister who, although hit by shrapnel during the withdrawal, denied it until blood was seen to be filling out his breeches above his pigskin gaiters. He wrote home that his men 'showed great steadiness for raw troops'.

Back once again in the support line, the naval battalions remained there until the evening of 2 May when they were withdrawn and returned to their trenches above 'W' Beach.

The following morning the Turks attacked again, once more concentrating their main onslaught against the right of the Allied line where the French troops had shown the tendency to waver in the face of a dogged assault. Once more the Ansons were rushed into the breach alongside the French, and once again the example they showed rallied their allies. Over the next two days, attack after attack was beaten off. On the 5th, the bone-tired Ansons were withdrawn, but not for a rest – the front line was being reorganised for another big attack against the Turkish lines.

It was clear to everyone that, after the failure of repeated attacks against the Allied line, the Turks were going on the defensive. They could be seen reinforcing their positions along the whole length of their line. If the campaign was not to stumble into the stalemate of the Western Front, an attack had to be made at the earliest opportunity to deprive the enemy of the chance to dig himself in to an immovable position.

General Hamilton had, by the beginning of May, received reinforcements. The 42nd Division had arrived from Egypt and, although still not properly organised, was able to send a brigade to support the 29th Division. Two brigades had arrived from Anzac Cove, one Australian, and one of New Zealand troops. These were formed into a composite division with the addition of a third brigade known as the Composite Naval Brigade. This group was made up from the Drake Battalion, the Plymouth Battalion, and the 1st Battalion of the Lancashire Fusiliers, all placed under the command of General Paris. The 2nd Naval Brigade was attached to General d'Amade's French Expeditionary Corps and placed under his command. Altogether there were 25,000 men in the Allied line on the morning of 6 May.

The first objective of the attack was the enemy front-line trenches in front of the village of Krithia. Secondly, the 29th Division was to advance and take two low hills to the north-west of Krithia, and thirdly, the whole force was to advance on Achi Baba from the west, south-west, and south. The Composite Naval Brigade had the centre of the line and the 2nd Naval Brigade were to advance alongside the French as they attempted to reach the top of the Kereves Dere slopes on the right.

The Second Battle of Krithia began at eleven o'clock in the morning. The Hood and Anson battalions, on the left of the French line, began to press ahead of the troops on either flank. The French were quickly pinned down on the ridge of Kereves Dere on their right and, on their left, the Lancashire Fusiliers were being heavily shelled. By 12.30, the two battalions had gained 600 yards, but their losses had been severe. The man who had commanded the Hood Battalion from the very beginning, Lt-Col. Arnold Quilter, was killed as he led his men in the very first assault. The Ansons had also suffered. The Prime Minister's nephew, Sub-Lt Melland, would never see England again, and Sub-Lt Tisdall was killed as he stood on the parapet of a newly captured trench, looking for the enemy. Just before the battle, Tisdall had written a poem he had entitled 'Norfolk':

I'll go to Norfolk at the summer's close
And see again the hillsides gilt with grain,
The glassy fords, the woods, the turnip rows,
The dim sad purple of the marsh again.

I'll see the great farms and small villages.
The towering churches where few people prayed,
The ruined abbeys in whose quires the breeze
Sings sadly of an unreturning day.

And there I'll walk long miles and swim and run,
And look for hours on the flowers that grow
Purple on the sea-crowned marshes in the sun,
And hope to change the world, it needs it so.

But fate had declared otherwise, and a Turkish bullet ensured that only Tisdall's spirit returned to his beloved county. Regarded by the Brigade's chaplain as 'one of England's bravest men', Tisdall's extreme courage had almost passed unrecognised. After the heat of the landing at 'V' Beach, all that could be remembered of Tisdall himself was that he was 'one of those Naval Division gents'. Not one to talk about his actions himself, it took considerable research to establish his identity and it was almost a year after his death before his award of the Victoria Cross was announced.

By 3.30, General d'Amade was forced to order the Hood and Anson battalions to dig in where they were. They were so far ahead of the other troops that serious gaps had occurred in the line. The Drake Battalion were then ordered forward to occupy the gaps and dig in.

The fighting ground to a halt mid-afternoon. The right of the line had made little progress towards capturing the Kereves Dere ridge, and the left had made hardly any progress at all towards their objectives. Despite exhaustion among the troops, the attack had to be continued the next day.

The first advance on the following morning was to be undertaken only on the left of the line but, as the day wore on, the 29th Division made little progress despite being reinforced by the New Zealand Brigade. At 4.45, the order was given for an advance along the whole front. The Commanding Officer of the Drake Battalion, Cdr Campbell, had been put in charge of the Composite Division's front line and given the responsibility for making sure that the flanks of the Division kept in touch with advances made on either the right or left of the line. Any gap that occurred would be almost bound to let the Turks through with disastrous consequences.

Once again, the weary British and French troops pushed against the enemy defences. Well-sited machine guns with wide fields of fire slashed across the attackers, and hidden artillery rained down shrapnel shells. As darkness stole across the battlefield and the fighting died down, the 29th Division had advanced 300 yards, the French had gained a few yards of the Kereves Dere slopes, and the 2nd Royal Naval Brigade had pushed forward for almost 100 yards. In the centre of the line Commander Campbell had succeeded in his prodigious task of keeping his flanks in touch with the uneven advance and was awarded the Distinguished Service Order for his efforts.

Although there had been some slight advances made over the two days, the achievements were not enough to warrant ending the battle. For the next stage, the Australian Brigade were withdrawn from the Composite Division in the centre and, during the night, moved to the right to stiffen the French.

As the sun rose on 8 May, the assault by the French and Australians smashed into the Turkish defences. The Anzacs advanced an amazing 600 yards while the French cleared the Kereves Dere ridge of the enemy. The Hood and Howe battalions moved up with the advancing troops to extend the line to the left, but a gap still existed on the left flank of the advance and a Turkish counter-attack headed straight for it. In consequence, the Drake Battalion were rushed forward to hold the line. The Turks were determined in their assault, but the Drakes hung on doggedly until the Plymouth Marines came up alongside them. From then on the line was secure. During the fighting, Lt Cdr Freyberg had been wounded in the stomach and evacuated to a Field Hospital on the beach. Another casualty was Lt Asquith who had received a bullet through the left knee. A press correspondent, interviewing Asquith's platoon after the battle, noted:

> He was immensely popular with his men, for he sought no special privileges as an officer, but cheerfully shared their discomforts.
>
> He was absolutely fearless,' one of them declared to me, 'and used to sit on the edge of the trench smoking a cigarette and eating bully beef and biscuits with us as happy and contented as a sandboy.
>
> On one occasion, shortly after landing, when we were very hard pressed by the Turks, he strolled up and down in our trench, under fierce shrapnel and rifle fire, encouraging us and keeping us together in a wonderful manner. I don't think he would have been wounded so soon – it was only a week after landing – if he had not been so utterly indifferent to danger.
>
> Although he was hit, rather badly I believe, in the knee, he absolutely refused to be carried away on a stretcher, but limped painfully away, saying stretchers were required for more urgent cases. I believe a transport picked him up later. He seemed quite heartbroken at having to leave us so soon.

Six weeks later, after recovering in hospital in Egypt, Asquith rejoined his platoon.

During a lull in the fighting in the early afternoon of 8 May, a figure, assumed to be a Turkish sniper, was seen to the front of the Portsmouth Battalion trenches. A shot rang out and the man fell. Still he moved and, just as another shot was about to be fired, someone shouted out that the man was British. Lance Corporal Robert Coubrough hauled himself out of the trench and crawled over to the man as snipers fired at him. Coming alongside the wounded man, Coubrough was astonished to find that the casualty was Edward Roland, an Able Seaman from the Hood Battalion who had been first wounded on 4 May – four days earlier. In the four days that had passed since being shot, Rowland, a former County Durham miner who had transferred to the RND from the Durham Light Infantry, had managed to stay alive, only to be shot again by his own side. As Coubrough prepared to drag Roland to safety, the seaman was hit again, this time by a Turkish bullet. Fearful of causing more damage, the Marine told Roland to just stay where he was and stick it out until darkness, before he crawled back to his own trenches. With the sun well over the horizon, Coubrough returned with a stretcher party and brought Roland in to safety. Sadly, the seaman died that night from his wounds.

Although the campaign was now more than two weeks old, the Commander-in-Chief still had his headquarters at sea. Onboard the *Arcadian*, General Sir Ian

Hamilton weighed up the situation. Desperate to push on, he felt that the losses he had sustained – 6,500 men at Cape Helles alone – made any further attempts to advance futile. He signalled Kitchener requesting at least two more divisions, 'otherwise I am afraid we shall degenerate into trench warfare with its resultant slowness'.

Digging in was already taking place an along the line. Turkish attacks were frequent and savage. On the 10 May, one such attack against the French almost succeeded in breaking through until a counter-attack by the Plymouth Marines pushed the enemy back. Turkish snipers, men of bravery and high courage, harassed the troops as they tried to secure their positions and 'sniper drives' were repeatedly organised to clear the area of these marksmen. Lt Cdr Boissier of the Howe Battalion, who had ripped apart biscuit tins to line Rupert Brook's grave, earned the Distinguished Service Cross for his exploits during these operations. (This danger from snipers did not prevent Sub-Lt Herbert of the Hawke Battalion from, later, taking his naval officer brother, Sidney, up to the front line where his brother's white uniform excited much sniper interest.)

On 12 and 13 May, the Royal Naval Division brigades were relieved by the Manchester Regiment of the 42nd Division. The battered battalions retired to an area south-west of the Achi Baba Nullah where a small grove of stunted trees was to become their next camp. Some of the battalions had lost half their strength over the last few days, and the survivors were desperately tired as they dug themselves holes in the soil in which to shelter and gain some rest.

The 2nd Naval Brigade had left the command of General d'Amade on 10 May and, on the 14 May, the gallant General paid them a visit at the rest camp. The seamen presented him with a machine gun they had captured from the Turks, and when he addressed the assembled battalions he read from a copy of a letter he had sent to the Commander-in-Chief. It read:

> In accordance with your orders I am returning the 2nd Naval Brigade to the Composite Division. It is my pleasant duty to place on record how much I have appreciated the brilliant military qualities, the devotion to duty, the courage and the intrepidity of the three valiant battalions – Anson, Howe and Hood – of which it is composed. It is a great honour, and a great satisfaction to me to have had during the 6th, 7th, 8th and 9th of May, the devoted and ever ready collaboration of Commodore Backhouse, an officer who has inspired his troops with those noble qualities to which every French soldier who has seen them at work renders homage.

The day prior to General d'Amade's visit, the battalions who had been engaged in the fighting at Anzac Cove also arrived at the rest camp. For none of them, however, was there to be a protracted period of relaxation. Reorganisation of the front line meant that each Division was to have its own sector. The left of the line, across Gully Ravine, belonged to the 29th Division with Cox's Indian Brigade; the 42nd Division had the Krithia Nullah; the Royal Naval Division, Achi Baba Nullah; and the French, the ridge of Kereves Dere to the Dardanelles Straits.

When the reorganisation was complete, and the Divisions were manning their own trenches, a series of night raids were made that pushed the front line as far as ½ mile forward. On 18 and 23 May, the 2nd Naval Brigade took part, the 1st Naval Brigade on the 24 May, and the Marine Brigade on the 27 May. In some places the RND line was now only 200 yards from the enemy's advance positions.

During the May battles, one of the Division's chaplains, the Reverend Bevill Close, had become concerned that the wounded were not being removed from the battlefield as speedily as they should have been. It took a minimum of two men to carry a man on a stretcher, and his wounds could be made worse by lifting him on to an examination table. To counter this, the Chaplain designed a stretcher supported above a single, central, bicycle wheel. This meant that the stretcher could not only be operated by a lone stretcher-bearer, but the lowering of four legs from the corners of the frame turned the stretcher into a stable, waist high, examination, or even operation, table. The device was widely adopted, becoming known as the 'Close Stretcher Carrier'.

On the 28 and 29 May, three new battalions arrived on the peninsula. The Hawke, Benbow, and Collingwood battalions had sailed from England in early May with an élan equalling that of the earlier battalions. Their transports were armed with machine guns against submarines, and lifeboat drills were carried out during the day. In the evening, Battalion orders were sung in the manner of Gregorian chants to the assembled men by a trio consisting of Sub-Lts Watts, Davies, and Markham – the entertainment provided by singing the orders being widely understood to be the only way to get the men to pay attention to their contents.

The officers, while drinking in their messes during the pleasant evenings of the voyage, had solemnly intoned the words written by Sub-Lt Herbert and based on a speech by the Prime Minister:

We shall not sheathe the sword which we have not lightly drawn,
Until Belgium has recovered all, and more than all, that she has sacrificed,
Until France is adequately secured against the menace of aggression,
Until the rights of the smaller nationalities of Europe have been planted upon an unassailable foundation,
Until the military domination of Prussia is wholly and finally destroyed.

The transports reached Lemnos on 22 May only to find the Mudros boom closed. After an anxious night, which could have seen them as easy prey for enemy submarines, they were allowed in to the huge harbour to join 112 ships already at anchor. Whilst they had waited outside, the Collingwood Battalion officers trimmed their hair back to a short stubble in the hope that their example would be followed by their men. It certainly provided huge amusement at the following day's church parade when the order 'Off Caps' was given.

With the arrival of the fresh battalions, the Division resumed its original organisation. The 1st Naval Brigade was made up of the Hawke, Benbow, Drake, and Nelson battalions; the 2nd Naval Brigade was composed of the Collingwood, Howe, Hood, and Anson battalions; and the Deal, Plymouth, Portsmouth, and Chatham battalions completed the Marine Brigade. For the first time since Antwerp, the Royal Naval Division was complete on the field of battle.

The next large-scale attack was planned for 4 June. After a long bombardment that was supposed to drive the Turks from their advanced trenches, the whole of the Allied front line was to move forward and capture the first three lines of enemy trenches. The Royal Naval Division had been ordered to send the Royal Marine Brigade and the 1st Naval Brigade, with the exception of the Drake Battalion, to form a general reserve. The attack on the Turkish lines opposite the RND trenches was to be carried out by the 2nd Naval Brigade with the Drake Battalion in reserve. Commodore Backhouse arranged his order of attack with the Hood Battalion – now commanded by Lt-Col. Crauford Stewart – in the centre, the Howe on the left flank, linking up with the Manchesters of the 42nd Division, and on the right, next to the French, the Ansons. The Collingwood Battalion, new to the shock of battle, was to be in support. The three experienced Battalions were to attack the first and second enemy trenches. They would then be followed by the Collingwoods, who were to advance and take the third Turkish line.

The preliminary bombardment of the Third Battle of Krithia opened at eight o'clock in the morning of 4 June. For over three hours, gradually increasing in ferocity, naval guns pounded the Turkish trenches. At 11.20, the firing died away and, all along the front, the troops cheered and shouted while waving their bayonets above the trench parapets. This feint was answered by a crescendo of machine gun fire. The bombardment had appeared to have little effect on the defenders. Ten minutes after it had ceased, the bombardment was reopened hoping to catch the Turks as they manned their trenches in response to the ruse.

At midday the ships stopped firing and the first to advance towards the enemy were four of the RND's armoured cars. Weighing 4 tons and constructed on a Rolls Royce Silver Ghost chassis, the cars had Maxim machine guns mounted in turrets, and carried a crew of three Royal Naval Air Service officers and men. The first of the vehicles had been landed in May and the commander of the unit,

Lt Cdr Wedgwood, had been desperate for an opportunity to put them into use against the Turks. With grappling irons attached to a pole protruding from the rear of the cars, the plan was to reverse the cars towards the enemy, hook their defensive barbed wire, and drag it clear, leaving the way open for the advancing troops. As the cars backed towards the Turkish lines, the men waiting to advance from the British trenches waved their rifles and shouted, 'Come on the Navy!' – a cry answered from inside the cars with 'Belt it in!' But it was all to no avail. In addition to coming under intense small-arms, machine gun, and shell-fire, the ground over which the cars had to pass proved impossible to negotiate – one car fell in to a shell-hole with such force that its turret simply fell off. There was no other alternative but to leave the field, their mission unsuccessful.

As the armoured cars retired, the Allied line advanced in attack. The Howe, Hood and Anson battalions left their trenches and were met by a vicious hail of fire, the like of which they had yet to experience. Within seconds, half the officers had become casualties and fallen dead or wounded. Machine guns swept great gaps in the mass of advancing men. Still they pressed forward, and reached the first Turkish trench only to find it had been evacuated by the enemy and contained only the dead and dying. Although the first line had been taken, it was of little use to the attackers. To their surprise and consternation, they found that the trench was at least 10 feet deep and, when they had jumped into its bottom, they were unable to fire on the Turks in the next line. They tore at the high parados lining the rear of the trench with bayonets and entrenching tools, hoping to bring down its packed soil and sandbags, but found it built mainly of Turkish corpses.

Lt Stuart Jones, the Ansons' senior surviving officer, rallied the remnants of his battalion and led them out of the deep trench in an attack on the Turkish second line. The Hood and Howe followed his example. Soon 800 yards of the enemy's second line had been captured. But it was a tenuous hold. There were only twenty officers and 300 men to defend the gain against a counter-attack until the Collingwoods arrived. Even worse, on the right of the line, where the French should have been advancing along the ridge of Kereves Dere, the only movements that could be seen were Turkish troops retaking their front-line trenches, and Lt Shaw-Stewart running across the French front shouting 'Avances! Avances!' and waving his walking stick at the retreating French. But the French assault had collapsed and now the right flank of the naval battalions was unprotected. Already men were falling back as firing began to break out from the slopes and high ground.

At 12.15, Commander Alexander Spearman climbed over the parapet of his battalion's trench and, brandishing his revolver, cried, 'Come on Collingwoods, don't leave me now!' A steel-tipped wave of proud and eager men burst on to the battlefield and flooded towards the enemy. It was a target of which no Turkish machine gunner had dared to dream. All the enemy guns turned on the Collingwoods as they charged across the open ground towards the first line of trenches. Cdr Spearman died before he had gone more than a few yards from the trench. His adjutant, Lt Cdr Wallace Annand from South Africa, was killed the instant he clambered over the parapet, leaving at home a son, Richard, who would go on to earn a Victoria Cross. Another officer who lost his life in the charge was Sub-Lt Oscar Freyberg, the younger brother of Lt Cdr Freyberg of the Hood Battalion. The machine guns raked the Collingwoods, and streams of bullets slashed into the advancing men. Twenty-six officers and 900 men of the Collingwood Battalion had left their trench to enter the battle; only 300 were left to drop into the shelter of the first enemy-advanced trench. Behind them sprawled a khaki sea of dead and wounded. Some of the survivors made an effort to reach the second, and even the third, line of enemy trenches, but the machine guns continued to exact their dreadful toll.

Soon it became impossible to continue holding back the Turkish pressure on the right flank, and the Turks could be seen preparing for a counter-attack against the thinly held second line. The experienced officers of the Hood, Howe, and Ansons began to withdraw their surviving men, but the Collingwoods had become disorganised and were scattered along the entire front – some even still advancing towards the enemy. To Chief Petty Officer William Carnall, it appeared that he was the senior survivor of the Collingwood Battalion. He had seen the other battalions starting to withdraw and, for lack of any other instructions, decided to gather the remnants of his battalion together and follow their example. Back and forth along the line he ran shepherding the dazed men back to their own front lines.

On another part of the line, Leading Seaman Arthur Blore was part of a party of Ansons digging a communication trench just in front of the newly captured Turkish second line. Coming under fire, his officer was shot and killed. At the same time, he could see that the Collingwood attack had broken down and it was clear to him that the Ansons still holding out in the Turkish line would have to withdraw. Getting together twenty-two men he advanced to the line and ordered the men to make their way back to their own start line. As he did so, a Turkish machine gun opened fire along the trench. Calmly taking aim, Blore shot back with his rifle, killing two of the enemy. He continued to fire, preventing other Turks from manning the gun until the men behind him had all left the trench. He then climbed out and ran for his life back to his own lines.

For the whole length of the Division's shattered line, with their officers dead or wounded, ratings continued to engage the enemy. Chief Petty Officer Homer of the Howe Battalion, with the men around him pinned down by a Turkish machine gun, advanced in a series of sprints across open ground until he could bring his rifle to bear on the enemy gunners. From his new position, he killed or wounded the gun crew, continuing to do so when replacements were sent to man the gun. By his action, the Howe Battalion were able to move forward to a more protected position. Able Seaman Pierce of the same battalion, along with other men, dropped in to an enemy trench only to come under severe small-arms fire. Many around him were wounded and it soon became clear that the position could not be held. Pierce continued to hold the trench until the wounded were clear, before leaving himself, carrying a wounded man. Chief Petty Officer Stear of the Anson Battalion, came across a group of men from the Collingwood Battalion. Their officers were dead or incapacitated, and none had had the slightest experience of the type of savage fighting that was going on around them. Stear took over the group, rallied them, and led them forward in a charge straight at the enemy. Chief Petty Officers Homer and Stear were awarded the Conspicuous Gallantry Medal; Chief Petty Officer Carnall was awarded the Distinguished Service Medal. All were immediately given commissions. Leading Seaman Blore and Able Seaman Pierce were both awarded Conspicuous Gallantry Medals.

By 1245, three quarters of an hour after it had started, the battle was over. The largest gains had been made by the 42nd Division, despite the Manchesters' right flank being uncovered by the Naval Brigade's 350-yard withdrawal. But the losses were appalling. More than 7,000 British and French had lost their lives for a sandy bulge in a line less than 3 miles long. The 2nd Naval Brigade had been savagely mauled, and the Collingwood Battalion had marched into oblivion. Over 500 men of the new battalion had died in the battle. Out of twenty-six officers, sixteen lay dead on the battlefield, and eight were wounded. Only two had come through unscathed. The twenty-seven-year-old composer and pianist, Sub-Lt Denis Browne, who had helped to bury Rupert Brooke, would write no more for *The Times*. Before he succumbed to his wounds, he wrote to Edward Marsh:

> I've gone now too: not too badly I hope. I'm luckier than Rupert because I've fought. But there's no one to bury me as I buried him, so perhaps he's best off in the long run.

Lt Compton Mackenzie, already a well-known writer, had been given a commission in the Royal Marines and attached to General Paris's staff. Sent as a liaison officer with General Hunter-Weston, he was with a senior staff officer when the shocked survivors of the Collingwood Battalion walked slowly past with a shambling, halting gait – their eyes hollow with the horror of what they had experienced. The senior officer turned to Mackenzie and, pulling his arm, said quietly, 'Let's get out of their way, they won't want to see us just now.' The red collar tabs on their uniforms indicating their status as staff officers, would not have been a welcome sight for men who had seen their companions fall in wholesale slaughter.

Despite such severe losses, the main battle was still continuing, and the Drake and Benbow battalions were put into the front line. The Chatham Battalion was ordered from its reserve position and fought on the left flank of the 42nd Division until 7 June. The ground gained was held and the Turks prevented from making a breakthrough with their counter-attacks.

Sub-Lt A. P. Herbert was deeply affected by the carnage in which he had been involved and, unstinting in his despair, he wrote –

This is the Fourth of June
Think not I never dream
The noise of that infernal noon,
The stretcher's endless stream.
The tales of triumph won,
The night that found them lies,
The wounded wailing in the sun,
The dead, the dust, the flies.

The flies! Oh God, the flies
That soiled the sacred dead.
To see them swarm
from dead men's eyes
And share the soldier's bread!
Nor think I now forget
The filth and stench of war,
The corpses on the parapet,
The maggots on the floor.

In the days following the 4th of June disaster, General Paris took stock of the Division. It was clear to him that, as no reinforcements were available, nor looked likely to be forthcoming, the losses sustained had impaired the whole divisional organisation. He therefore decided that the Naval Brigades would have to be reduced to three battalions each. The Benbow and the remnants of the Collingwood battalions were disbanded and the survivors absorbed by the Hood, Howe and Anson battalions of the 2nd Naval Brigade.

Then the news of the casualties reached Winston Churchill; he expressed his deep sadness over the tragedy to his brother, Jack, who was fighting with the army on Gallipoli:

Poor Naval Division. Alas the slaughter has been cruel. All are gone whom I knew.
It makes me wish to be with you.

The Royal Naval Division's sector was now defended by the Royal Marine
Brigade and the 1st Naval Brigade. Commodore Backhouse and his exhausted
seamen were sent to the island of Imbros on 19 June for a week's rest. On the
25th they were inspected by General Hamilton who, knowing the First Lord's
affection for the RND, sent Churchill an encouraging message:

You would not recognise the men if you saw them again now. They have filled out
and got a splendid, bold, martial appearance that would delight your heart.

Two days later, the 2nd Naval Brigade was back on the peninsula. In their
absence, the fighting on the Achi Baba Nullah front had continued. The night of
19 June had seen a desperate engagement by some men of the Hawke Battalion.
'A' Company had been ordered to attack an enemy trench in the centre of the
divisional front. As they charged across the open ground, Turkish flares soared
into the night sky and bathed the front in light. Many of the attackers fell to the
machine guns that immediately opened fire on them. Despite the fierce action,
the Hawkes rushed the trench and drove out the defenders. They then began
to consolidate their position, preparing to receive reinforcements and repulse
any counter-attacks. But, as the dawn lent daylight to the scene, the men in the
captured trench were horrified to see that not only had they no field of fire to
the rear of the trench due to rising ground, but that they could also be easily
subjected to enfilading fire on both their flanks. The situation worsened when it
was discovered that, under cover of darkness, a party of Turkish bombers had
occupied on old trench close to them. Shortly after dawn, the Turks began to
hurl their crude but effective grenades into the captured trench, and the casualties
began to mount. Just before six o'clock, a platoon from 'C' Company dashed
across the gap to reinforce the defenders but, within minutes, more than half
of them had become casualties. The position was clearly untenable, and when a
withdrawal was ordered. nineteen officers and men lay dead in the dust in and
around the evacuated trench, seventy-four were wounded.

Three days later the 1st Naval Brigade was relieved by the Marines who
were ordered to attack and take the same trench the Hawkes had held and
lost. 'A' Company of the Portsmouth Battalion made the assault and captured
the position. This time the reception was even hotter than before and, in less
than an hour and a half, the Marines were forced to fall back to their original
position.

During their time in the trenches, the Royal Marines had been supported by an unusual addition to the Division. Eight officers and over 200 other ranks of the Royal Naval Division Cyclist Company had arrived from England. However, with hardly an inch of ground suitable for the use of cyclists, they supported the battalions before specialising as the 'Divisional bombers' – making hand grenades out of redundant jam tins.

When the Marines, in their turn, were relieved by the 1st Naval Brigade, the Anson Battalion, fresh from their rest on Imbros, were sent forward to man the trenches between the 1st Brigade and the French on the right, On the early morning of 5 July, the Turks launched an attack against the French lines. There seemed to be little enthusiasm for the assault despite the encouragement of two German Officers. However, about twenty Turks entered a trench defended by a company of Ansons. They were swiftly ejected and the position retaken. The whole event, however, came as something of a shock to the Anson Company Commander whose trenches had been invaded. During the whole period of the engagement, he had been in his dugout enjoying a breakfast of Maconochie rations and apricot jam and had been totally unaware of the drama being enacted a few feet from his, no doubt, well-earned repast. For a long time after this incident, the seamen of the Anson Battalion had their sense of humour tested when being asked if they had 'enjoyed their breakfast'.

It was shortly after these engagements that General Paris went to see the Army Corps Commander, General Hunter-Weston – the meeting illustrating the difference between naval and military attitudes. The exchange was witnessed and recorded by Lt Mackenzie, still serving as the RND's liaison officer. Hunter-Weston told Paris of a recent attack he had ordered. 'Many casualties?' enquired Paris.

Hunter-Western looked puzzled for a moment before answering in an almost angry tone, 'Casualties? What do I care for casualties?'

At this, Paris rose to his feet, 'I must be getting back.'

The Army General returned to his puzzled look, 'You'll stay to tea?'

'No, thanks,' replied Paris, this time in a growl of contempt as he turned on his heels and left.

As reinforcements failed to arrive on the peninsula in sufficient numbers to enable a large offensive to be mounted, the campaign had, as General Hamilton had feared, developed into a stalemate of trenches. From the Aegean to the Dardanelles, lines of trenches snaked across the foothills of Achi Baba. The links between the front line, support, and reserve trenches, rest camps and the beaches were provided by long, broad communication trenches. Many of the trenches had been given names by the troops in the different sectors; the front line was Main Street, Hope Street or Rue de Paris; the Eastern Mule trench, Oxford

Street, Regent Street, Plymouth Avenue, and the, optimistically named, Avenue de Constantinople were communication trenches. Points where several trenches converged were given such names as Holborn Circus, Clapham Junction, and Leicester Square.

When the landings had first taken place, the peninsula had been a green and fertile region. Spring flowers had just begun to bloom, scarlet poppies vied with blue cornflowers in adding brilliant bursts of colour to golden cornfields, and the clear April air had held the invigorating scent of wild thyme. Two months later, all that remained from the front line to Cape Helles were a few stunted trees and shrubs struggling to survive in earth that had been rubbed bare by the passage of thousands of men.

With the Mediterranean summer had come disease to attack the weakened troops – terribly punishing diseases, such as enteric fever, typhoid, and dysentery, which produced inertia and stupor even in the fittest of men. Even worse, however, for many who served on Gallipoli were the flies. Huge, horrible, blue-green creatures that descended on the living and the dead alike. No food could be eaten without becoming covered by them, they settled instantly on wounds, and, beneath the ground, their maggots grew fat on decaying corpses. The Turks were almost loved in comparison with the detested flies.

In fact, the Turks had proved to be honourable and chivalrous opponents. During a truce arranged to bury 4,000 Turkish dead, a Turkish officer, pointing to the vast number of corpses laying beneath a sweltering sun, said to a British officer, 'At this spectacle, even the most gentle must feel savage, and the most savage must weep.' Captured Turks would smile and point out the advantages their side had on the front line, and even suggest ways that the British might get round them.

There had been changes in the military dress worn by the RND and other units engaged in the Gallipoli fighting. With the searing summer temperatures, long trousers had become uncomfortable and so 'shorts' became 'rig of the day' – the knee-length shorts often being obtained by the simple measure of applying a pair of surgical scissors or a pocket knife to a normal pair of service trousers. The tropical field helmet – though a useful protection against the harsh sun – had turned out to be impractical on the battlefield. As the wearer dropped full length on the ground and raised his head to sight and fire his rifle, the rear helmet projection would hit his back between the shoulder blades and tip the front peak over his eyes. Instead, the peaked forage cap, or a rolled-up woollen comforter, was worn, often with a handkerchief or other square of cloth attached to protect the neck from the sun.

Food, usually in short supply, was, at best, monotonous, at worst inedible – and usually had to be cooked by the man himself. Breakfast was more often than not a lump of salt bacon, tea with sugar, and a 'hard tack' biscuit. At dinner, the bacon was replaced with bully beef which, in the heat, turned to a runny mush and, unless eaten immediately, became rapidly 'fly stew'. Supper consisted of cheese and biscuit, consumed, yet again, in a battle with the flies. Variety was occasionally provided by the issue of 'Maconochie Rations' – tins of sliced carrot and turnips in a thin gravy. At other times, the men would break up their biscuits and add boiling water to produce a porridge-like consistency which was sweetened by adding Tickler's plum and apple jam.

Parcels from home containing food and extra clothing were always very welcome. If such a parcel arrived for a man who had been killed, the parcel would be opened and the contents shared among the men of his platoon.

Water was always scarce. There were a few streams and wells on the peninsula, but those in possession of the Allies were well-known to 'Johnny Turk' who would lay down artillery and small-arms fire whenever any activity was seen in their area. By far the most water came by sea and had to be collected by working parties using biscuit tins. The tins, unfortunately, were made of a highly polished metal so promptly revealed the position of the water carriers and caused them, once again, to come to the attention of enemy fire.

One of the most popular activities, despite being in the open and well within range of the enemy guns, was the Sunday church service. Attendance was voluntary, and many men drew comfort from the singing of old hymns such as 'Oh God, Our Help in Ages Past', and 'Nearer My God to Thee' in the knowledge that the same hymns were being sung by their families in parish churches throughout Britain. Such services on the battlefield usually ended with the singing of 'When the Roll is Called Up Yonder.'

Even more popular than the church services was the daily issue of rum. Rum was issued to all sections of the British forces on Gallipoli but, being part of the Royal Navy, the Division was entitled to its daily 'tot'. Collected on a platoon basis from a site under the supervision of a duty officer, the rum was just as subject to illegal schemes as any ship at sea, and required the same amount of initiative to keep ahead of the authorities. An example of such enterprise occurred in the Drake Battalion when the rum ration failed to materialise when expected. Chief Petty Officer William Flook of the Drake Battalion's 'D' Company decided to go and find out what had happened. He was not long in coming across the answer. The rating sent to collect the rum had decided to sample some of the potent drink and was found slumped in a drunken heap. Flook could have put the man 'in the rattle' (i.e. on a charge), but he had not been rated CPO for his dull thinking. He dragged the man into an abandoned dugout and hid the remaining rum under nearby sand bags. On his return to the lines, he reported the man concussed by a shell and sent to the rear, with the rum being destroyed in the explosion. He then organised a resupply of the day's ration. After some time, he returned to the man, woke him up, and brought him back with the remaining rum – which was shared out to a grateful platoon.

During the early days of July, the RND, weakened by casualties and sickness, were withdrawn to their rest camp, with the Divisional Sector being handed over to the newly arrived 52nd Division. The Anson Battalion began to train in pack mule work, a task brightened by such army orders as 'if a mule breaks its leg, it is replaced forthwith by an intelligent NCO or Sapper'. Beach party duties were undertaken by the Deal Battalion Marines. Although called 'rest camps' the collection of dugouts, 'funk holes', and – where the scroungers had been successful – corrugated iron shelters were far from being a quiet haven where battle-weary troops could obtain respite from the rigours of war. Not far from the reserve trenches, the camps were well within range of the Turkish artillery, and even casualties from small-arms fire were commonplace. The Turks constantly fired their rifles and machine guns over the heads of the opposing front lines and many men were accounted for by 'overs' scoring hits well behind the trenches. On the Asiatic side of the Dardanelles, an 11-inch mobile gun nicknamed 'Asiatic Annie' kept up a random firing that roared over the whole of the Allies' area.

Early in the morning of 12 July, after a heavy bombardment lasting 1 ½ hours, the 52nd Division and, on their right, the French, attacked the enemy. By the end of the day, the flanks had made some progress, but the attacks from the centre had been severely repulsed. On the battlefront many men of the King's Own Scottish Borderers and the Highland Light Infantry lay dead. So desperate had the fighting become that the 52nd's reserves had been brought forward. A new reserve had to be found, and the only troops available were the exhausted seamen and Marines of the RND.

Beneath a darkening Turkish sky, the Plymouth, Portsmouth, Chatham and. Drake battalions moved up once more into the front line trenches. Behind them, the Nelson, Hawke, Hood, and Howe battalions were placed on immediate standby. As the night progressed, the Nelsons were ordered forward to join the front line battalions.

During the morning of 13 July, the 52nd Division continued to press forward its attack. By midday, the first two enemy trenches had been taken, but a third trench, shown clearly on the maps of the attackers, could not be found and many men were cut down by machine gun fire simply because they had advanced too far into enemy territory searching for the third trench.

At three o'clock in the afternoon, Brigadier General Trotman, in temporary command of the RND in General Paris's absence on Mudros, decided to send forward the Chatham, Portsmouth and Nelson battalions to find and attack the third trench. The Drake and Plymouth battalions would remain in reserve. Unfortunately, the message failed to reach the Chatham Marines in time so, at

4.50 p.m., the Portsmouth and Nelson battalions advanced with a third of their intended force missing. As they passed through the captured second Turkish line, the scenes at the battlefront became more and more confused. Large groups of men milled about not knowing where to go or what to do. Many just sat or kneeled, stunned and shocked by the events happening around them; others were violently sick as they sheltered against the blackened, decaying corpses the Turks had used to line their trenches. The dreadful stench, swarming flies, and debilitating disease combined on the battlefield in an appalling cauldron of misery.

The Nelson Battalion pressed forward and linked up with advanced units of the 5th Battalion of the Highland Light Infantry. The advance had been costly in casualties and left them with little option but to lie in a shallow depression and try to hold their ground. The Portsmouth Battalion had attacked in vigorous style in seeking the missing third trench, but their élan had been their undoing. After a short space of time, Captain Gowney, the hero of the train attack during the retreat from Antwerp, was the only officer in the entire battalion who had not been wounded. Nevertheless, after falling back for a few yards, the Marines dug themselves into a slight depression that afforded only inches of shelter. Neither battalion had any means of communication that could be safely used either between each other, or to other units in their rear. The Chatham Battalion had by now advanced and were occupying the first two Turkish trenches, but a wide gap still existed between them and the Portsmouth Marines 200 yards in front on their left.

The situation had to be consolidated as quickly as possible. Darkness had already fallen and a determined enemy counter-attack stood every chance of breaching the thinly held line. With Cdr Campbell injured and invalided home, the Drake Battalion, under their new temporary commanding officer, Lt Cdr H. D. King, moved forward with orders to link up with the Chatham Battalion on the right and the Nelson on the left. It was a hazardous undertaking that could easily have gone wrong in the darkness, and required discipline, initiative and enterprise. The Turks were keeping up constant small-arms fire across the whole sector, and considerable casualties were inevitable. Yet, by dawn, the task had been achieved. A new front line stretched completely across the divisional front, and work could begin on digging communication trenches to the old front line. For his leadership and organisation on the night of 13–14 July, King was awarded the Distinguished Service Order and promoted to Commander, a promotion confirming his command of the Drake Battalion.

During the entire battle, there had always been the risk of a strong Turkish counter-attack and in the reserve trenches Sub-Lt Herbert's response to the threat was to issue to his platoon the masterly understatement, 'Remember, regard all Turks with the gravest suspicion.'

On 24 July, it was decided that the gallant, but badly mauled, 52nd Division should hand the sector back to the Royal Naval Division. The Royal Marine Brigade took the left of the line, and the 1st Naval Brigade the right. The 2nd Naval Brigade formed the divisional reserve.

In a newly won part of the line, the constant harassment by the enemy was just part of the pressure upon the new occupants. The dead had to be buried, trenches repaired, communication trenches dug, and saps commenced. The strain on the already exhausted Naval and Marine Battalions was enormous. It was soon realised that the time spent in the front-line trenches would have to be shortened, and the interchange of reserve and front-line battalions become more frequent.

During one of their turns of duty in the front line, the Hood Battalion, now commanded by Lt Cdr Freyberg, was given the task of forcing back a barricade erected across a communication trench linking the naval trenches with the new Turkish front line. For several days the Turks had been advancing the barricade down the trench towards the British. It was soon to be more a threat than a nuisance.

The company detailed for the attack was commanded by Lt Charles Lister who personally led the assault. Despite a savage resistance by the defenders, the seamen stormed the barricade and swept the enemy from their positions. Even close-range artillery fire ripping down the trench could not quell the rush. By the time the attack had lost its momentum, 35 yards of trench been gained, the barricade forced back and now in British hands. But the cost had been high. Bodies of the dead carpeted the trench from the front line to the newly-gained obstacle; Lt Lister lay wounded in the stomach by a shell fragment.

As July came to a close, it became clear to everyone present that the Royal Naval Division had reached, if not passed, its limit of endurance. It was vital that they should be relieved. After the June battles, their strength had fallen to 7,349 of all ranks; by the end of July, 5,167 remained, of which only 129 were officers. Even those who still manned the trenches were far from fit for active service as disease continued to weaken them. On 25 July, the front-line trenches of the divisional sector were taken over by the Army's 33rd Brigade. A week later the Division retired to its rest camp handing the remainder of their part of the line over to the 42nd Division.

The weary seamen and Marines settled down in the dugouts of their rest camp. They were still liable to be bombarded by the enemy's guns, especially the erratic and wide-ranging 'Asiatic Annie', but the pressure of the front line, although only just over a mile away, was lifted, giving them days of relaxation in which to bathe in the Aegean and to struggle back to something approaching health. Their morale was high despite their losses. It was just as well, for a new, almost shattering, blow was about to fall upon them.

The Admiralty, which had always reserved its right to have first call upon the Division's resources, demanded the return of 300 stokers to the Fleet. In addition Commodore Oliver Backhouse and his staff were required for duty at sea. The RND, which at one time had twelve battalions in three brigades, and with its severe losses had been stretched taut to keep ten battalions, now had no option but to reduce to eight battalions in two brigades. The Royal Marine Brigade ceased to exist and the Division underwent a period of reorganisation.

The Deal, Portsmouth, Chatham, and Plymouth battalions were merged into two new battalions retitled the 1st and 2nd Royal Marine Battalions. To these were added the Anson and Howe battalions to form a new 2nd Royal Naval Brigade with General Trotman as Brigade Commander. The remaining naval battalions, Hood, Hawke, Nelson and Drake, made up the new 1st Royal Naval Brigade under General Mercer.

As the reorganisation in progress, the Anson Battalion, now fully trained in the handling of pack mules, and the 2nd RND Field Ambulance boarded transports and sailed north. There they joined with forces gathering to land on the peninsula at Suvla Bay, a landing place a few miles above Anzac Cove.

It had been rumoured for some time that a further landing would be taking place. The impasse at Anzac and on the Helles front had to be broken and, among all the arguments put forward, a landing in the north had been the most favoured. The odds on success looked attractive. The landing beaches were low and level. Only low mounds barred the route inland, and a salt lake behind Suvla Bay was dry in the summer months. As the landings were taking place, the Anzacs would launch attacks against Lone Pine Ridge and the heights of Chanuk Bair, eventually joining up with the territory to be captured at Suvla. Another attack against Krithia would keep the Turks busy to the south.

Against the hopes was the reality that most of the troops who were making the landing were raw recruits from Kitchener's Army making their first contact with the enemy. The senior officers were all elderly regular army men known as 'dug-out' Generals. In command was Lt General the Honourable Sir Frederick Stopford who was sixty-one years old and had been in retirement since 1909. His Chief Staff Officer, Brigadier General Reed VC had won Britain's highest award for valour in South Africa, but his ruling passion was heavy artillery bombardments. He seemed prepared to discuss little else.

At 9.50 on the evening of 6 August, troops, packed into newly designed landing craft nicknamed 'beetles', and commanded by Cdr Unwin VC, headed towards the darkened shore. Within minutes, the first boats had grounded on the beach and the soldiers were stepping, almost unmolested, onto the beaches. The opposition was minimal, only one casualty was incurred, and soon 7,000 men were safely ashore. The soldiers began to move inland across what appeared to be empty countryside. On the right of the landing, opposition was met at a Turkish advance post called Lala Baba, but the position was taken after some losses had been sustained. After more than two hours of roaming about trying to find the enemy, the troops simply halted their advance and waited for someone to tell them what to do. A few miles away to their right, the Anzacs were winning seven Victoria Crosses in hand-to-hand fighting on Lone Pine Ridge.

By the end of August, after a period of appalling inactivity and muddle, the Suvla Bay and Anzac Cove areas had been linked up. Most of the progress had been made by the Anzac troops in a series of savage encounters with the enemy. The New Zealanders had reached the top of Chanuk Bair, but had been driven off with great loss. The same had happened to the Australian Light Horse in their gallant attack on Battleship Hill. None of the high ground that would have given access to the straits ever fell to the British forces.

The month had not passed without incident for the RND Battalions at the Cape Helles front. From 15 August they had been back in the line, this time in a new sector. The new divisional frontage stretched from Gully Ravine on the left to, on the right, the Krithia Nullah. Their main communication trench was now the Eastern Mule Trench, their front line, the Rue de Paris. Much of the sector consisted of old Turkish trenches whose walls were packed with the rotting corpses from both sides of the conflict. Huge clouds of the loathsome flies filled the air, and the ground heaved with their maggots. Disease constantly thinned out the ranks, yet it was only the most desperately ill who could be allowed to leave the area for a short chance to recuperate. For those who remained, there was plenty of work to take their minds off their ghastly environment. The Divisional Engineers, who had earned the highest praise wherever they had been put to work, toiled night and day digging a new front-line trench, constructing drainage systems, and improving communications.

In order not to appear completely on the defensive, operations still had to be carried out against the well-entrenched enemy. Barricades, often of decaying bodies, had to be attached and forced back down the communication trenches linked to the Turkish front line. 'Bombing' raids were carried out by the Divisional Cyclists using their home-made grenades assembled from old jam tins filled with scraps of metal and fitted with an explosive charge. The device had a fuse through the top, which, to be lit before it was thrown. Another improvisation, often used through lack of trench mortars, was a large catapult that hurled the home-made bombs roughly in the direction of the Turks. Rumour elsewhere had it that the contraption was made and sold by Gamages, a well-known London Store.

Many hours had to be spent by officers crawling in advance of their own front line, reconnoitring enemy positions, a hazardous, but necessary, undertaking at which Lt Cdr Asquith of the Hood Battalion, and Lt Blyth of the Drakes, excelled.

Equally, the Turks were not content to remain on the defensive, and on several occasions, enemy raids had to be beaten off – often with considerable loss among the defenders. One such loss during this period was Lord Ribblesdale's son, Lt the Honourable Charles Lister, who had helped to carry the body of Rupert Brooke to its final resting place. He died on a hospital ship near the end of August, aged twenty-eight.

The seriously wounded of the RND, and those whose disease-ridden bodies rendered them incapable of even the most minor of tasks, were sent to Alexandria. There, while resting prior to returning to the peninsula, or being prepared for the journey home, they were looked after by members of the Admiralty Information Service. The founder of this organisation, and its guiding light in Alexandria, was Violet Asquith, the daughter of the prime minister, and sister of Lt Cdr Asquith of the Hood Battalion. The AIS kept a check on the condition of the wounded naval men and informed their families of their progress; the Red Cross carried out a similar service for the Army.

Back on Gallipoli, attempts were made to brighten the lives of the men in the RND. One of the Divisional Chaplains, the Reverend Bevill Close, through some unfathomable miracle, managed to produce some footballs. He organised a league between the battalions that was followed with great and keen interest. The games were played whenever possible on the rare spaces of 'dead ground' out of sight of Turkish riflemen, but such areas were not always available and, on many occasions, matches took place in full view of the enemy. Yet never once did the Turks open fire on the players, either through an interest in the sport itself or, perhaps, through an amazed disbelief at such antics on the very edge of the battlefield.

The Army had tried its hand at producing a magazine entitled the *The Peninsula Press* (popularly known as the 'Dardanelles Driveller') which, after a few copies, disappeared from the scene. The RND decided to produce its own broadsheet, which it called *Dug-Out Gossip*. The first Editorial read:

We are born … Unlike the 'Dardanelles Driveller', we are here to stay, so long as the stationery lasts.

We intend to be as unlike as it is possible to anything that has yet appeared in the journalistic line south of Achi Baba.

We shall cater for no tastes but our own. If our sense of humour does not appeal to you, this is simply your misfortune.

We do not crave for a large circulation, nor other people's advertisement. We advertise ourselves. Contributions (other than the subscription) from outsiders are not required, but if insisted on, will not be published.

SUBSCRIPTION – Well, we leave that to you. In case of a sudden, hurried, and long advance we may at any time have to delay publication.

The Editor

On the social front, a mixture of lime juice and rum, referred to as the 'Achi Baba cocktail', was drunk in preference to the usual chlorinated water whenever possible.

Although the morale of the RND remained high throughout this period on Gallipoli, their casualties continued to mount and, in September and October, more than 4,000 men were killed or had to be evacuated through wounds or sickness. Reinforcements had now begun to arrive from the Divisional Depot at Blandford, but not in high enough numbers to keep the divisional sector manned to a strength that could keep back a determined enemy attack. After consultation with the Commander-in-Chief, General Paris was able to secure the reinforcement of the RND with two battalions of the London Regiment.

In order to accommodate the newcomers, it was decided to build a new divisional rest camp behind the divisional sector and evacuate the old Achi Baba Nullah rest camp. As winter on the peninsula could be cold and wet, and as a protection against shelling, the new rest camp was planned to consist of deep dugouts connected by trenches. Variations in construction schemes had proved fruitless, as the only corrugated iron available was too thin to be of any use, and any wood on the Cape Helles front had long since disappeared. Little could be brought over from the old rest camp, as the main means of shelter there had been simply tarred blankets.

Little could be done to help with the increasingly miserable conditions, but that did not mean that no-one tried. Back in England, the following appeared in the *Eastern Daily Press* on 16 October –

Mrs H D King, wife of the Officer Commanding Drake Battalion RND, urgently appeals to the public for help in sending our comforts of all sorts to the men of the above battalion which has been fighting continuously on the Gallipoli Peninsula since the historic landing in April last.

Ever since the Spring, the Drake Battalion Comforts Committee have been sending out parcels of comforts regularly each week to the men of the battalion.

With the approach of winter, the needs for the comforts increase, and, therefore, greater support is required.

The funds are now running short, and contributions of money in aid thereof, as well as gifts of all kinds, including warm underclothing, particularly shirts, socks, scarves, and helmets, will be gratefully received and acknowledged by Mrs H D King, The Dales, Sheringham.

The men had long grown accustomed to living in 'dugouts', both in the trenches and in the rest camps. Lt A. P. Herbert – who was to show an astonishing talent for light verse – wrote 'The Dug-out' for the *Dug-Out Gossip*:

> It was my home, not ringed with roses blowing
>
> Not set in meadows where cool waters croon;
>
> Parched wastes were round it, and no shade was going,
>
> Nor breath of violets, nor song bird's tune;
>
> Only at times from the adjacent dwelling
>
> Came down with Boreas the quaint, compelling
>
> Scent of the Tenth Platoon.

Work on the new rest camp continued through the first weeks of November and, by the evening of 26 October, all the trenches had been dug and two of the dugouts completed. Then came a devastating blow, this time from Nature herself.

The approach of winter had been amply forecast by short, sharp gales over Cape Helles. Flocks of ducks flying south had provided sport for the soldiers. No-one, however, was prepared for the events that took place in the last week of November. On 26 November, the heavens opened and a deluge poured down upon the peninsula. Water streamed down the sides of Achi Baba and turned the trenches into torrents of rushing water that caused the sides to cave in and swept barricades of rotting corpses away. By the end of the night, the Allies had lost 200 men by drowning. But there were more horrors to come. The next night, the wind turned and became a northerly gale producing a savage snow blizzard. On the following morning, 18 degrees of frost had set in. For three days, the thermometer failed to rise above 22 degrees Fahrenheit. Ice covered the flooded trenches and dugouts, and men froze to the ground. Many had only sodden blankets to protect them against the onslaught, and several died from exposure. On the Anzac-Suvla front, 10,000 men had to be sent from the front lines, suffering from exposure and frostbite. The peninsula had not experienced such weather for at least forty years.

By the morning of 30 November, the gale had died down and the temperature once more began to climb. Some flooding resulted as the ice melted, but this was easily endurable compared to the previous extremes of discomfort. The break in the weather had even brought a bonus. Disease had been brought to a halt, and the bitterly loathed flies had been swept from Gallipoli.

The first few days of December saw the RND desperately repairing their trenches and re-erecting barricades. The new rest camp had to be bailed out, and the construction continued. They worked until 5 December, when the Division was ordered to take over part of the French sector. The 84th Brigade was to take over the rest camp and the trenches from Gully Ravine to Krithia Nullah.

The move, completed by 17 December, had been viewed by both officers and ratings with some consternation. It was a strongly held belief that the conditions in the French trenches and rest camps were, to say the least, primitive. When the recently evacuated French rest camp was reached, however, it was found, by comparison to their earlier accommodation at Cape Helles, to be almost palatial. The French had had none of the supply problems that had plagued the British forces on Gallipoli. The officers' quarters even had wooden floors and furniture. It was with wry amusement that the RND battalions noticed that the corrugated iron roofing that covered much of the dugouts, and was so different to the flimsy British issue, was marked 'Made in England'.

On Monday 21 December, the RND heard the half-expected, though nonetheless exciting, news that all the Anzac-Suvla forces had been evacuated. 83,000 men, 40,000 of them in the last two days, had slipped silently away and left the Turks facing empty trenches. Not one man had been lost as the troops had made their way down to the beaches and the waiting boats.

Three days later, on Christmas Eve, General Sir Charles Munro, who had relieved Sir Ian Hamilton in October, gave orders that preparations for the evacuation of Cape Helles were to be commenced forthwith. 35,000 were to try and repeat the success of the Anzac-Suvla evacuation.

23–25 December had seen heavy shelling by the Turks, and an attack by the now greatly reinforced enemy had been expected. When it failed to materialise, the evacuation preparations began to get underway. Stores were moved down to the beaches, evacuation routes planned, and periods of silence at night were enforced to accustom the Turks to quietness along the front.

On 30 December, General Paris received confirmation that the evacuation would take place within a few days.

The French were the first to go. By 1 January, the RND had taken over the whole of the French sector and now had their right flank resting on the Dardanelles cliffs. The 1st Royal Marines, the Hood, Drake and Howe battalions took over the front-line trenches, the Hawke and 2nd Royal Marines had the reserve line, while the Anson and Nelson battalions, along with the two London Regiment battalions, were at the rest camp.

Gradually, men and materials were shipped away from the toe of the peninsula. As the troops gathered on the beaches, a bugler was placed on the ruined battlements of the Sedd-el-Bahr fort where he sounded the note 'G' whenever he saw the yellow flash as 'Asiatic Annie' opened fire. This gave the soldiers time to take cover.

6 January was known as 'X' day, the day of the calculated risks of reducing the remaining troops to the barest minimum. 'Z' day, when the last of the troops were to be embarked, was to be 8 January.

The two battalions of the London Regiment left on the night of 6 January and, by the early hours of the 7th, there were fewer than 19,000 British troops left on the peninsula facing twenty-one Turkish Divisions. It was just at that moment that the Commander-in-Chief of the Turkish Army, Liman von Sanders, launched a ferocious assault against the British lines.

At two o'clock on the morning of the 7th, a terrific bombardment broke out along the Turkish front. Nothing like it had been experienced from the first day of the landings. For four and a half hours, the peninsula rocked with the fury of heavy artillery fire. In response, the return fire was slow and weak, as much of the British artillery had already been taken on board the evacuation vessels. A squadron of Royal Naval ships hurriedly formed up on the left of the line and soon effective naval gunfire support began to pound the enemy trenches. Nevertheless, just after midday, the Turkish infantry advanced en masse against the thinly defended British lines.

In the Royal Naval Division sector, all the reserves had been brought forward to meet the attack and, in common with the other three divisions remaining in the line, opened fire with such desperate fury that the first-line advancing Turks were brought mercilessly to a halt. As the next wave left their trenches, they too were shot to oblivion by defenders who knew they were so close to getting away from the deadly trap that Gallipoli had now become. As the British troops gripped their hot rifles ready for the next onslaught – an amazing thing happened – the Turks refused to advance. Despite all orders and threats from their officers, the enemy had had enough. Nowhere was the British line breached.

During the night of 7–8 January 1916, the Hawke Battalion and the 2nd Royal Marines joined the Nelsons and Ansons at the rest camp. This left just the 2,000 men of the Howe, Hood, Drake and 1st Royal Marine battalions to man the three trench lines at the front. In the first line, 845 men and eight machine guns were deployed, in the second 300 men and two machine guns, and, in the third, 460 men with three machine guns. In addition, over 200 men from the RND Field Ambulance remained at the front. Any attack from now on was certain to be a bloody affair.

When they reached the rest camp, two companies of the 2nd Royal Marine Battalion were ordered to take their places in a defence perimeter line around the embarkation beaches.

'Z' day arrived and brought with it the hoped-for calm weather. The Turks, blithely unaware of what was going on in front of their own lines, did little more than let loose a few, desultory rounds of small-arms fire, or let loose an occasional shell from 'Asiatic Annie', which did no harm. Meanwhile, as the remaining British troops watched the setting sun turn the peaks of Samothrace to purple for the last time, the battalions at the rest camp began their quiet march to the beaches and the waiting destroyers.

By nine o' clock it was the turn of the front-line defenders. Leaving only a skeleton force, they moved down the communication trenches and nullahs surrounded by an uncanny silence. They were onboard the evacuation vessels by 11.45. Only then did the remaining troops begin to filter away. As they went, they erected barricades, connected up mines, and charged booby traps to slow down any last-minute Turkish attack. On reaching the beaches, they found the wind had begun to whip up the water and it was with bated breath that they grouped around the piers waiting for picket boats and 'beetles' to ferry them out to the waiting ships. By 3.30 on the morning of 9 January, the last of the British forces had stepped off the hostile beach. The Anzac-Suvla miracle had been echoed at Cape Helles – no one had been killed in the evacuation, and not one man had been left behind.

The last men of the Royal Naval Division to embark were General Paris and his staff. As their evacuation ship, HMS *Grasshopper*, steamed toward Imbros, huge detonations ripped along the deserted British lines and the night sky was lit by dazzling flashes from exploding shells and flares. Beneath the shaking ground, bodies of thousands of British soldiers trembled alone in alien soil.

Wild thyme, myrtle, and camel thorn would soon cover the land once tramped to dust by the passing feet of many soldiers. The straits would remain closed until the war's end, and Russia would be forced to develop her northern ports of Archangel and Murmansk; only to be let down by the inefficiency of the Russian railway system. Winston Churchill, his reputation seriously damaged by the turn of events, left the government and had no major political role for the remainder of the war.

But, for the troops, the conflict continued. The British and Empire army units of the Expeditionary Force had gone to Alexandria and Cairo prior to being sent to other theatres of war. The RND, returned once more to Admiralty control and directly under the orders of Admiral de Robeck, were sent to the isle of Lemnos and arrived at Mudros harbour on 10 January. The island was cluttered with stores and munitions intended to support a long stay on Gallipoli, and the first of the seamen's tasks was to assist with the re-embarkation of all the equipment. After a few weeks, all that remained were the empty store-houses and the Division itself.

While decisions were being made regarding the RND's future, the 1st Brigade were given the job of garrisoning the islands of Lemnos, Imbros and Tenedos. The Hawke and Drake battalions took over Imbros while the tiny Tenedos went to a single company from the Hood Battalion and volunteer gunners from the Hawkes and Drakes, who took over three anti-aircraft guns from the Royal Naval Air Service.

The 2nd Royal Naval Brigade found itself facing the enemy once more – this time the Bulgarians.

Bulgaria had joined the Central Powers at the beginning of September 1915. German victories against the Russians and the stalemate on Gallipoli had persuaded King Ferdinand that his best option lay with the Germans. Between 3–5 October, two divisions, one French and one British, landed at Salonika in neutral Greece (it was hoped this landing would persuade the country to declare for the Allies). Two days later, German and Austrian forces crossed the Danube and invaded Serbia. On the 11th, Bulgaria marched into Macedonia. King Peter's Serbian army was utterly smashed and sent reeling back across the mountains of Albania, eventually to take refuge on Corfu. The Allies at the Salonika front had made an advance but, nothing achieved, returned to cover Salonika with a 60 mile defensive line, its right flank on the Gulf of Stavros.

It was to this right flank that the 2nd Brigade had been dispatch. Although the line was thinly held, there was very little threat from the enemy who stayed mainly behind the Greco-Serbian frontier, 25 miles away. Between the two fronts, the Greeks, still clinging to their neutrality, had deployed several divisions. There were occasional clashes between reconnoitring cavalry patrols, and, on one occasion, three German aircraft flew over the 2nd Brigade dropping bombs, the only casualty being a Greek pig.

The 2nd Royal Marines managed to get away from the monotony of digging trenches and filling sandbags by relieving a battalion of the Rifle Brigade in the mountainous forward area. They returned to the Gulf of Stavros on 8 April, where they and the other battalions were inspected by General Paris. By the 17th, the entire brigade had been relieved and re-embarked for Mudros.

With Gallipoli behind them, and no longer needed at the Salonika front, the Royal Naval Division was to prepare for warfare closer to home

Sub-Lt Vere Harmsworth, the son of Baron (later 'Viscount') Rothermere, the owner of the Daily Mail. An escaper from internment ind Holland, Harmsworth was killed in front of Beaucort-sur-Ancre 13 November 1916.

Lance Corporal Walter Parker VC.

CHAPTER V

Courage in the Mud,
but One Was Shot at Dawn

By the beginning of 1916, the Western Front had become a static line of trenches that stretched from Switzerland to the Channel. Offensives the year before at Ypres – where the Germans had introduced poison gas into the war – Aubers, Neuve-Chapelle, and Loos had all failed to break the stalemate. On 6 December 1915, the newly appointed commander of the French forces, sixty-three-years-old. Marshal Joffre, held a conference of all the Allied commanders at his Chantilly HQ. There it was decided to plan for a large offensive by Franco-British forces in the area of the River Somme to take place in the summer. The German High Command, however, had been doing some planning of their own.

The Chief of the German general staff, General Erich von Falkenhayn, considered that his most important task of 1916 was to wear the French army down by a constant pressure on one point of the French defences. He chose the fortress city of Verdun.

Surrounded by natural defence lines of hills and ridges, Verdun had defied invaders since the fort was first built in the seventeenth century. It had become a symbol to the French people of absolute defiance against all odds. Falkenhayn had chosen his spot well; he knew that the French would defend the citadel with a ferocious, reckless, determination.

On the other hand, the French had never really considered the probability of an attack against Verdun and, even if such an attack should occur, the collapse of the Belgian forts had shown that such defences could easily be reduced by modern artillery. Consequently many of the fortresses' heavy guns had been removed for use in the offensives of 1915.

By the beginning of February, the Germans had brought up 1,200 guns to bear on the city. Almost half were of a large calibre, and thirteen were the giant siege mortars that were known as 'Big Berthas', and that had done great damage when used against Antwerp and elsewhere. Helped by the removal of church steeples that could have assisted French artillery spotters, the preparations had been carried out in complete secrecy.

The initial attack was held up for nine days because of heavy snowfalls, but at dawn on 21 February, the Crown Prince, the commander of the German forces facing Verdun, gave the order that started a nine-hour bombardment, the like of which had never before been seen on the Western Front. At four o'clock in the afternoon, the bombardment lifted and the German troops, advancing in small groups and infiltration parties, attacked over the obliterated French trenches. Yet, despite the destruction, the defenders fought with such vigour that the attackers were forced to fight for every inch. However, on 25 February, a twenty-four-year-old Lieutenant, Eugen Radtke, leading a small patrol, found one of the vital outlying defences, Fort Douamont, almost undefended, and took it without the loss of a single man.

While Germany acclaimed the capture of Fort Douamont as a great victory, in France the news assumed the proportions of a terrible national disaster. Joffre was now forced to look at Verdun through different eyes – the honour of France was now at stake. The citadel could not be allowed to fall regardless of the lives that may be lost. Falkenhayn's challenge had to be met.

General Henri Philippe Pétain was the man chosen by Joffre to be the saviour of Verdun. The choice was a wise one. Rejecting a directive that Fort Douamont must be retaken, Pétain ensured that the remaining forts were sufficiently garrisoned and provisioned prior to turning his attention to his lines of communication. Soon, the only road into Verdun was packed with convoys of lorries carrying supplies for the citadel. Constantly under shellfire, the road was kept open by companies of engineers who repaired the damage as soon as it occurred. The lifeline became known to the defenders, and to the rest of France, as 'The Sacred Way'.

For the next three-and-a-half months, the battle was fought on the desolated land in front of the fortress citadel while the Germans continued to pour shells into the shattered ruins that Verdun had become in the name of French honour.

The first signs of pressure being taken off the troops at Verdun came in June. Russian forces under General Brusilov had sent the Austro-Hungarians staggering back in the east and Falkenhayn was forced to send troops from Verdun to the aid of his crumbling allies. Although, later in the month, the Germans were to succeed in taking another fort using the new phosgene gas, their successes were almost at an end. By the 23rd they had reached their furthest point of advance. Two days later the rumble of heavy artillery announced the start of a new Franco-British offensive that straddled the River Somme.

For five days the artillery bombardment shelled the German lines, turning the surface into a devastation that obliterated trenches. But, deep in well-prepared dugouts, the Germans waited for the attack they knew would come.

At seven o'clock on 1 June 1916, the bombardment lifted and, beneath the bright sun of a summer's day, almost 100,000 British soldiers left their trenches and marched towards the enemy in long dense lines. Each man carried a pack weighing at least 66lbs, but often reaching as much as 90lbs. They advanced at a steady pace, led by young officers carrying pistols cocked and ready. Most of the British soldiers were raw and inexperienced, either Territorials or from Kitchener's 'New Army', and they advanced knowing that the German defences must have been destroyed by the five days of heavy bombardment.

However, as the troops got within 100 yards of their objective, a withering fire broke out from the enemy positions and the waves of advancing men were scythed down with appalling ease by German machine gunners as they emerged from their dug-outs and sited their weapons among the shell-holes. Despite being cut down in rows, the British, in a remarkable display of mass courage, continued to press their attack until they were within range of their hand grenades. Beneath a pall of smoke that blacked out the sun, the fighting continued all day, but, by evening, the only British gain amounted to a small advance on the right of their line where the HQ of the German 62nd Regiment had been captured.

For this small gain, the British had scarred an entire generation. Their casualties amounted to 57,500, of which almost 20,000 lay dead before the German lines. Not since the Battle of Towton in 1461, when 28,000 Englishmen lay dead, had the British known such casualties. Never again during the course of the war would they have such high casualties on one day, but the killing would have to continue - the Battle of the Somme, once started, had to be completed.

When the battle was seventeen days old, the Royal Naval Division, under General Sir Archibald Paris – who had been made a Knight Commander of the Bath in recognition of his services in Gallipoli – took its place in the line in the Angres-Souchez sector, well to the north of the Somme battle-front.

The Division had arrived at Marseilles in the middle of May and had travelled by train to Pont-Remy. Their progress through France had been marked by cheering crowds who massed at the stations en route and pressed food and wine upon the grateful seamen and Marines. At Pont-Remy, the Division left their trains and marched to Longpre near Abbeville – an established concentration and rest area. Once again the RND was to be reorganised.

Before their arrival in France there had been a move to reduce the Division to six battalions. At one stage, the orders for this action had actually been issued but were later countermanded. Now, to a background of fierce controversy over the future and control of the Division, it was decided to bring its strength back up to three brigades with twelve battalions.

The War Office had for some time been casting covetous eyes at the RND and wanted to take the Division over completely. This would, of course, have meant that the distinct naval characteristics of the Division would have been completely destroyed. The majority of the Admiralty might not have seen this move as too much of a loss, being somewhat bewildered to find themselves responsible for a major land fighting force. The new First Lord, Sir Edward Carson, was, however, determined not to lose control over the Division completely. Eventually a compromise was worked out. The Admiralty would continue to look after pay (which was higher than the Army), allowances, records, and the awarding of commissions. The War Office took responsibility for training, discipline, recruiting, and equipment.

Some effects of the new division of control were felt immediately. The khaki sailor's hat with its gold-lettered cap tally had to go, its place being taken by the army's peaked forage cap. This brought forward a new problem. Whilst the officers and Chief Petty Officers had always worn naval peaked caps and consequently had cap badges denoting their rank, there were no cap badges for the remaining seamen. This problem did not affect the Royal Marines, whose 'Globe and Laurel' cap badge had been in existence for some time. The necessary cap badges were swiftly and handsomely produced. The Hawke Battalion was given a rearing bird of the same name over the motto 'Strike'; the Hood gained a crow and anchor over the word 'Steady'; the Anson, a coronet pierced by a spearhead above the motto 'Nil Desperandum'; while the Howe Battalion was given the naval crown. The Nelson Battalion had a bows-on view of HMS *Victory* in full sail; and the Drakes, a sailing ship on top of the world surrounded with oak leaves, surmounted by a crown, all above the motto 'Auxillo Divino'. All the battalions had curved brass shoulder titles with the battalion's name and a new Divisional emblem – a red anchor on a blue background within a red circle - was worn on the upper sleeve.

The problem of rank recognition between the army and the navy had also to be resolved. The officers of the RND had, from the time before Gallipoli, worn army rank on their shoulders in addition to their naval rank – thus a Lieutenant of the RND, being equivalent to a Captain in the army, wore two rings ('stripes') on his cuffs and three 'pips' on his shoulders. Ratings were required to assume the insignia of their equivalent army rank: a Leading Hand wore two Corporal's stripes on his right sleeve and Petty Officers the three stripes of a sergeant. Chief Petty Officers took on the role of Staff Sergeant and Sergeant-Major and wore a crown on the right cuff. To fill the gap between Private and Corporal, for which no naval equivalent existed, the new rating of Able Seaman (Higher Grade), (AB (HG)) was introduced.

Attempts had been made to bring the Division up to its required strength of twelve battalions by drafting men from the Divisional Depot at Blandford, but the depot had been stretched to its limits just keeping up with the losses already incurred by the two brigades. It was, therefore, decided that the third brigade would be supplied by the army. In order to make this easier, and to fit in with army custom, the 1st and 2nd Naval Brigades had to be renumbered. The 1st Brigade – Anson, Howe, 1st Royal Marines, and 2nd Royal Marines - became the 188th Brigade. The 2nd Brigade – Drake, Nelson, Hawke, and Hood – became the 189th Brigade. The new brigade would be the 190th and consist of the 1st Battalion of the Honourable Artillery Company, the 7th Battalion of the Royal Fusiliers, the 10th Battalion of the Dublin Fusiliers, and the 4th Battalion of the Bedfords. With Brigadier General Mercer promoted to become Adjutant-General of the Royal Marines, Brigadier General Trotman took over the 190th Brigade; Brigadier General Robert Prentice, the 188th; and Brigadier General Lewis Phillips, the 189th.

To bring the Division up to full strength other units were added or increased. They were the Divisional Train; the RND Engineers; the light, medium, and heavy trench mortar batteries; machine gun companies (who had as their badge crossed machine guns with the letters 'RND' below); Field Ambulances; the Mobile Veterinary Section; the Sanitary Section; the Ordnance Section; and the Ammunition Column. The Cyclists Company, despite their valuable work as bomber-makers on Gallipoli, was broken up and dispersed among the other Marines. To make up for the lack of field artillery that had cost so many lives at Gallipoli, the 315th, 317th, and 223rd Field Artillery Brigades joined the Division under Brigadier General A. H. de Rougemont.

A Pioneer Battalion had been provided by the 14th Battalion of the Worcestershire Regiment. The pioneers had been raised at the personal cost of Col Sir Henry Webb and were now under the command of Lt-Col. Gascoigne (formerly of the Seaforth Highlanders). Although primarily employed in the building of roads and the construction of trenches and other fortifications, the pioneers were also fully trained troops able to hold their own in the front line.

The Royal Naval Division had become an imposing affair.

In June, the Division, with the exception of the 190th Brigade, who were still completing their initial training, moved to the Angres-Souchez sector to complete their training in the new kind of trench warfare that was current on the Western Front. Instead of a strongly fortified front line with a support and reserve line to the rear, the new system had a thinly defended front line, often no more than a series of outposts. The second line was only strong enough to hold back a small or local attack, the main line of resistance in strength being the third line. Changes to the defensive arrangements were not the only differences to their Gallipoli experiences that the RND were to experience. Instead of the Wolsey sun helmets, they were supplied with the new 'tin hat', a steel helmet based upon a medieval English pattern. Whilst there remained a problem with flies, they were not as bad as those encountered during the summer at Gallipoli. Body lice, on the other hand, were every bit as bad, and the rats infinitely worse. The Divisional Transport, which on Gallipoli had consisted of little more than a few wagons and a Field Ambulance, now had to be mastered in a way that could allow the Division to be moved en masse from one part of the line to another. Officers had to accustom themselves to riding on horses as a means of mobility. There was also the new menace of gas warfare, and trenches, which were substantially built but acted as drains for the surrounding fields. It only took a small amount of rain to turn the trenches into rivers of deep mud. There were even new weapons – the Lewis Gun and the Stokes Mortar – that had to be mastered. On the other hand, now that they were on the Western Front, they were issued with the new Lee-Enfield rifle.

Gaining this new experience and knowledge was not without its interesting moments. When the scholar, composer, and athlete Lt 'Clegg' Kelly, of the Hood Battalion, was sent to an infantry depot to learn about the new system of trench warfare, he not only turned up sporting a full beard, but demanded that, being the Senior Service, the Royal Navy had precedence over their military colleagues when on parade.

With their training completed, the RND battalions entered the line alongside battalions of the 47th Division. Although the sector was considered 'quiet' when compared to the fighting that continued to the south, across the Somme, the enemy was by no means asleep. During a patrol between the lines on 14 June Lt Elliot of the 1st Royal Marines was hit and badly wounded. For two days a Marine private, also named Elliot, and others of his patrol tried to get the officer back to their own lines. The officer died of his wounds on 16 June and Private Elliot did not get back into his own trenches until the 18th. He had been between the lines for four days without food and was awarded the Distinguished Conduct Medal for his attempt to save the life of the officer.

During this period, Lt Ivan Heald, who before the war had been a reporter with the *Daily Express*, discovered his own means of diversion. He would crawl across no-man's land to the enemy's barbed wire and tie empty tins among the strands. Attaching a long length of string to his handiwork he returned to his own trenches where he would then amuse those around him by jerking on the string causing the tins to rattle and the enemy to open fire against an invisible target. As if such antics were not enough to keep him occupied, Heald later transferred to the Royal Flying Corps and was killed in a training accident, his loss mourned by all who had known him.

In the main, however, life among the ruined mining villages and slag heaps of the Angres area did not cause a great deal of concern to a division who had come through Gallipoli with honour. For several weeks, the battalions moved from reserve to support and to front-line positions singing 'Till the boys come home' as they marched along. Whilst in the front line Lts Asquith and Heald, usually in company with one or more ratings, would crawl around no-man's land in the dark reconnoitring the position of the enemy (at times no more than 25 yards from their own front line). Apart from the occasional flare or burst of machine gun fire their nocturnal roaming escaped detection by the enemy. Lt Kelly preferred a different approach. Having crawled close to the German trenches, he would start singing lines from Wagner's opera *Siegfried*. Frequently, the singing was taken up by a German and, when this happened, Kelly would try and persuade the soldier to leave his trench and voluntarily become a prisoner of the British. The tactic never worked, but provided an entertaining distraction in both trenches. When not attempting to subvert the Germans with Wagner, Kelly – who, among other highly regarded compositions had written an elegy in memory of Rupert Brooke – worked with the Hood's military band, at one time putting on a performance of Tchaikovsky's '1812 Overture' to a background of guns firing in Souchez Woods. After a period in the front line or in the support trenches on the dominating high ground of Lorrette Spur, there was often the opportunity to visit the pleasant villages to the rear for a glass of wine and a small degree of comfort.

It was during this time that the Army High Command, apparently uncomforted by the singular individualism of a unit entitled the 'Royal Naval Division', ordered that the RND be henceforth known as the '63rd (RN) Division'. The original 63rd Division had been a Northumbrian Territorial division that had been disbanded. Now the divisional number, augmented by the initials 'RN' was imposed for the sake of military regularity. This early attempt at enforcing conformity never sat easily with the Division who continued to refer to themselves by the original and well-loved title.

On the night of 6 September the RND battalions handed over their trenches to the 37th Division. However, four days later, the Anson Battalion was ordered to carry out a raid on the enemy lines to try and gain information about the troops immediately opposing their sector. Two officers and twelve ratings carried out the raid with imposing competence, capturing a member of the 103rd Saxon Regiment. The long training period had achieved its aim. The Division was now ready to take its place in the heat of battle on the Western Front.

They spent the last days of September back at the concentration area billeted in the pleasant Artois villages between Arras and Bailleul. The 190th Brigade, its training completed, joined the Division and, for the first time in its history, the Royal Naval Division prepared to move as a single unit. They were moved southwards, towards the still-continuing Battle of the Somme.

By 1 October the German front line had, in places, been driven back up to 8 miles from its position of three months earlier. At the northern flank of the advance the line ran from east to west, north of the villages of Thiepval, Coucelette, and Gueudecourt. The western extremity of this new line rejoined the old front line where the River Ancre had carved a valley through the rolling countryside. Here the enemy line continued on its old north–south axis running before the villages of Beaucourt-sur-Ancre, Beaumont Hamel, Serre, and Gommecourt. Despite continuous pressure against the villages immediately to the north of the Ancre – Beaucourt-sur-Ancre and Beaumont Hamel – the German defenders had repulsed all the attacks mounted against them. Although casualties had been enormously high in these attacks, the pressure could not be allowed to fall off. A new assault was planned to take place in November, this time with the Royal Naval Division bearing the brunt.

The Division arrived at the villages of Varennes and Forceville, which lay some 4 miles behind the Serre-Beaumont sector of the line, on 4 October. There they were told to make all preparations for the coming attack. Three days later the 190th Brigade was moved forward into the trenches between Serre and Beaumont Hamel to get a feel for the front line.

The ground the Division now faced was different to the shattered buildings and mining debris of the Angres area only in the sense that it was far, far, worse. Constant shelling had reduced many of the buildings to little more than brick-coloured stains. Trees existed only as splintered trunks, and trenches were badly knocked about. Worst of all was the trampled and shell-blasted sea of mud that stretched in all directions – at least as far as could be seen in the perpetually falling rain. If any of this would affect the Division's morale, a much worse blow was about to descend.

The 190th Brigade had been on the front line for a week when the Divisional Commander paid them a visit. As he walked along the line with a senior staff officer, a shell landed beside them. The staff officer was killed outright, and Sir Archibald Paris lay seriously wounded.

As the news went round the Division, everyone was stunned. The General was an immensely popular and respected leader. Neither his personal bravery, nor his military expertise had ever been in doubt. Since before Antwerp, he had been the Division's guide and staunch defender, and his loss was a heavy blow to bear. Heavier, indeed, than the most pessimistic would have believed possible.

The ruined villages behind the lines provided little shelter for the troops against the deteriorating weather, while those who manned the trenches merely existed in miserable squalor. None of this, however, had greatly affected the morale of the RND, but the loss of General Paris had come as a shattering blow. On top of the appalling conditions and heartfelt tragedy, the new Divisional Commander arrived on the scene.

Major-General Cameron Deane Shute had served in the Welch Regiment and the Rifle Brigade. He was widely acknowledged to be a brave, but unimaginative, man, whose firm belief in unchangeable Army militarism was utterly rigid. He let it be known immediately that he had no time for naval traditions or trappings. He was part of the Army, and the Division would become part of the Army – whether it liked it or not.

In the days that followed, when they should have been preparing for the impending attack, the Division resisted wherever possible the attempts by General Shute and his staff officers to abolish naval custom, with its flexibility within which individualism might flourish, and replace it with military severity.

It did not take Shute long to run foul of naval tradition. During an inspection he came across Sub-Lt Clifford Codner of the Hawke Battalion, a former miner who had joined the RND in January 1915. In August the same year, he had spent one day as a Leading Seaman before, within twenty-four hours, being advanced to Petty Officer. He stayed at that rate for just two months before being awarded a commission as a Sub-Lt. Having formally requested 'leave to grow', he was granted permission to grow a beard. Such a sight was anathema to Shute, who promptly demanded the offending article's removal. Codson, however, stood his ground and refused. After a flurry of communications and the taking of advice, Shute was forced to withdraw his demand. The Division rejoiced at Codson's victory, and the Hawke Battalion's Lt A. P. Herbert celebrated by writing a poem under the title of 'The Battle of Codson's Beard':

I'll tell you a yarn of a sailor-man, with a face more fierce than fair,
Who got round that on the Navy's plan by hiding it all with hair;
He was one of a hard old sailor-breed, and had lived his life at sea,
But he took to the beach at the nation's need, and fought with the RND.

Now Brigadier-General Blank's Brigade was tidy and neat and trim,
And the sight of a beard on his parade was a bit too much for him:
'What is that,' said he, with a frightful oath, 'of all that is wild and weird?'
And the Staff replied, 'A curious growth, but it looks very like a beard.

And the General said, 'I have seen six wars, and many a ghastly sight,
Fellows with locks that gave one shocks, and buttons none too bright,
But never a man in my Brigade with a face all fringed with fur;
And you'll toddle away and shave to-day. But Codson said, 'You err.

'For I don't go much on wars, as such, and living with rats and worms,
And you ought to be glad of a sailor lad on any old kind of terms;
While this old beard of which you're skeered, it stands for a lot to me,

For the great North gales, and the sharks and whales, and the smell of the good grey sea.
New Generals crowded to the spot and urged him to behave,
But Codson said, 'You talk a lot, but can you make me shave?
For the Navy allows a beard at the bows, and a beard is the sign for me,
That the world may know wherever I go, I belong to the King's Navee.'

They gave him posts in distant parts, where few might see his face,
Town-Major jobs that, break men's hearts, and billets at the Base;
But whenever he knew a fight was due, he hurried there by train,
And when he'd done for every Hun –they sent him back again.

Then up and spake an old sailor, 'It seems you can't 'ave 'eared,
begging your pardon, General Blank, the reason of this same beard:
It's a kind of a sart of a camyflarge, and that I take to mean
A thing as 'ides some other thing wot oughtn't to be seen.

'And I've brought you this 'ere photergraph of what 'e used to be
Before 'e stuck that fluffy muck about 'is phyzogmy.'
The General looked and, fainting, cried, 'The situation's grave!
The beard was bad, but, KAMERAD! he simply must not shave!'

And now, when the thin lines bulge and sag, and man goes down to man,
A great black beard like a pirate's flag flies ever in the van;
And I've fought in many a warmish spot, where death was the least men feared,
But I never knew anything quite so hot as the Battle of Codson's Beard.

Shortly after the arrival of the new Divisional Commander, the Divisional Sector was moved south from the Serre-Beaumont Hamel trenches to a 1,200-yard-wide front facing Beaucourt-sur-Ancre with its right flank resting on the River Ancre. The trenches the 188th and 189th Brigades took over from Portuguese troops were in a terrible state. Poorly constructed, they had become rivers of mud in which the men waded knee-deep. There were no dugouts in which to shelter from the almost continuous shelling, and the communication trenches had been dug right across the face of a ridge giving the enemy gunners ample time to aim at any movement along their length. General Shute (soon referred to by the seamen as 'Schultz the Hun') decided that the line had to be straightened out and assembly trenches dug prior to the attack.

This onerous task, combined with the continuous carrying of stores and ammunition to the front line by the battalions stood down from the trenches, threatened to exhaust the men at just the time when they should have been resting. Many of the battalions had already been reduced from 700 to 500 men through illness brought on by the gruelling labour recently undertaken. Even worse, Shute decided that the whole job had to be done on a single night, that of 20 October. To achieve this, two shifts of working parties, each shift numbering 500 men, would be used. In the event, the large numbers of men moving along the front at night unnerved the Germans, who opened fire with artillery. One mortar round fell close to Lt Cdr Asquith, burying him and rupturing both his eardrums. Much to his annoyance, his injuries were used as an excuse to send him home to recover – not because of any failings on his part but, being the prime minister's son (and with a brother already killed on the Western Front), no-one wanted the responsibility of placing him at risk.

Those who remained were utterly exhausted, a situation not improved during the first few days of November when the rain turned into snow, and a bitter cold added to the hardships.

Neither conditions nor exhaustion had any effect upon Shute's attempt to bring the Division into his idea of military order. As he and his staff carried out their initial inspection of the new trenches, a staff officer reported that he had found evidence of human body waste in a corner of a trench. Shute fired off a succession of bombastic complaints in every direction. In reply, the normally amiable Lt A. P. Herbert wrote a poem entitled 'That Shit Shute':

The general inspecting the trenches
Exclaimed with a horrible shout,
'I refuse to command a division
Which leaves its excreta about.

But nobody took any notice
No-one was prepared to refute,
That the presence of shit was congenial
Compared with the presence of Shute.

And certain responsible critics
Made haste to reply to his words
Observing that his
Staff advisors consisted entirely of turds.

For shit may be shot at odd corners
And paper supplied there to suit,
But a shit would be shot without mourners
If somebody shot that shit Shute.

Herbert's words were put to the tune 'Wrap Me up in My Tarpaulin Jacket' and sung the entire length of the British front line.

On 9 November, against all expectations, the dawn brought with it a high, bright, yellow sun that gave the air a sparkle. There had not been a morning like it for weeks and it happened to be the morning when the staff officers paid a visit to study the area for the forthcoming attack. During the afternoon, when the staff officers had left, the rain began to pour down again, but everyone knew it was too late. Sure enough, on the following day, the orders confirming the attack came through. The advance would take place on Friday 13 November.

The Royal Naval Division's task in the battle was to force the German front line back beyond the village of Beaucourt-sur-Ancre. To assist them in their attack the new tactical development known as the 'creeping barrage' would be used. The old method of heavily bombarding the enemy trenches prior to an attack, a method that had been used during the early part of the Battle of the Somme, was discovered to have some serious defects. The Germans had become highly skilled in preparing deep dugouts to protect their troops from the shelling and, once infantry began to advance against their line, they emerged from this protection, set up machine guns in the newly created shell craters, and proceeded to slaughter the attackers.

The 'creeping barrage' laid down a curtain of shells just in front of the advancing troops, lifting step by step to allow the advance to continue. As it lifted from the enemy trenches, the attackers followed immediately with rifle, bomb, and bayonet before the defenders could surface and set up a defensive line. Two important rules had to be observed by the attacking infantry. Firstly, once the bombardment lifted from the enemy line and began to roll on to the next objective, the line had to be secured to prevent the enemy from emerging from behind the infantry as they followed the advancing barrage. This was dealt with by advancing in waves which passed through each other as the enemy trenches were being secured. Secondly it was vitally important to keep up with the barrage, thus depriving the enemy of an opportunity to man or create defences before the attacking troops arrived upon them.

The first objective of 13 November was the German front-line system which consisted of three lines of trenches. The third trench line had been designated the 'Dotted Green Line'. From that position, the ground dipped away into a narrow valley through which ran Station Road linking Beaucourt railway station – to the south of the village – and Beaumont Hamel. The road was guarded by trenches, while among the railway sidings at the station were several dugouts that were linked underground to rear positions, and had to be taken during the course of the advance.

Beyond Station Road, the far side of the valley sloped up to a heavily defended ridge. This defensive line was known as the 'Green Line' and was the Division's second objective.

The third objective, the 'Yellow Line', ran across a hill in front of Beaucourt and continued westwards, parallel with the 'Green Line', through low ground. It was known that this line had also been well entrenched by the Germans and would have to be taken before the village itself could be captured. The fourth objective was a vague line which ran beyond the village and was known as the 'Red Line'. The successful outcome of the battle was taken to be the formation of a defence line along the final objective.

At 5.45 on the morning of the 13th, the attack would be opened by the artillery barrage as it began to creep towards the 'Dotted Green Line'. The line of exploding shells was to be closely followed by four battalions, each battalion advancing in four waves. On the right, with their right flank on the Ancre, was the Hood Battalion under their new Commanding Officer Lt-Col. Freyberg (who, because of his German name, was known by his fellow officers as 'Fritz'). On his return from Gallipoli, he had transferred from the RNVR to the Army, but still chose to belong to the Division he had served with since the earliest days. With Lt Cdr Asquith sent home with damaged ears, the Hood's new second-in-command was Lt Cdr Egerton who was already the holder of a Distinguished Service Order. On the left of the Hood was the Hawke Battalion whose Commanding Officer, Lt-Col. Wilson, had been made a Companion of St Micheal and St George for his services in Gallipoli. To the left of the Hawkes was Cdr Ramsey Fairfax's Howe Battalion. Between them and the 51st Highland Division, who were to attack Beaumont Hamel, were the 1st Royal Marines under Lt-Col. Cartwright.

The first four battalions were to be followed by four more, who as the 'Dotted Green Line' was being secured, would pass through the first battalions, follow the barrage, and attack the 'Green Line'. At 7.30 a.m. the barrage was to lift and move towards the 'Yellow Line' followed closely by the first four battalions, whose place in the trenches of the 'Dotted Green Line' would be taken by the four battalions of the 190th Brigade.

By 8.30 a.m., it was considered that the 'Green Line' would have been secured by the second-wave battalions, and they would be able to follow a lift in the barrage that would enable them to advance to the 'Red Line'.

The second wave of battalions was made up of, behind the Hood, the Drake Battalion under Lt-Col. Tetley; following the Hawkes were the Nelsons led by Lt-Col. Burge. Lt-Col. Saunders' Anson Battalion followed the Howe, and the 2nd Royal Marines, commanded by Lt-Col. Hutchinson, were behind the 1st. Orders were given that the various Battalion Headquarters were not to move forward to join the other companies until the first objective had been taken.

The night of 12–13 November was cold and misty. Snow lay over parts of the ground as the battalions moved quietly forward into their places for the attack. Any problems caused by the change in command had been pushed aside, and morale was a high as ever as they lay or crouched on the open ground behind the trenches. Ahead of them, on ground that sloped gently upward, were the three lines of trenches of the 'Dotted Green Line'. In some places the enemy was 250 yards away, in others less than 200. But all that could be seen was the early morning darkness softened by the mist.

Suddenly, and unexpectedly, German artillery opened fire and high explosives fell among the rear battalions. In a very short time, the Drake, Hawke, and Anson battalions had all lost their Commanding Officers among the numerous dead. There was nothing the survivors could do but take what shelter they were able to. In the meantime, a signal arrived at the front line from Divisional Headquarters. It demanded a 'nominal role of all the officers and men in your unit who can speak Chinese'.

At 5.45 a.m. the enemy fire was answered by the Divisional Artillery as it laid down a curtain of fire along the front. As the line of explosions began to creep towards the enemy, the waves of sailors and Marines clambered over the parapets of their trenches and followed the barrage. When the four lines of men from the first battalions had left, the second battalions followed, ready to move through the first objective. On the right, Lt Col. Freyberg and his Headquarters had chosen to disregard the order keeping them in the rear until the first trenches had been taken, and had advanced with the rest of the battalion. Behind them, the Drake Headquarters, now without their Commanding Officer, followed their example and walked into no man's land when their battalion moved forward. They were followed by Sergeant Meatyard of the Royal Marines ignoring all that was going on around him and concentrating on unwinding the large, heavy coil of telephone wire that was to prove a vital communication link with the rear.

On the right of the attack, German shells fell between the opposing trenches, but most fell in the rear area of the support lines. A few exploded in the centre of the advance but, on the left, where the 1st Royal Marines were about to reach the first German trench, the enemy bombardment rained down on the attacking troops and caused enormous casualties.

The survivors never faltered in their advance, but their reduced numbers could not carry their attack through the three lines of trenches. When the 2nd Marines arrived – incredibly dribbling a football between themselves – they expected to pass on beyond the 'Dotted Green Line'. Instead they found savage hand-to-hand fighting raging in the first and second trenches.

In the centre of the advance, the Hawke Battalion set off followed immediately by the Nelsons – who had also chosen to ignore their orders to wait for the first objectives to be taken. From a forward shell-hole, the Adjutant of the Hawkes, Lt Cdr Douglas Jerrold, watched the advance –

> Every variety of shell was dropping, but we only saw the lines of infantry, first of our own men, then of the Nelson Battalion, disappearing into the mist in perfect order and sequence. Any barrack square in Christendom would have been dignified by such an exhibition of precision. Here, for hundreds of simple and Christian men, was their hour of opportunity. Here all grievances were forgotten and all enmity healed … Eight lines of men passed me so closely that I could see every expression on their faces as they faded into the mist, and among all those men walking resolutely to wounding or death, I saw not one expression of fear or regret, or even of surprise.

But the Howe and Hawke battalions' assault was to be seriously blunted by fierce resistance from a redoubt packed with machine guns. Some men from the Howe had managed to get into the first trench and were engaging the enemy at close quarters. Hundreds of men, however, from the Hawke Battalion lay dead and wounded in front of the redoubt. Time and time again they had attacked it with rifle and grenade, but the deadly machine guns had swept them all away. Others tried to go round the obstacle to attack it from the flank or rear, or to follow the barrage, thus keeping the advancing line intact. Twenty-one-years-old Lt the Honourable Vere Harmsworth, although already wounded, rallied his men and dashed into the first trench to the right of the redoubt. Killing the opposition they encountered, the seamen, following their officer, charged down a communication trench into the second line. Once more the enemy was driven back. Leading his men onto the third line, Harmsworth was emptying his revolver into a group of German soldiers when he was shot and killed. The example had been made, however, and the first and second waves of the Nelson Battalion smashed their way through on the flanks of the redoubt. Despite their success, the third and fourth waves of the Nelsons stormed the formidable redoubt and lost many men without achieving their aim.

On the right of the attack, the Hood Battalion had advanced closely behind the creeping barrage led by the striding figure of their Commanding Officer. They had dealt with the enemy dugouts as soon as the barrage had moved on, and had captured nearly 600 prisoners. They regrouped beyond the 'Dotted Green Line' and waited for the Drake Battalion to advance through them to take the 'Green Line'. But the Drakes had suffered heavy casualties, having lost their way in the mist and darkness. Their advance had swung to the left, and they had found themselves mixed up with the Hawkes; many fell to the machine gun fire from the redoubt. Only small detachments made their way to the waiting Hood Battalion, with less than five minutes to organise before the barrage moved on to the 'Green Line'.

Lt-Col. Freyberg, although by now wounded, took stock of the situation. The Drake Battalion, few in number and with most of their officers dead or wounded, would not be able to advance alone. In addition to them, there was his own battalion, one company of the Honourable Artillery Company, who had advanced with him, and a group of ratings from the Hawke Battalion who, when all their officers had been killed, had fought their way through the enemy trenches and had reached the first objective alongside his men. He decided to lead the entire, mixed, force against the 'Green Line'.

When the barrage moved on, the mixed force followed closely behind. As before, when the trenches and dugouts along Station Road were cleared by the curtain of shellfire, they were promptly attacked by the advancing troops. On the right of the line, at the railway siding, the gifted Australian academic and composer, Lt Cdr 'Clegg' Kelly, who had helped to carry the body of Rupert Brooke beneath the blue skies of Skyros, died in the darkness and mud by the Ancre as he led an attack against a machine gun. His men finished the job, destroying the dug-outs and trenches that threatened their flank.

The combined force pressed on up the slope towards the 'Green Line' and, at 6.20 a.m., the Division's second objective was taken on the right of the advance. Over 400 officers and men regrouped beyond the 'Green Line' ready for the next lift of the barrage. In the attack on the second objective, they had taken another 400 prisoners, and Freyberg had been wounded a second time.

Another part of the Division had also reached the 'Green Line'. Some detachments of the Anson Battalion under Lt Cdr Gilliland had passed through the 'Dotted Green Line' where the Howe was still engaging the Germans, and advanced over Station Road and into the 'Green Line'. There he was joined by a small number of Marines from the 1st Royal Marines who had managed to fight their way through the strongly held German positions. A larger detachment of the 1st Marines had swung to the left and were now fighting alongside the Gordon Highlanders of the 51st Division.

The battle to secure the Division's first objective was still continuing. The major problem continued to be the redoubt, which had repulsed all attempts to destroy or capture it. The Commanding Officer of the Hawke Battalion lay seriously wounded in front of its guns. Between leading bombing attacks on the enemy, Cdr Ramsey-Fairfax was consolidating the ground already won by his Howe Battalion.

At 7.30, with the light of dawn beginning to filter through the mist, the barrage lifted and began its move towards the 'Yellow Line'. It was followed in two places by units of the Royal Naval Division. On the right Freyberg led his combined force, while on the centre left of the attack Gilliland advanced with his Ansons and Marines. Neither knew of the presence or success of the other.

Both of the attacking forces reached the 'Yellow Line' with relatively light casualties, as the Germans had, for the most part, withdrawn. Freyberg, on high ground in front of the village, pulled his troops back slightly as the barrage continued to play along the 'Yellow Line'. He then sent his left flank back to join up with the Hawkes, Nelsons, and Drakes still fighting on the first objective, thus preserving his lines of communication and. preventing the enemy from coming round behind.

There was a different situation found by the Anson and Marines in their advance to the 'Yellow Line'. When they arrived they found it to be on low ground, dominated by high ground to the right and the village on the right front. Coming under heavy fire, Gilliland, who believed that his force was alone on the 'Yellow Line', decided to withdraw once more to the 'Green Line' area.

At this stage of the battle, General Shute decided that, if he was to exploit the success of the advance on his right, he had to get the Division's left and centre at least on to the 'Green Line', if not on the 'Yellow Line'. Such a decision was a sound one, but one that disappointed Freyberg and his force, who were eager to sweep forward and attack Beaucourt itself.

Meanwhile the fighting was still continuing along the left and centre of the 'Dotted Green Line'. By mid-morning, a detachment of Ansons and Marines, led by Captain Gowney, forced their way into the third enemy trench and began driving the Germans along its length in both directions. His excellent work was almost undone by Divisional Headquarters who, not knowing that he and his men had taken a substantial part of the third line, ordered it to be bombarded. However, by midday, Gowney had established barricades across the trench, which prevented the enemy from re-entering.

Lt Cdr Ellis of the Ansons managed to reach the 'Green Line' with one rating. There he found Gilliland and his party who, throughout the morning, had been strengthened by members of the Howe, Hawke, and Nelson battalions who had fought their way through. Upon learning that Freyberg and his force were on the 'Yellow Line', they followed Ellis back to the position they had earlier vacated in the belief that they were too far forward. Once they were in position again, Ellis returned to Divisional Headquarters to keep the staff informed of the progress in that sector.

The Divisional Commander decided to press on with the attack at dawn the following day. He arranged to have the 111th Infantry Brigade brought round to the Divisional front to assist with the assault on Beaucourt, and ordered six tanks

– a brand-new weapon which had first been used against the enemy two months earlier – to be ready for the morning.

During the night Gilliland's party spread out to their right along the 'Yellow Line' and linked up with Freyberg's forces. By 4 a.m., Gowney's Ansons and Marines had reached the 'Green Line', and had made contact with the battalion of Gordon Highlanders on their left.

The arrival of dawn found a state of considerable confusion on the right of the line. Two battalions of the 111th Brigade had moved up and occupied 500 yards of the 'Yellow Line' on the left of Freyberg's force. He was then joined by the 13th Battalion of the King's Royal Rifle Corps, who were followed by the remaining three companies of the 1st Honourable Artillery Company. Shortly afterwards, the 7th Royal Fusiliers arrived expecting to find that an advance against Beaucourt had already been made.

At that point the enemy began to heavily bombard the right of the British line with the result that many units became detached from their battalions. Soon the entire sector facing Beaucourt became disorganised and in a critical condition. Freyberg, realising that action had to be taken immediately to prevent the complete break-up of the forces in his area, gave the order to advance at the rush. With him at their head, the entire force rose with a cheer and charged at the village. Within minutes, Beaucourt-sur-Ancre had fallen. The vigour of the attack completely overwhelmed the defenders and swiftly put their machine guns out of action. Over 800 prisoners were taken. The Commanding Officer of the Hood had been wounded for a third time during the attack, but he began immediately to consolidate his gains.

Back on the 'Dotted Green Line' the redoubt still held up the advance in the centre. Lt Campbell, the actress's son, returned to the original front line to lead the newly-arrived tanks against the strong-point. Walking ahead of the leading tank, he directed it over the broken ground to the best position for the tanks to bring their 6-pounder guns to bear on the fortification. After a short, sharp, bombardment, the redoubt and its flanking trenches surrendered. 600 prisoners were led into captivity by the Dublin Fusiliers as the centre and left of the Division moved forward onto the 'Green Line'.

By mid-afternoon the British line had reached the Division's fourth objective – the 'Red Line'. The flanks had been secured and contact with British forces over the River Ancre had been made by means of the railway bridge to the east of Beaucourt.

As Freyberg discussed the formation of the village's defences with Captain the Honourable Lionel Montague and Major Norris – the second-in-command of the Hawke Battalion – the Germans opened a bombardment against Beaucourt. A shell exploded near the three officers wounding them all. This was the fourth wound that Freyberg had received since the start of the battle. This time he was seriously injured, but he refused to be moved until he had been through all the force's dispositions with the Hood Battalion's second-in-command, Lt-Com. Egerton. Two months later Lt-Col. Bernard Freyberg was awarded the Royal Naval Division's third Victoria Cross by King George V at Buckingham Palace. The citation read, 'For most conspicuous bravery and brilliant leading as a Battalion Commander.' After describing his actions on the day, it ended by saying, 'The personality, valour, and utter contempt of danger on the part of this single officer enabled the lodgment in the most advanced objective of the corps to be permanently held.'

Two days after the start of the battle, on 15 November, the Division was relieved by a brigade of the 37th Division, with the 111th Brigade remaining in support. The survivors marched back to the ruined, rat-ridden village of Englebelmer.

The naval brigades had suffered badly with 3,000 men killed and wounded. Only fifteen officers and 630 men of the 189th Brigade were able to march off the battlefield, and only twelve officers and 554 men of the 188th. The Hawke Battalion had only three officers and eighty ratings who had come through unscathed. In the Anson Battalion, just one officer, Lt Cdr Ellis, was not among the casualties.

The Royal Naval Division, which had grown accustomed to the sneers of senior army officers about its ability in the field, had in one day advanced further and. taken more prisoners than any division of the British Army since the start of the war. Among the prisoners the Division had taken were two Major-Generals.

There was, however, an incident during the battle that threatened to tarnish the memory of the fallen, and the achievements of the Division as a whole. Cardiff-born Sub-Lt Edwin Dyett of the Nelson Battalion came from a military and naval family. Both his grandfathers had risen to high rank in the Army, and his father was a ship's master in the merchant navy. It was known, however, that he had inherited few of the qualities of his forebears. Lacking presence and leadership skills, he had failed to make an impression on his fellow officers. In fact, he was regarded with suspicion, having once reported another sub-lieutenant who was entertaining a woman in his room. With his lacklustre bearing in mind, the Nelsons Battalion's Commander, Lt-Col. Tetley, ordered Dyett to remain at the battalion Headquarters with other headquarters officers – each of whom could be called forward should the situation demand it.

All the battalion headquarters had been ordered to remain in position until their respective battalions had achieved their first objective. The Hood and the Drake headquarters, however, ignored the order and moved forward at the same time as their battalions. What happened next remains a mystery on which very little light can be shone. As the headquarters staff advanced, Dyett walked forward with Lt Truscott. Eventually, they arrived at Beaucourt-sur-Ancre station where they found another Drake Battalion officer, Sub-Lt Herring, who had rounded up a number of scattered and lost RND men. Herring was also aware of the situation on the battlefield, including the fact that a large number of Drake Battalion officers were dead or wounded. On hearing this, Truscott rounded up about twenty-five of the Drake's men that Herring had brought to the station, and set off to find the rest of the battalion. As he left, he noticed that Dyett and Herring were engaged in a heated discussion. Herring later claimed that he had told Dyett of the situation and demanded that he joined the battalion on the battlefield. Dyett, however, according to Herring, said something vague about returning to brigade headquarters for instructions. Nothing more of Dyett was seen for two days until he was discovered by the returning battalion at the headquarter billets at Englebelmer. When it was learned that he had not reported to the brigade headquarters as he had claimed to be his intention, he was arrested and charged with cowardice. At his court martial, he refused to defend himself, or present any evidence, apparently under the impression that he would not be found guilty. The court, however, decided differently and not only found him guilty, but also sentenced him to death. The President of the trial, bearing in mind that Dyett was wholly unsuitable for the duties and responsibilities of a battalion officer, and noting the fact that he had requested for a transfer to seagoing duties, recommended that the sentence be reduced to a prison sentence. The Divisional Commander, General Shute, agreed, but the Commander-in-Chief, Field Marshal Haig, found himself in a very difficult position. Not only was Dyett distantly related to Haig's predecessor, Field Marshal French, but he was aware that there was discontent among the troops over the number of executions that had been carried out among the army's other ranks, but little sign that the same rigour was being applied to officers. He decided that the sentence should stand as passed by the court martial. Sub-Lt Edwin Dyett, aged twenty-one, was shot at dawn by men from his own battalion on Friday 5 January 1917. His last words were 'Well, boys, goodbye. For God's sake, shoot straight.'

CHAPTER VI

The Taking of Gavrelle and the Divisional Horse Show

Just a few days after the Royal Naval Division had captured Beaucourt-sur-Ancre, the Battle of the Somme shivered to a halt. The worst winter in thirty-six years dampened down the fighting beneath a freezing layer of snow and ice.

To recover from their work on the Ancre, the Division spent the last two months of 1916 out of the battle zone at a rest camp near Rue. Reinforcements from Blandford arrived and were quickly trained to take their place alongside the veterans.

The losses incurred by the battalions allowed army officers to be appointed to many senior positions. Among the officers commanding the battalions of the 189th Brigade, only one remained from the Royal Navy. Lt Cdr Nelson took over the battalion bearing his own name. However, despite the changes, coupled with a proposal seeking to persuade officers and ratings to transfer to army engagements (with a drop in pay), the Division still held firmly on to its naval customs wherever possible. By the middle of January 1917, the Royal Naval Division was ready to return to the front line.

In London, however, a row was brewing over the control of the RND. Not unnaturally, the Army Council felt that, as the Division were acting in all respects as soldiers, they should come under the Army's control. The Admiralty, on the other hand, delighted with the Division's performance, rejected the Army's suggestion. To try and sort matters out, a meeting at the House of Commons was chaired by the Secretary of State, the Earl of Derby (who had served with the Grenadier Guards during the Boer War). The reasoned argument put forward by the Army soon crumbled in the face of a counter argument led by the First Lord of the Admiralty, Sir Edward Carson – who had led the prosecution against Oscar Wilde. If the Army succeeded in taking control of the RND, the Royal Navy would demand the return of the entire naval element of the Division. That, of course, meant not only all the naval officers, seamen and stokers, but also the

Royal Marines, who were very definitely part of the Royal Navy. No agreement was reached at the meeting, but a message from the War Office soon informed the Admiralty that any idea of transferring the RND to the Army had been 'abandoned' as having 'no advantage'.

The start of the new year had seen many changes in the control and conduct of the war. Lord Kitchener had gone down with HMS *Hampshire* when the ship was mined off the Orkneys. Joffre had been made a Marshal of France and promoted out of the leadership of the French Army. His place had been taken by General Nivelle who had won fame at Verdun. Von Falkenhayn had been replaced by Hindenburg and Ludendorff. During the winter, the new German High Command had ordered the creation of a strongly fortified defence line, to be called the 'Siegfried Line' behind their present front line. Often as far as 25 miles behind the most forward trenches, the new defence system – which became known to the Allies as the 'Hindenburg Line' – would shorten the German front line by 20 miles. 'Operation Alberich' would release thirteen valuable divisions. Little of this affected the RND as it returned to the Ancre Valley once more. On the nights of 18 and 19 January, they, once again, took their place in the trenches.

The new divisional sector straddled the narrow river. The 189th Brigade moved into the line beyond Beaucourt, while the 188th took over trenches across the river on their right where, directly to the brigade's front, the village of Grandcourt lay – still in the hands of the enemy. The 190th Brigade went into reserve and had the arduous and hazardous task of supplying the front-line battalions.

Although the weather continued to be bitterly cold, and no great offensives were taking place, local engagements still broke out up and down the line. Six days after taking over the front line, the Hood Battalion's outposts were attacked by the enemy coming down the frozen river. For a while the Germans managed to get into the Hood's trenches but, after a brisk hand-to-hand struggle in which one officer and seven ratings were killed, they were ejected and thrown back.

On the other side of the river, the 2nd Royal Marines made two raids to capture enemy outposts. The first one, using only one officer and two Marines, was successful, but the second failed against a more alert enemy.

At the end of January, the 189th Brigade were relieved by the 190th and told to prepare for a new assault. Under cover of darkness, they were to attack the enemy trenches 300 yards in front of their own, sited on a ridge commanding the river and Grandcourt on the opposite bank. The Hawke and Hood battalions were to lead the attack, with one company of the Nelsons to assist the Hawke in securing a defensive flank on the left. The Hood, on the right of the attack, would have to deal with some enemy outposts on their right flank as they advanced, but it was generally felt to be a routine trench attack. Accordingly, Brigade Headquarters considered that the assault, from beginning to end, would last eight minutes.

At nine o'clock on the evening of 3 February, the first waves of the assault moved into the forward positions beneath a bright moon and with a sharp frost in the air. A popular figure had reappeared in the Hood's lines. Lt Cdr Asquith, on hearing of the impending attack, and being utterly miserable in an enforced staff job, had decided that, as a Staff Officer, he ought to learn something about the effects of an artillery barrage. On this flimsy pretext, he presented himself to the Hood's new Commanding Officer, Lt-Col. Munro, and had been granted permission to take part in the assault.

When the artillery barrage opened up at eleven o'clock and began to creep towards the enemy trenches, the first waves of attackers followed closely behind. Clearing the first trench, the barrage continued on towards the second, revealing a strongly fortified machine gun post in front of the advancing Hawkes. Important lessons had been learned during the attack of Beaucourt and, instead of trying to take the position by frontal attack, the battalion separated into two groups, a large proportion going to the left with the remainder joining up with the battalion on the right.

The Hood, who, as usual, had begun the attack in splendid style, came under attack from the enemy outposts on its right. The platoons on the right flank of the battalion advanced to meet the threat as they had been ordered. The rest of the battalion, instead of continuing towards the first enemy trench, thought that a general change in direction had been ordered and swung to the right.

In a very short time the entire Hood Battalion was at right angles to the direction it should have been going in. Just at that moment, when firm leadership and understanding of the situation was most needed, the Commanding Officer of the Hood was shot and badly wounded.

But fate, and a white lie, came to the aid of the Hood. Lt Cdr Asquith promptly took charge of his old battalion. In the middle of a darkened battlefield, with the enemy in front and on the flank, he not only realigned the whole battalion, but led them in successful attacks against the first and second lines of trenches.

The coming of dawn found both the Hawke and Hood battalions in the two trenches, but separated from each other by the machine gun position which, the Brigade Headquarters insisted, was nothing more than a solitary machine gun with its crew sited in a shell crater. On the left flank of the attack, the Nelsons were prevented from joining up with the Hawkes by another machine gun-supported strong point.

As the morning progressed, several attacks were made against the enemy keeping the Hawke and Nelson battalions apart, but each time they were beaten back. However, during the mid-afternoon, in yet another attempt, Leading Seaman Wheeler of the 189th Light Trench Mortar Battery earned promotion to Petty Officer and was awarded the Distinguished Conduct Medal after single-handedly closing with the strong point and destroying it with a trench mortar. With the left flank now secured, there remained only the fortified position between the Hawke and the Hood.

It was decided to send the Drake Battalion to assist in attacking the remaining strong point, and to fill any gaps in the line. Making their way forward, they came under artillery fire from the flanks of the captured trenches. Many of the Drakes, caught in narrow communication trenches, became casualties. When the shelling stopped, the enemy counter-attacked on both flanks. The attack on the left was halted by the Divisional machine gunners who had managed to set up a defensive screen, but on the right, the enemy broke through and was only driven out after savage fighting.

By eight o'clock on the evening of 4 February, Lt Cdr Asquith – still in temporary command of the Hoods – decided it was dark enough for another attempt to destroy the strong point and link up the two battalions. Leading a company of the Drake Battalion through the damaged trench system, Asquith and his men came under fire, and he was hit and wounded. The attack had to be called off. No-one else knew the ground in the dark, and a patrol that went forward to try and locate the fortified position ended up behind the German lines.

Finally, at dawn the party of Hawkes, led by Sub-Lt Bowerman, who had already earned a Military Cross in the battle for Beaucourt, rushed the strong point and captured it. The supposed solitary machine gun and its crew sited in a shell crater turned out to be a well-protected dugout with a garrison of thirty-two men.

Instead of taking eight minutes to complete, the battle had seen over fifty hours of fighting and the Division's casualties amounted to twenty-four officers and 647 ratings. Two enemy officers and 225 men had been captured, along with two machine guns. Three Distinguished Service Orders were awarded, one to Asquith (once again wounded and sent back to a staff job) another to Lt Cdr Shelton, the Antwerp 'refugee', for his excellent work in consolidating and keeping intact the left flank and the third to Surgeon H. B. Padwick of the Hawke Battalion for his vital work among the casualties during the enemy bombardment. That night the 189th were relieved by the 190th Battalion. In addition to Leading Seaman Wheeler, three other Distinguished Conduct Medals were won in the action. Able Seaman Macaulay, killed three of the enemy, wounded another, and captured their machine gun, bringing it back to his own lines. Petty Officer Mallet of the Machine Gun Company, brought up his machine gun under very heavy fire and manned it continuously throughout the entire engagement, and Able Seaman

Price, although wounded and buried in an explosion, dug himself out, then spent an hour under heavy fire digging out five other men.

On the far side of the river, on the same night as the relief was taking place, two patrols from the Howe Battalion advanced towards Grandcourt. Encountering no opposition, they continued right into the ruined village itself. The enemy had gone. The patrols reported back to Cdr Ramsey-Fairfax who, in turn, informed the 188th Brigade Headquarters. It was an historic moment. The Royal Naval Division was the first part of the Allied forces to report the start of the German retreat to the Hindenburg Line. 'Operation Alberich' had begun.

On the morning of 2 February, the Marine Battalion entered Grandcourt. On the other side of the river, the Honourable Artillery Company advanced their line several hundred yards up the valley to Baillescourt Farm, thus bringing the line north of the river opposite the line established by the 188th Brigade in front of Grandcourt. They had captured over eighty prisoners in their advance, but had suffered the loss of, among others, their commanding officer, Col Boyle.

A few days later, the 188th Brigade was relieved south of the river. They moved across the Ancre valley to join the other two brigades and took their place in the trenches ready to take part in an attack on Miraumont, their own objective being a sunken lane near the crest of the slopes overlooking the level ground to the south-west of the village.

By 5.45 a.m. on 17 February, the Anson Battalion had established advanced posts along the north bank of the river, and would provide protection for the right flank of the Howe Battalion as they advanced. The 1st Royal Marines were to attack on the left of the Howes with their left flank partially protected by the Hawkes and the 2nd Marines who would remain in the trenches on the left. The Hood Battalion was in reserve.

As the barrage began to move forward, the Germans opened a bombardment on the Division's front lines. Although some shells fell among the Howes, the 1st Marines got the worst of it and suffered high casualties. No one however, suggested that the attack should be called off, and the two battalions followed the barrage side by side.

The Howes achieved their objective with only light casualties, their right flank being protected by the Ansons and the river. The Marines reached and took their objective, but suffered heavily through having their left flank come under strong fire from the enemy. Captain Pearson had a marked effect on the outcome of the battle when he saw a group of Germans attempting to site a machine gun that would fire straight down the sunken lane. Running at the enemy, he killed two before being joined by Lt Sanderson, and between them, killed another five. At this the survivors of the gun crew withdrew. Pearson was awarded a Military Cross for his action. Eventually, two companies of the Hood were sent forward to assist in creating a defensive flank and the new line along the lane was soon consolidated. The 1st Royal Marines had over 400 casualties; the Howe lost two officers and twenty ratings.

The next morning, the Germans mounted a strong counter-attack, but the Divisional Artillery laid down a bombardment so accurately that the attack was blunted before it reached the RND lines. Those of the enemy who survived the shelling were easily dealt with by the 188th and 190th Machine Gun Companies. Three days later the 188th Brigade handed over the new line to the 190th.

The victory on 17 February caused the Germans to speed up their withdrawal. On the 25th, the 190th Brigade occupied Miraumont without a shot being fired. The following day, the brigade, with the exception of the Bedfords, were ordered to attack a strongly fortified trench, north of the town. It was fully expected to be a desperate affair with the German rearguard hanging on grimly. But most of the enemy had left and, by nightfall, the 190th had secured the trench along with a few prisoners.

On 19 February, General Shute handed the Division over to Major General C. E. Lawrie. The new Commanding Officer, although an experienced army officer, was prepared to let the merits and achievements of the RND speak for themselves and be of greater importance than a rigid observance of military custom. The change was universally welcomed.

At the beginning of March, with the Germans retreating in front of their sector, the RND were relieved and sent to a camp near Ovilliers, 5 miles to the south.

To the east of the advancing Allied front line, 'Operation Alberich' was well under way. As the Germans retreated to the Hindenburg Line, they destroyed everything that could be of any possible use to the allies. So appalling, and so comprehensive, was the destruction, that Crown Prince Rupprecht refused to sign the orders authorising the operation. But it went on nevertheless. Buildings were demolished, all the trees cut down, roads and bridges destroyed, and wells contaminated. Booby traps were littered over the whole area.

The line to which they retreated had been prepared with great thoroughness. Dugouts were deep and well equipped, machine guns sited behind concrete defences, and light railways brought up supplies from the rear. In front of the defenders lay a bleak desert resulting from their destructive retreat. Only at one point, at its northern end – in front of Arras – did the Hindenburg Line follow the old front line, and there, it was decided, the next major British offensive would take place.

The Royal Naval Division's time at Ovilliers should have been a period of rest after their fighting in the Ancre valley, but the German retreat had dictated otherwise. In order that supplies could keep up with the troops in pursuit of the enemy, new roads and railways had to be built through the devastated areas. As a result, the Division was constantly called upon to provide working parties for this vital, but exhausting, task. The men, many of whom came from the north-east of England, and had been coal miners prior to joining the Division, handled the work as they had handled every task they had been given – with a combination of effort and skill, strengthened by traditional grumbling. For part of the time, other men of the Division were attached to the Canadian Railway Company, and assisted in the laying down of new railway tracks. It was a tiring time for men who had earned a long rest.

After the dull exertions of the first weeks in March, the Division learned, much to everyone's delight, that they were to return to the fighting, this time to trenches north of Arras. Lt-Col. Freyberg had returned to take command of the Hood Battalion, and the former adjutant of the Drake Battalion, Cdr Sterndale Bennet, now became its commanding officer. The popular twenty-three-year-old grandson of the renowned English composer, Sir William Sterndale Bennet, had earned a Distinguished Service Order at the Battle of the Ancre. Lt-Col. Lewis had taken command of the Nelson Battalion.

The new French Commander-in-Chief, General Robert Nivelle, had planned for a massive Anglo-French assault to take place in the spring of 1917. The British were to launch an attack around the Arras region, and this would be followed by a huge French thrust further to the south in which Nivelle intended to advance 10 miles on the first day.

The German retreat in February and March had eliminated most of the objectives of Nivelle's offensive, but he continued to insist that the plan still held. Eventually, however, he decided to concentrate the French assault further to the east across the River Aisne.

The front along which the British were to attack measured 15 miles, and ran from Givenchy-en-Gohelle, a village south of Liévin and north of Vimy Ridge, to a point some 8 miles south of Arras.

When the Royal Naval Division arrived in late March, they found, much to their disappointment, that they were not to enter the coming battle as a single unit. The Divisional Artillery was detached and sent to join the 3rd Canadian Division facing Vimy Ridge. The 188th Brigade were sent further north, where they were attached to the 5th Division opposing Liévin. The remaining two brigades became part of the XIII Corps who were the general reserves.

On 4 April, almost 3,000 guns opened up a barrage bigger than the one that heralded the Battle of the Somme. For five days the bombardment continued while the British forces prepared themselves for the assault.

At 5.30 a.m. on 9 April, the attack began through driving sleet and snow, behind a creeping barrage which was the most precise seen since the tactic was developed. By mid-morning the Canadians, assisted by the RND Artillery, stood on the crest of Vimy Ridge looking down on the plain of Douai. In the centre of the advance, in front of Arras, most of the objectives were taken but, at the southern end of the assault, the attacks had been blunted by the defences of the Hindenburg Line.

On 12 April, patrols from the 1st Royal Marines discovered that the enemy had evacuated Angres and Liévin and, on the following night, the Marines took over the abandoned positions. Also on the 12th, it was decided that the XIII Corps should come out of general reserve and relieve the left flank of the XVII Corps south of Vimy Ridge.

Leaving the Ansons and 1st Royal Marine Battalion in the Angres area the RND, minus its artillery, relieved the 34th Division, west of the village of Gavrelle (itself some 4 miles north-east of Arras). The village, in the hands of the elite Prussian Guards and the 66th Wurtenburger Fusiliers, had resisted several heavy attacks by the 34th Division prior to their handing over the sector to the RND.

The first task facing the 189th and 190th brigades when they entered the trenches was to straighten out the line they held. On the right, outposts of the 189th were well advanced and could be used as a front line from which to launch an attack. The 190th, on the other hand, were too far back and had to be brought forward until they were level with the 189th. The first attempt was made in broad daylight, and without artillery support, on the morning of 15 April. The Royal Dublin Fusiliers and the Bedfords left their trenches and advanced over the broken ground. It was a brave attempt, but it failed due to the intensity of the enemy artillery and machine gun fire, which was far heavier than had been expected. The following night, these two battalions were relieved by the Honourable Artillery Company Battalion and the Royal Fusiliers who were to attempt to straighten out the line that night. Under cover of darkness, the outposts were successfully pushed forward. For the next two nights the attacks continued until, by the morning of the 19th, both brigades were in contact with each other on a line less than 200 yards from the enemy.

As the battalions prepared themselves for the impending main attack, bad news came from the south. The French had failed in their attempt to break through and, in consequence, German defence on the Arras front began to stiffen. Nevertheless, it was imperative that the pressure be kept up to prevent the enemy's reserves from being sent south to take part in any counter-attack.

The RND itself received a sad blow where pleasure was mixed with the disappointment. Lt-Col. Freyberg VC was promoted to Temporary Brigadier General on 20 April – the youngest officer in that rank in the British Army. The next day, he was appointed to take over the 173rd Brigade of the 58th (London) Division. His career had been meteoric – it was less than three years since he had joined the Royal Naval Division as a Royal Naval Volunteer Reserve Lieutenant

But it was a promotion richly deserved, and was applauded by all who knew, and had served alongside, him. The Division would be poorer for his going, but he had played a key role in the formation of its character and élan, something that would remain while the Division existed.

Freyberg's departure from the Division had created a serious problem. Who could take over the Hood Battalion? Clearly an army officer could not be brought in to lead the men into the coming assault with no knowledge of their conduct or capabilities. But there was someone in the area who not only had that knowledge, but also had repeatedly earned the admiration and loyalty of every officer and rating in the Hood Battalion. Cdr Asquith, now recovered from wounds he had received in the January fighting, was serving on the Intelligence Staff of General Allenby's Third Army. When asked by Brigadier General Phillips, the 189th Brigade Commander, to obtain permission to rejoin his old battalion, Asquith moved so fast that he took over the Hood the very next day.

The assault on Gavrelle was to take place on St George's Day, 23 April. The first battalions to go 'over the top' would be, on the right, the Drake and Nelsons of the 189th Brigade, with the 7th Royal Fusiliers and 4th Bedfords on their left. They were to take the Division's first objective – the German trenches in front of the village. After a rest of fifteen minutes, they were then to advance to the second objective, the main street running north–south through the village centre. At this point, there would be a halt to reorganise and allow the Hood Battalion to come up and join on the left of the Drake. These two battalions were then to advance to the Division's third objective, a line 300 to 600 yards beyond the village.

The two 190th Brigade battalions would be backed up by the 1st HAC as necessary, and ammunition and other supplies would be brought up by parties from the Dublin Fusiliers and the Hawke Battalion. As the Divisional Artillery was still in the Vimy Ridge area, the barrage would be provided by the 34th Division's artillery. The Anson and the two Marine battalions, who had rejoined the Division, were the divisional reserve, while the Howe formed the reserve for the 189th Brigade.

At 4.30 on the morning of the attack, the artillery began to lay down its barrage. Red and green flares arced through the night sky assisting the gunners in finding the range. Fifteen minutes later the curtain of shells began to move forward, and the advancing troops, by now completely accustomed to this form of attack, followed closely behind.

It was inevitable that, once the attack got under way, the enemy artillery would open fire on the Division's front-line trenches in an effort to prevent supporting troops from following on after the initial advance. With this in mind, Asquith chose to disregard the instruction to keep the Hood Battalion back until the Nelson had reached its first objective. Instead, he led his men out of the assembly trenches immediately the Nelsons had got clear. As they followed the lead battalion into the first German trenches, the enemy counter-barrage began to pound the trenches they had just left.

Within ten minutes, the Division's first objective had been taken. The barrage had worked well, and the casualties were light. A fifteen-minute pause followed while the attackers recovered their breath and prepared for the next stage of the assault.

Once more the barrage lifted, and the Nelson and Drake Battalions moved on, with the Hood following. On entering the ruined village, the method of fighting had to change. Several machine guns in well-sited positions had to be destroyed, and snipers hiding among the debris had to be hunted down. During this random skirmishing, many units of the advancing battalions became mixed up while pursuing and attacking individual targets. It was with great difficulty that the Hood and Drake Commandedrs reorganised their battalions ready for the advance to the final objective. To their left rear, the Fusiliers and Bedfords began to form a defensive flank against heavy machine gun fire pouring down from a strong point known as 'Railway Post'.

At the appointed time, the barrage began to creep forward to the third objective, with the Drakes on the right and the Hoods on the left following closely behind. After an advance of about 250 yards through Gavrelle the battalions reached the Oppy–Plouvain road which ran north and south through the ruined village. This road was crossed on the Hood's left flank by the Fresnes–Arras road running east–west. As the battalions took precarious shelter in shell craters, the Battalion Commanders took stock of their position.

To the front of them the countryside was wide open. Directly in front of the Hood Battalion were two enemy trenches, the first less than 150 yards away. At 300 yards away another line of trenches could be made out, this one crossing both battalion fronts. On the left of the Hood Battalion, across the Fresnes road, a ridge ran parallel to the highway. From this ridge, the enemy could cover every movement made by the two battalions. A large windmill had been built on top of the ridge which had been the final objective of the Bedfords who were still held up by the enemy on their left flank. 100 yards down on the left hand side of the road sat the ruin of the mayor's house.

The battalions had not been there long before it was decided that an identification raid should be organised to learn the identity of the enemy units in the opposing trenches. A Sub-Lt and a leading seaman from the Hood Battalion were ordered to carry out the actual raid, while two parties, made up of a leading seaman and two able seamen in each, were to advance on either flank to act as decoys. In accordance with the usual custom, the ratings were given a tot of rum before they began the raid, and the officer – very young and inexperienced – was given a more than adequate drink of whisky.

As the raid got under way the drink began to have an effect on the officer who, much to the consternation of his accompanying leading seaman – a tough Tynesider named Kelly, began to charge down an enemy communication trench. Kelly, understanding the situation well, and seeing that the only outcome of such an action would be death or capture for both of them, concentrated on keeping the enemy at bay by hurling hand grenades in all directions. Eventually, Kelly managed to persuade the officer that the only option open to them was a quick dash back to their own lines. After ducking and weaving across no man's land, Kelly dropped into the shelter of the Hood's trenches, where on reporting to Asquith he discovered that the young officer had not been seen. 'Failing' to hear his Commanding Officer's order not to do so, Kelly once again climbed from the trench and headed towards the enemy. He found the officer lying in a shell crater and suffering from the full extent of the pre-raid whisky. Despite heavy small-arms fire from the enemy, Kelly lifted the officer up and brought him safely back to their own trenches.

For his actions that day, Leading Seaman Kelly was awarded the Military Medal, presented to him by the Mayor of Jarrow, along with ten pounds, a gold 'Albert' watch chain, and a gold watch from the 'People of Jarrow Hero's Fund'.

Still unsure of the enemy positions and numbers along his front, Asquith then decided to take a look for himself. Taking a small party of men with him, he crawled down a shallow ditch, which led to the right flank of the first enemy trench. The party had not gone far when their cover petered out and they came under fire. Soon casualties were sustained and the party was forced to return. They cut across the front of the battalion and made their way down the Fresnes road towards the enemy's left flank. Making good progress, they reached the Mayor's house where, upon entering, they were astounded to find the German garrison fast asleep, Asquith rounded up the bemused enemy and had them escorted back into Gavrelle. He then ordered up a Lewis gun and some snipers, which he installed at the top of the house under the command of a Sub-Lt whose orders were to keep the enemy in the first trench busy. When he returned to the rest of the battalion he found that the situation had worsened considerably. The Germans had begun shelling the Hood's part of the Oppy–Plouvain road. The casualties were high, and his two senior company commanders had been killed.

It was clear that the battalion could expect to be subjected to a counter-attack at any time, particularly from the enemy forces centred around Railway Post, who were holding the ridge and the windmill on the Hoods' left flank. Asquith decided that it made more sense to have a strongly defended position on the rear than to risk losing all to a strong enemy attack on his present position. Accordingly, he sent an entire company back to reinforce the trenches in front of Gavrelle, which had been the Division's first objective. He was left with no more than 100 seamen with which to consolidate his position and beat off any attack.

At 9 a.m. Asquith met Lt-Col. Collins Wells, the Commanding Officer of the Bedfords, at the crossroads. The Bedfords had suffered badly from the attacks on their left flank, and Collins Wells had only been able to collect some sixty of them to bring forward. Nevertheless, he offered to strengthen the left flank of the Hood Battalion. This agreed upon, Asquith then requested Lt-Col. Lewis of the Nelsons to send forward two platoons to back up the Bedfords. The platoons were dispatched immediately.

While the small force desperately tried to form some kind of defensive position from which they could resist a counter-attack, the enemy were trying to push patrols forward. As each attempt was made, they came under fire from the Lewis gun and rifles in the mayor's house, and were forced to retire. But, as the morning progressed, the party holding this vital position was killed one after the other by return fire from the enemy. Soon only Leading Seaman Charlton remained alive. He earned the Distinguished Conduct Medal by continuing to man the gun, holding back the Germans until lack of ammunition forced him to retire, bringing the gun with him.

The expected counter-attack came at one o'clock, after a heavy bombardment. The counter-bombardment caught many of the German troops as they came across the open ground, and the remainder was stopped by rifle and machine gun fire.

The wounded were taken back into the village, where Staff Surgeon William McCracken was performing wonders under desperately poor conditions. He had set up a base in a cellar, where he worked continuously despite the heavy bombardment. He was assisted by his stretcher-bearers, and a party of German Red Cross men that he had captured during the initial advance into the village. Throughout the whole of 23 April he evacuated more than 120 officers and men. Among those badly wounded during the heavy shelling on the first objective, was Lt A. P. Herbert, Adjutant of the Hawke Battalion.

At 4.30 p.m., a message arrived at the front-line position. Brigade Headquarters had ordered an advance to be made on the Division's third objective – the German trenches in front of the Hood. As they were only holding on to the ground they had already gained by sheer dogged determination, any thought of a further advance was out of the question. Asquith, Cdr Sterndale Bennett of the Drake, and Lt-Col. Lewis decided the best thing to do was to ignore the order.

Shortly afterwards the Brigade staff formed a true understanding of the situation and, during the evening and early morning, they sent forward the Howe

Battalion to relieve the Hood, and moved the Nelsons up to the left flank, facing the ridge to support the Bedfords. The remainder of the night passed in relative quiet, without incident.

The activities of the enemy on the morning of the 24th made it quite clear that they did not consider Gavrelle to be given up for good. Large concentrations of troops could be seen gathering in front of the Division's lines. At midday, the heaviest shelling the Division had ever experienced broke out along the front line. For three hours, the whole front shuddered beneath the massive bombardment, until three o'clock when the barrage lifted and moved on to the trenches in front of Gavrelle. As the bombardment travelled behind them, the defenders could see the German infantry advancing to attack. The first wave was obliterated by the counter-barrage, but the second and third waves reached the RND trenches. Time and time again the Germans managed to get into the Division's lines, but were repeatedly driven out. Cdr Bennett was everywhere, urging on his Drake Battalion. Not once was the line breached and, by 5.40, the attack had ground to a halt. That night, the 188th Brigade, the Anson, Hawke, 1st and 2nd Royal Marines; took over the line from the 189th and 190th brigades.

The battle for Gavrelle had cost over 1500 casualties and planted British troops on a line that was to remain unchanged for more than a year. Asquith was awarded a bar to his DSO. Staff-Surgeon McCracken was recommended for the award of the Victoria Cross by Asquith for his work on the 23rd but, in the end, received the DSO.

There still remained the Germans on the ridge to the left of the bulging salient created by the RND's advance. In order to take this position, the 1st Royal Marines were to advance on the right flank of the Army's 2nd Division as it attacked Oppy. If successful, their advance would bring the front line level with a position north-east of Gavrelle, where the 2nd Royal Marines would be launching their attack. It was likely to be a particularly dangerous affair, as both the Marine Battalions would be attacking with one flank unprotected – a situation caused by a gap that separated them.

The advance began at two o'clock on the morning of the 28th. The 1st Royal Marines pressed on towards the enemy front line, losing many men due to the mass of barbed wire the Germans had erected in front of their trenches. When they managed to get into the first trench, they were cut down from their unprotected right flank by the enemy in Railway Post, the same strong point that had held up the Fusiliers and Bedfords in their attack on the 23rd. The fire from the well-sited machine guns was so intense that the Marines and other units of the 2nd Division were forced to fall back. During the fighting Lt-Col. Cartwright, the Commanding Officer of the 1st Royal Marines, fell mortally wounded. More than 500 casualties had been sustained.

Unaware that the withdrawal was taking place, a company of the HAC, under the command of twenty-year-old former Boy Scout Lt Reginald Haine, attacked the strong point three times. On each occasion they were driven back. Haines then ordered his trench mortars to attack the strong point before leading a fourth rush at the enemy – this time he succeeded in capturing it, along with two machine guns and fifty prisoners. But, unsupported on either flank, Haine and his men were forced to give it up when subjected to the full force of a massive German counter-attack. They did not fall back far, setting up machine guns ready to repel the continued German attack they knew would come. From then on, and well into the darkness of the night, the HAC men refused to budge, and held their ground, fending off repeated attacks.

Meanwhile the 2nd Royal Marines were attacking the ridge on the left flank at Gavrelle with its dominating windmill. Against furious opposition, the Marines continued their advance and, eventually, a platoon under the command of Lt Newling were able to dash forward and capture the windmill.

As the Germans could be expected to mount heavy counter-attacks to recapture this important position, a company of the Anson Battalion was sent forward to form a defensive flank. The counter-attacks did not take long in coming. Three times during that day the Marines had to hold on grimly against heavy assaults thrown at the windmill, but each time the enemy was driven back. When nightfall came on the 28th, it was decided that most of the positions gained on the ridge could not be held against an overwhelming enemy whose strength had been totally misjudged. A withdrawal from all the gains except for the windmill was organised to take place during the darkness of the night of 28th–29th.

Somewhere during the organisation of the withdrawal, a breakdown in communication had occurred, and the Ansons, still forming a defensive flank, were not told. Consequently, come the dawn, the Ansons found themselves totally isolated. The situation was further complicated by the fact that they had captured 250 of the enemy during the previous day. Fighting desperately, they began to pull back while Petty Officer Scott earned himself a Distinguished Conduct Medal by taking just fifteen men and driving the German prisoners back to the Division's lines. By midday the windmill position was secured, and the Ansons had reached safety.

During the early hours of the morning on the same day, a composite battalion, made up from the 190th Brigade's Fusiliers and Bedfords, were loaned to the 188th Brigade for an attack on the same positions that had cost the 1st Royal Marines so dearly the day before.

The attack went in at 4 a.m., and the first German trenches were quickly taken. There still remained, however, the strong point that had done so much damage to the Marines. Once again the HAC, under Lt Haine, launched an assault on the Railway Post and, again, drove the enemy out. Although this time they were given support, and succeeded in holding on to the strong point, the Germans kept up a tremendous pressure for the remainder of the morning by heavily shelling the area and sending in counter-attacks.

During one of these counter-attacks, following in the wake of a particularly heavy bombardment, 2nd Lt Alfred Pollard, of the 1st HAC, led four men down a trench leading northwards from Railway Post in a head-on counter-attack against the advancing Germans. Pollard was no stranger to danger. He had risen from the ranks and, as a sergeant he had already earned the Distinguished Conduct Medal. During the fighting at Ypres, he was awarded a Military Cross after being commissioned. Throwing hand grenades as he charged forward, he caused many casualties among the enemy, who broke before his onslaught and fled in disorder. He not only retook the ground that had been lost, but even gained extra. For their absolute disregard for danger, their exemplary conduct, and the example they provided for their men, Haine and Pollard were awarded the Royal Naval Division's fourth and fifth Victoria Crosses.

That night, the Division was relieved by the 31st Division. They had earned a brief rest period, which was spent in and around the small village of Roclincourt, north of Arras. From the time they had taken over the lines facing Gavrelle on 15 April, their casualties had amounted to 3,794 – more than forty officers, and 1,000 ratings and other ranks, had lost their lives. There remained, available for duty in the trenches, 203 officers and 6,000 men.

During the rest period, there were some important changes in the command structure of the Division. Lt-Col. Hutchinson of the 2nd Royal Marine Battalion was promoted to Brigadier General and assumed command of the 190th Brigade. He was succeeded by Royal Marine Lt-Col. Ozanne. Brigadier General Phillips was promoted and command of the Brigade went to Brigadier General Coleridge. The 1st Royal Marines came under the command of Lt-Col. Wainwright, and Cdr West, who had been second in command of the ill-fated Collingwoods at Gallipoli, took over the Howe from Cdr Ramsey Fairfax who was invalided home. The Hawke Battalion, whose previous Commanding Officer, Lt-Col Whiteman, had been killed on 23 April, was taken over by Cdr Ellis.

The Division returned to the trenches around Gavrelle on 19 May, after a period of work on the rear communication trenches. Back in the front line their task was of almost the same nature. The defences of the position they had won the month before were still in need of consolidation. By the time they were relieved once more by the 31st Division on 10 June, the whole position, but in particular the vital high ground of the windmill, was ready to play its part in the next phase of the war on the Arras front.

The Division returned once again to the dull but vital work of constructing defences and communications. But it was not all work. On 14 June, it was decided to hold a

Divisional Horse Show. The 1st RM Battalion won the prize for the best Battalion Transport with their water cart, mobile cooker, and limbered wagon drawn by a pair of horses. They also won the prizes for the best mule wagon and packhorses under the command of a non-commissioned officer, and for the best overall wagon. Seen as a just reward – or penalty – for their victory, the Royal Marines were then inspected by their Colonel in Chief, Admiral Lord Charles Beresford (or 'Charlie B' as he was known to all and sundry). To further the spirit of competition, the Divisional Commander, Major General Lawrie, presented the Division with four silver bugles to be competed for in cross-country running, football, boxing, and bayonet fighting. Not surprisingly, the Royal Marines won all three sporting competitions, while the 1st Battalion of the Honourable Artillery Company took the bugle for the bayonet combat. In the meantime, the 5th and 31st Divisions were to launch an attack along the front between Gavrelle and Oppy, a village to the north, on 28 June. Communication trenches had to be dug down a long slope that led from the old front-line positions to the new. The work was completed under the direction of the Divisional Engineers.

The attack was successful, the first-line trenches were taken, and the Germans driven back into Oppy. With the dominating position of the Gavrelle windmill in British hands, there was no chance of an enemy counter-attack being launched with any hope of success.

Before they returned to the front line, the RND had to undergo one of its periodic reorganisations. The 10th Dublin Fusiliers left the 190th Brigade to reinforce the 16th (Irish) Division, and their replacements, the 5th Battalion of the King's Shropshire Light Infantry, would not be arriving until 20 July. At the same time the 1st Battalion of the Honourable Artillery Company left the Division and was replaced by the 1st/28th Battalion of the London Regiment (known to all as the 'Artists Rifles') who were still in need of training. Consequently, when the Division returned to the trenches on the Gavrelle-Oppy front on 4 July, they had just two brigades, with the two army battalions being attached to the 189th.

Although the Division's front line was thinly held, the Germans had gone onto the defensive. Local raids were made by the different RND battalions, mainly for identification purposes, but often the attackers found the defenders had evacuated the trenches and positions. The newly arrived Army battalions joined the Royal Fusiliers and the Bedfords later in July, and the 190th Brigade was reconstituted. It was an ideal time to introduce the newcomers to the Division and its methods. On 25 September, the Division was relieved by the 47th Division and boarded trains that took them north to Cassel where they arrived on 2 October. Nearby, the Third Battle of Ypres had been continuing for nearly three months, and the Royal Naval Division was to take part in the advance on Passchendaele.

CHAPTER VII

Passchendaele and Welsh Ridge

The Flanders campaign had begun before dawn on 7 June 1917, when nineteen mines exploded beneath the German lines in front of Wytschaete and Messines. Over a million pounds of explosive had been used, and the sound was heard and the vibrations felt in London, 130 miles away. Over 10,000 German troops were killed by the blasts and, during the advance that immediately followed, another 7,000 were taken prisoner.

With the Messines Ridge in British hands, the way now lay clear for an attack on the Passchendaele Ridge, which ran north-east from the new front line. By mounting massive assaults along its length, and from Ypres to the west, the British Commander-in-Chief, General Haig, believed he could make a breakthrough that, with the help of an amphibious attack on the coast, would capture the North Sea ports of Ostend and Zeebrugge.

The Battle of Messines had been a good start to the operation, and the dry summer weather favoured the more mobile kind of warfare that would be necessary for a successful outcome. But then the delays began. The Prime Minister, Lloyd George, took several weeks before he and his Cabinet gave permission for the advance to take place. Haig then decided that the 5th Army, rather than the 2nd Army – who were already in position – should attack from Ypres, and so more time was used in putting General Gough's army on the left of General Plumer. There was also a delay while the French contribution to the coming offensive, General Anthoine's 1st Army, took its place between Gough and the Belgians.

An air offensive began on 11 July, and air superiority had been achieved by the end of the month.

The first advance of the Third Battle of Ypres took place on 31 July. The day went well for the attacking troops, and most of their objectives were taken despite heavy German counter-attacks. Then the weather broke. Belgium began its wettest August for thirty years.

With the rain came the mud. The base of the western slopes of Passchendaele Ridge rapidly became waterlogged, its drainage-system, developed over centuries, destroyed by shelling.

In mid-August another advance was made. This time the gains were smaller than the first, mainly due to the German tactic of a massed counter-attack to drive back the enemy. General Plumer then took charge and, in three operations, took the Menin Road Bridge, Polygon Wood, and the village of Broodseinde. The weather had moderated during the first two advances, but the main feature had been Plumer's insistence that the artillery kept up with the infantry through each phase of the advance, and his holding back troops to match the German counter-attacks.

By the time Broodseinde had fallen, October had arrived and brought with it a cold damp winter. Generals Gough and Plumer wanted the campaign brought to an end. There was no hope at all of reaching the North Sea ports before the winter had set in, but the Commander-in-Chief considered that the remainder of Passchendaele Ridge had to be captured in order to stabilise his lines.

This was the situation that faced the Royal Naval Division when they relieved the 9th Division on the night of 24 October.

The divisional sector ran from Wallemolen Cemetery north-west to the Lekkebokkerbeek, a streamlet running east-west, with the Canadian Corps on their right flank. The 9th Division had only been able to make an advance on each of the sector flanks, leaving the enemy still in possession of the ground facing the centre of the divisional front. It was this line that the Division, brigade by brigade, was to attack during the last days of October.

The ground over which the attacks were to be made reflected all the horrors known on the Passchendaele front. The shelling and the weather had turned the whole area into a cratered, treeless swamp. Men, animals and equipment sank into the oozing mud that covered the entire landscape. The 14th Worcestershire Battalion, the divisional pioneers, struggled to make assembly trenches out of connecting flooded shell holes. They ran out communication cables under shellfire, dug out gun emplacement that promptly filled with water, and laid down duckboards. The duckboards were the only way that men and supplies could get up to the front, and columns of men using these wooden tracks made easy targets for a watchful enemy. To step off the duckboards was to court disaster in the slime. Shell craters often contained many feet of water and to slide into one could mean death by drowning. In addition, the Germans were using mustard gas for the first time in the war. A gas mask was only partial protection, as the gas also blistered any exposed skin. It tended to liquidise on the ground and persist for days, thus burning anyone who tried to seek shelter in any depression where it had collected.

Trenches, in the Somme or Arras sense of the word, were totally out of the question. The front line was merely a string of outposts, usually positioned in waterlogged craters, each being dependent upon itself for protection. The support line was rarely much better. Communication trenches simply did not exist, and the only means of moving up to the front line was by single file along the duckboards.

These were the conditions under which the 188th Brigade was to attack at dawn on 26 October.

In front of their front line, ranging from 500 yards on the left and 2,000 yards on the right, a flooded stream, the Paddebeek, ran right across the direction of advance. In front of the Paddebeek, six enemy posts were the first objectives of the attacking battalions. On the left of the advance, the 1st Royal Marines were to attack a succession of posts known as Berks Houses, Bray Farm, and Banff House. These ruins were almost lined up at right angles to the front line. The Ansons on the right had Sourd Farm (a fourth post in the line being attacked by the Royal Marines), Varlet Farm – about 200 yards to their immediate front – and the remains of a trench known as Source Trench, 200 yards further on. These taken, a second wave of battalions, the 2nd Royal Marines on the left and the Howe on the right, were to pass through the first battalions, cross the Paddebeek, and advance on the Division's second objectives. On the right, the Howe was to take two more posts, Source Farm – just across the Paddebeek and on the far right of the sector – and, 500 yards past the stream, the ruins of Tournent Farm. The 2nd Royal Marines on the left were to advance at the same rate, keeping the line straight, and destroying any opposition in their path.

The rain had been pouring down since midnight when the advance began at 5.45 a.m. Floundering through thick mud and skirting flooded craters made it difficult to keep up to the barrage, but the Royal Marines in particular were able to attack their objectives as soon as the barrage passed over them. By 7.20 the Marines had captured all the posts ahead of them, and, soon after, it was reported that the Ansons had done the same although they had actually missed Varlet Farm (which, fortunately, had been abandoned by the enemy), and taken another post situated in ruins 200 yards further on. At the start of the attack it was decided to increase the number of stretcher-bearers, and the wisdom of this decision was borne out by the high number of casualties caused by enemy machine guns sited along the far side of the Paddebeek.

Although the main objectives had been taken, there still remained a number of enemy outposts holding out in the centre of the advance. These had not been attacked because, once a company or platoon had reached and taken its goal, it remained where it was to defend the gains. Thus, posts whose positions were unknown were rarely attacked, as, once the advance got under way, the condition of the terrain prevented any swift redirection of the assault.

With the centre still being held by the Germans, the second wave of battalions advanced up the flanks towards the second objectives. On the right, the Howes pressed on towards Tournent Farm, engaging minor outposts on their way. The 2nd Royal Marines had crossed the Paddebeek and were heading for scattered outposts on the left. 'A' Company of this battalion, under Captain Peter Ligertwood, had made themselves small flags from red canvas nailed to sticks, to assist in identifying each other during the battle. Each flag had been blessed by the battalion's chaplain, and they were used throughout the action. Captain Ligertwood, despite being wounded three times, directed his men towards their target. Even when wounded a fourth time, this time mortally, he rose again to lead them. So inspired were his men by his leadership that they continued their attack until they ran out of ammunition and water.

Meanwhile, at 8 a.m., Cdr Asquith, whose Hood Battalion were standing by in case of a counter-attack, ordered up two companies from his battalion in preparation. As no reports were getting back from the battalion already engaged, he sent an officer forward to reconnoitre the situation. The officer reported back that the centre was still firmly held. Consequently, Asquith brought forward another company of Hoods.

The Canadians, on the right of the RND, reported that they had had no contact with the Anson or Howe Battalions. Asquith decided he had to take a look for himself. Taking Lt Garnham of the Divisional Artillery, and one seaman armed with a rifle, he set off towards the right flank. It meant an hour wading through the thick mud in full view of the enemy before he could reach the position captured by a party of Ansons under Sub-Lt Stevenson when they missed Varlet Farm. Just as Asquith and his party arrived, the Germans launched an attack against the outpost. After a brisk engagement the enemy were forced back. Pressing on to find the rest of the right flank positions, Asquith promised Stevenson that he would have a relief platoon sent up at the first opportunity. He then took his party further forward and found the foremost outposts achieved by the two battalions. Explaining the position to them, he then had them get in touch with the Canadians on their right. As a result of this, the Canadians were able to make a considerable advance knowing that their left flank was protected.

With Asquith's report in the hands of the Brigade HQ, the staff had a far better impression of events on the battlefront, and it was decided that there would be no further attacks that day. During the late afternoon, the enemy launched a counter-attack on the right of the advance, which for a while threatened to cause a retreat, but a company of the Hood Battalion moved forward and assisted in driving the Germans back.

As the light faded, and it became slightly safer for troops to move about, the Hood Battalion moved forward to relieve the Howes and Ansons on the right. On the left, the Hawke Battalion advanced to relieve the two Royal Marine Battalions. When Cdr Ellis arrived near the outposts that had been the Division's first objective he found that the Marines had given them up and were returning. The Marines, without water and without ammunition, had hung on until the very last moment, but had been forced to return before heavy enemy counter-attacks. Ellis decided to try and retake all the positions in front of the Paddebeek. In doing so, Lt Bartholomew earned the Military Cross as he led his company in recapturing Berks Houses, Bray Farm, and Banff House. Contact was then established with the Hood Battalion.

In the meantime, the Hoods could not be sure of establishing their forward line of outposts until the situation of Sub-Lt Stevenson and his Ansons could be ascertained. A group sent forward to investigate reported back that they had been fired on from the position, which suggested that it had fallen to the enemy. Asquith again decided to take a look for himself. When he arrived, he actually found Stevenson still holding out, but with only seven men left alive. Asquith returned to his own battalion and led forward a platoon to relieve the Ansons. The Hood's line was then secure.

The Divisional front now contained five major strong points taken by the 188th Brigade. Only on the right of the line had the enemy outpost not been secured, mainly due to a concrete pill-box in Source Trench, which housed a small garrison and a machine gun. All the ground across the Paddebeek had been lost to heavy enemy counter-attacks.

Once again Surgeon McCracken did excellent work among the many wounded as they lay in the mud exposed to the enemy. He was awarded a bar to his DSO.

On the 28th, the 188th Brigade was relieved by the 190th with its army battalions. The night before, the Army Commander, General Gough, had sent Brigadier General Prentice, the 188th Brigade Commander, the following message:

> Please convey to all ranks engaged in today's operations my very great appreciation of their gallant efforts; they have my sincere sympathy, as no troops could have had to face worse conditions of mud than they had to face owing to the sudden downpour of rain this morning. No troops could have done more than our men did today, and given a fair chance, I have every confidence in their complete success every time.

Now it was the task of the 190th Brigade to cross the Paddebeek, and attack the objectives that had been the second goals on the 26th. The Bedfords had the left of the advance; the Royal Fusiliers, the centre; and the Artists Rifles, the right.

The attack began at 5.50 a.m., but had not gone far before disaster struck. The German counter-barrage fell squarely on the advancing battalions. The casualties sustained were very high for such an early stage in an attack, but once reorganised, the soldiers pressed on. The delay, however, had lost them the protection of the barrage. Once the curtain of fire had passed over them, the task of the German machine gunners defending the Paddebeek proved ridiculously easy. As the Bedfords and the Fusiliers waded through the knee-deep mud, they were shot to pieces, and their assault brought to a halt well short of the Paddebeek.

On the right, the Artists Rifles struggled forward to reach Source Trench, but the machine gun in the pillbox cut them down long before they could get anywhere near it. By mid-morning, an entire company of the Artists had been destroyed.

The Canadians, on the right of the RND, had, with superb courage, managed to reach Source Farm, 400 yards beyond Source Trench. Their hold on this position was precarious, as their left flank, which the Artists had been unable to secure, was unprotected, and a request for reinforcements arrived at Brigade Headquarters. The reserve battalion was the newly arrived 5th King's Shropshire Light Infantry, and one of their companies was sent through the Canadian lines to assist. They were quickly followed by two more companies with instructions to attempt to take Source Trench by an attack from the right flank.

The attack by the two KSLI companies was repulsed by the Source Trench defenders just as the Artists had been. The position seemed unapproachable. The two companies then moved forward to join up with their other company at Source Farm. When they arrived, they found that, of the KSLI soldiers who had gone forward to attack Source Trench, only one officer and eight men had survived. Before night-time, however, they had managed to form a thinly held defensive flank that went round the Source Trench position and linked up with the surviving Artists holding out at Varlet Farm.

By now, the Division had lost almost a thousand officers and men in the two attacks and over 2,000 wounded. But the main objective, the Paddebeek, had still not been secured, and the minor objectives on the other side of the stream were still in enemy hands. On the night of 30th, and the early morning of the 31st, the 189th Brigade relieved the 190th.

With the arrival of the new battalions, the Hawke on the left and the Nelson on the right, a new method of attack was to be tried. The idea had come from Cdr Asquith. He had watched the appalling loss of life taking place as the two earlier advances had waded through the mud to frontally attack enemy outposts guarded by machine guns. The immense casualties incurred by such methods were not warranted by the meagre gains obtained. And, far too often, the outcome was a total failure to achieve any advance at all.

The new method would mean small groups of men attacking a particular position under the cover of darkness. They would be led by officers and senior ratings, who had previously made a thorough reconnaissance of the ground over which the attack was to be made, and of the objective itself. Surprise and intelligent leadership were to be the key factors.

In the cold and wet of the early hours of the 31st, as the battalion changeover was being completed, Sub-Lt Brearly of the Nelson Battalion, crawled through the mud in front of the concrete machine gun position that had held up all attempts to take Source Trench. On the left of the front, Sub-Lt Perry of the Hawkes was doing the same thing around an enemy outpost that had caused the position at Banff House to be evacuated by the army battalions of the 190th. Both officers were to lead attacks on their respective targets the following night.

The operations got under way at 6.10 p.m. With darkness covering the battlefield, only the occasional flare threatened to give the attackers away as they moved towards the strongpoints. On the right, Brearly had split his force of eleven ratings into three groups, two led by senior ratings and the third by himself. Knowing the weak spots in the barbed wire protecting the pillbox, they crept through the gaps and closed with the enemy. With only yards to go, the Germans spotted the group coming in on their left and opened fire. Immediately, Brearly, advancing in the centre, led his men and the other groups in an attack on the right of the position. Within seconds, the concrete outpost that had repulsed the onslaughts of whole companies had fallen to twelve men. One officer, eleven men and one machine gun were captured and several men killed, yet the attackers had not suffered one casualty.

On the Hawke Battalion front, Perry's party had met with equal success. They had captured nine men, killed two, and now held the outpost and its machine gun. Four hours later they even had a bonus, as an enemy ration party, unaware that the position had fallen, were promptly captured as they arrived with ammunition, water, and food.

The next night saw the capture of the only remaining enemy outpost of any importance on the Division's side of the Paddebeek by Lt Harris of the Drake Battalion, which had relieved the Hawkes at the front. With Sourd Farm captured, and the Hoods, who had relieved the Nelsons, advanced to the Paddebeek, the RND's first objective had, at last, been taken.

While the line was being secured, Asquith waded across the Paddebeek and reconnoitred the outposts around the next major strongpoint in front of his battalion – Tournent Farm. The main problem was that the ruined farm could not itself be attacked without the defensive outposts being captured first. And this action would inevitably warn the farm garrison.

When the situation was reported to higher authority, permission was granted for an attack to be made but, as a general attack was to be made shortly that would overtake Tournent Farm, the Hood's attack was to be called off if enemy resistance proved too strong.

The parties moved forward with Asquith in command. The outposts in front of the farm were swiftly captured, along with their garrisons and machine guns. Then the outposts on the right flank fell but, by now, all surprise had vanished and the large garrison at Tournent Farm began to put up a fierce resistance. By the end of the night, however, the Hood's front line had been advanced right up to the farm, and curved around its right flank, a highly satisfactory situation to hand over to their reliefs, for on the next night, when the farm itself might have fallen, the RND handed over the sector to the 1st Division.

The new method of attack, a flexible response to a changed situation, had more than justified itself. The 189th Brigade had achieved all the main objectives, with only 215 casualties, of which seventeen had resulted in death, compared to the 3,000 casualties of the 188th and 190th brigades.

The Division, minus the artillery, who were still in the field and earning warm tributes from all they had supported, returned to a camp near Ledeszeele. Whilst there, the Division learned of the death of Cdr Sterndale Bennett of the Drake Battalion, who had been wounded on 4 October. He was a popular officer, who had earned the respect of everyone who had served with him. The Drakes were now taken over by Cdr Pollock.

Lt-Col Lewis of the Nelsons had been gassed at the end of November, and for a few days the battalion had been led by Cdr Shelton, who as a Leading Seaman had escaped internment after Antwerp. But he too fell victim to gas, and command of the Nelsons now went to Cdr S. G. Jones who had once commanded the Ansons in Gallipoli.

This period away from the front lines was intended to be a rest period and a chance to train reinforcements prior to returning to the Passchendaele front. Events taking place to the south, however, were to dictate otherwise.

On 20 November, General Sir Julian Byng's Third Army launched an assault that ushered in a startling new era of warfare. At 6.20 a.m., immediately after 1,000 guns had begun to bombard the enemy, 381 tanks lumbered out of a 6 mile front and began to roll the German infantry back towards Flesquiéres and Masnières. All along the front, the stunned Germans fell back, only a pocket at Flesquiéres holding on for any length of time. The Hindenburg Line had proved no obstacle to the clattering monsters, and the infantry's task of 'mopping up' resulted in thousands of prisoners. By the second day, the British had advanced 5 miles into enemy-held territory and created a 3 mile wide breach in the German defences. It looked as if the major town of Cambrai was about to fall.

But the advance had been so fast that it took everyone by surprise. There were not enough reserves to keep the impetus going; all the tanks available had been used in the first assault, and many needed maintenance or had been destroyed by the enemy.

On the morning of 30 November, the Germans, strengthened by an extra Division newly joined from the eastern front where the Russians had withdrawn from the conflict, launched a determined counter-attack. Behind a brief, but sharp, bombardment of gas and smoke shells, they attacked the right flank of the salient. Another counter-attack at Bourlon Wood failed, but the right flank caved in until a brilliant counter-attack by the Guards Division at Gouzeaucourt halted the enemy. The only British reserves, the Cavalry, were sent in, but failed against the German machine guns. Gradually, the German pressure forced the British troops to abandon most of their gains until 7 December, when what had been a large salient that had posed a severe threat to the Germans had shrunk to a small bulge that skirted the northern edge of Flesquiéres and only provided a most precarious grip for the occupying troops. Such was the position when the Royal Naval Division relieved the 31st Division on 15 December.

The new divisional sector ran for nearly 7,000 yards along a low mound known as Welsh Ridge. Having originally been in German-held territory behind the Hindenburg Line, the defences were poor and primitive, and the first task of the Division during the long nights was to improve the trenches as much as possible before the inevitable attack. The front line, which ran along the forward slope of the ridge, was nothing more than a series of outposts that required to be connected up. The support line, a shallow trench, ran along the crest of the ridge, and the reserve line lay at the bottom of the steep rear slope. The lines were linked together by shallow communication trenches.

The 188th Brigade had arrived without a Brigade Commander, as Brigadier General Prentice had been invalided home. His place was taken by Brigadier General Coleridge who transferred from the 189th Brigade, which left that brigade without a commander. When it was learned who the new 189th Brigade Commander was to be, the appointment received the enthusiastic support of the entire Division. Cdr Asquith, who had earned a second bar to his DSO at Passchendaele, was promoted to the military rank of Brigadier General and appointed to the 189th Brigade.

The new Commanding Officer of the Hood Battalion was Lt Cdr Patrick Shaw-Stewart, one of the survivors of Rupert Brooke's burial party in far-off Skyros. The

Fellow of All Souls had requested to leave a staff job to get back to the RND.

Then, on 20 December, the Division heard of a tragedy that shook everyone from the most senior officer to the most junior rating. Brigadier General Arthur Asquith, while setting off on a reconnaissance, was seriously wounded. A German sniper had fired three rounds at him from close range. One had missed, one had slightly wounded his right leg, but the third smashed his left ankle. Asquith, in great pain, rolled across the shell-broken ground and dropped into his trench. Tended by Surgeon McCracken, there was no other option but to send him home for lengthy treatment. He had served the Royal Naval Division in an exemplary fashion from its earliest days. He had been a leader and innovator who had found glory in the most desperate and deplorable conditions. Fortunately, by his example, he had created a tradition in the Division that was eagerly followed by those who remained. But he was always to be missed. Lt-Col. Kirkpatrick of the Ansons took temporary command of the brigade, his battalion being taken over by Lt Cdr Archibald Buckle. The new Anson Battalion Commander had joined the Royal Naval Division as a petty officer and was commissioned in March 1915. Much to his frustration, he had been sent to the Blandford depot as a trainer and had proved so successful in that role that he was held behind as most of the Division was sent to Gallipoli. It was not until the Division arrived in France that he was allowed to join them in the field.

Over the Christmas period, snow fell heavily, and frost bit deep into the bodies of the men labouring to prepare the defences. On 29 December, the 190th Brigade had the left of the line, the 189th the centre, and the 188th the right. Two battalions manned the front line, with one in support and one in reserve. From left to right, the battalions deployed were the 5th KSLI, the Royal Fusiliers, Hood, Drake, Howe, and the 1st Royal Marines.

The early 'Hate' barrage, sent over by the Germans every morning, had been steadily increasing since Christmas Day, and at dawn on 30 December it was particularly heavy. As an attack could be expected at any time, the Battalion Cdrs toured their front lines to check that their men and positions were prepared to meet any assault following the bombardment. Lt Cdr Shaw-Stewart was wounded by a shell fragment during the first moments of the barrage, but still insisted on going forward. As he made his way along the Hood's trench, a shell landed near the parapet beside him. Within minutes, the twenty-nine-year-old Shaw-Stewart, a brilliant scholar who had been made a director of Baring's Bank at the age of twenty-five, was dead. When fighting in Gallipoli, he had written:

Was it hard Achilles
So very hard to die?
Thou knowest and I know not –
So much happier I.

Now he and Achilles were as one.

On the Howe sector of the front, Cdr West was making his way through a communication trench to his advanced positions when he too was killed by a shell. Another shell fell on his Battalion Headquarters, killing, among others, Lt Cdr Alan Campbell, who had led the tanks forward at Beaucourt-sur-Ancre. It was a tragic dawn for the Division, but worse was yet to come.

Suddenly the bombardment lifted and began to fall on the support line. As it lifted, the front-line defenders were horrified to see a horde of white-clad Germans rise from the position they had reached under the protection of the barrage. The enemy had made it to the barbed wire protecting the Division's front, and when the barrage lifted, they scrambled through and charged at the defenders. The troops in the trenches had no time to fire off more than a few rounds and yell warnings to others in the dugouts before the Germans had dropped into the trenches. From then on it became a nightmare of hand-to-hand fighting. Rifles were useless in such bloody close combat, but bayonets, trench clubs, entrenching tools, knuckledusters, fists, and boots were all used to bring down the opposition. After a savage, brutal battle, the first wave of attackers was subdued but, by then, the second wave was on top of the battered defenders.

On the right of the line, the Royal Marines held the enemy and drove them out of their trenches, but on the left the Shropshires and Royal Fusiliers had been driven back with great loss. Another breach had occurred between the Drake and Howe Battalions. The attack had been so swift and fierce that, in places, word had not reached the support companies of the front-line battalions that the attack had been made. The first indication the support company of the Hood Battalion had that the enemy was in their lines was when their cook, Able Seaman Brown, was confronted by three German officers while making his way along a communication trench. Recovering quickly from his shock, he killed one, wounded another, and took the third prisoner before being able to give the alarm. Sub-Lt Weir and Petty Officer Brown led a small party of men down the trench and began bombing the Germans back. After retreating for some distance, the enemy pulled down a barbed-wire 'knife rest' barrier, which blocked the trench and prevented the bombing party from reaching them.

With their communication to the front line cut off, the remainder of the support company had to climb from their rear trenches and advance over open ground. As they rushed forward, firing from the lost front-line trench caused many casualties and forced the remainder to take cover among the shell craters. At this, a bombing party in the communication trench climbed out, and attacked the enemy holding the next stretch from above. With the Germans driven back, they dropped once more into the trench and continued throwing their grenades. Just as they were about to reach the front line, the remainder of the company rose from their shelter and charged forward, the two groups arriving together. Once again it was a question of hand-to-hand fighting that only ended when the last German lay dead in the floor of the trench, or had fled back to his own lines.

By 8.30 a.m. the situation had been restored, and the Hoods, despite the almost total loss of two companies, were able to send assistance to the Royal Fusiliers on their left.

A serious problem had been created by the enemy getting into the front-line trench between the Drake and Howe battalions. Both battalions had reacted promptly by erecting barbed-wire barricades across the trench, which prevented the Germans from fighting their way along it. However, at the point where the enemy had gained entry, a communication trench led to the support lines, and the German troops rushed along it and reached the crest of the ridge before the Anson Battalion, who were in support, could organise a counter-attack.

The left of the divisional front had fallen back to the support line, and the reserve battalion, the 16th Artists, were told to prepare for a counter-attack at 2.15 p.m. The position on the right of the ridge, now in the hands of the enemy, would not be attacked until darkness had fallen, due to the steep slope the counter-attackers would have to climb from the reserve line. This attack was to have been made by the Anson and Nelson battalions, but the message to delay the counter-attack never reached Cdr Jones, who decided to mount his own assault at the same time as the Artists.

At the appointed hour, the Artists and Nelsons moved off to attack on their respective fronts. In the beginning, the Nelson Battalion found the going hard and, as the attack developed, it soon became clear that a daylight attack up the steep slope was impossible. The attack was called off to wait until nightfall.

The Artists, on the other hand, were at least able to launch their counter-attack down the slope from the crest of Welsh Ridge, although there seemed to be little advantage to be gained as they were met by a hail of fire from the enemy-occupied front line. By the time the advance had reached the halfway position, it had lost its impetus and the troops were told to take cover among the shell holes. They too would have to wait for darkness before continuing.

With dusk creeping over the scene, the Ansons' commander, Lt Cdr Buckle, explained his plans to retake the crest and front-line trench. There was to be no plodding towards the enemy machine guns in straight lines; once again a flexible response was more important than accepted military dogma.

At midnight, small parties of men made their way forward, listening intently for sounds of the enemy. Once the Germans had been located, the message was sent back and more seamen quietly joined the probing patrols. When the entire battalion had been silently deployed, a coloured flare soared into the black sky. It was the signal the Ansons had been waiting for. They sprang from their cover and hurled themselves at the enemy. The Germans were so surprised that not one shot was fired at their attackers. They retreated so rapidly before the pursuing Ansons that all the day's losses were regained with the loss of only three lives. Even the Commander-in-Chief, Sir Douglas Haig, was moved to refer to the work of Buckle and his Ansons as an 'admirably executed counter-attack'.

Midnight on the left of the front found the Artists preparing to attack their old front line once again. Just as the order was about to be given, a line of hand-thrown bombs exploded in front of them, followed by German troops launching their own attack. The Artists held their ground and, assisted by enfilading machine gun fire on their right flank, brought the attack to a halt. At 2 a.m., the Artists moved forward once more but, beneath a sky glowing with enemy flares, they were forced to go to ground yet again.

At dawn the enemy bombardment, particularly heavy on the left of the line, foreshadowed yet another attack on the Artists, who were lying between the lines in craters, or 'funk holes' they had chipped out of the frozen earth. When it came, the Artists and the enfilading fire on their right swept the open ground with a cool aimed precision that prevented all but a few from reaching the Artists' lines. Those who did reach the line died almost immediately.

The German attempt to seize Welsh Ridge had been broken. As the day progressed, the flanks of the new positions on the left were secured while, in the old front lines, the Germans could be seen changing the defences to face in the opposite direction. Two days later, the severely weakened Division was assisted by having its divisional frontage shortened. The 190th Brigade handed over the left of the line to the 53rd Brigade of the 19th Division.

During the last two days of 1917, the Royal Naval Division had faced the only major assault on the entire Western Front. It had cost them 1,420 casualties and had seen a loss of some of the Division's finest leaders. But they had prevented a force of more than fifteen enemy battalions from taking the vital heights of Welsh Ridge.

With the coming of the new year, the front quietened down. There was still the dawn 'Hate' to survive, and the occasional raid to capture a prisoner for identification and interrogation, but the most important task was the continued strengthening of the defences. After three weeks, the Royal Naval Division handed over the sector to the 2nd Division and retired to the rear areas.

Despite the exhausting action at the turn of the year and the back-breaking labour since, there was to be no rest period. Other divisions manning the front line in what remained of the Cambrai Salient, had to be assisted with the building of their defences, and working parties were sent out daily to lend assistance where it was most needed. Because of its losses the Division required considerable reinforcements, most of whom had to be rapidly trained to operate as parts of an active-service battalion.

The time for reorganisation was once again upon the Division. The Army had decided that infantry brigades were to be reduced to three battalions each. With the RND, this meant that the 5th King's Shropshire Light Infantry Battalion returned to the 19th Division, and the Nelson and Howe Battalions were disbanded, their personnel being absorbed by the remaining naval battalions. The 190th Brigade now consisted of the 4th Bedfords, the 7th Royal Fusiliers, and the 18th Artists. The 189th Brigade had the Hood, Drake, and Hawke battalions, and the188th was made up from the 1st and 2nd Royal Marines, and the Anson Battalion. In addition there were the Divisional Engineers, the Divisional Artillery, and the Divisional Machine-Gun Battalion. The 14th Battalion of the Worcester Regiment continued to give excellent service as the Division's Pioneer Battalion.

Towards the end of February, the Division was back in the front line. The new Divisional Sector lay some 4 miles north-west of their last position at Welsh Ridge. It guarded the northern flank of the same salient and ran along part of Flesquiéres Ridge. Before the Cambrai advance, the front now held by the Division had been the support positions for the Hindenburg Line. The Division's own support line now ran along the Hindenburg Line itself, while the reserves manned the old British front line. Still further to the rear, the original support line and the 'Green line' comprised the 'Rear Zone' of the 'V' Corps, of which the 63rd Royal Naval Division was part.

CHAPTER VIII

Storm Troopers and Retreat

By the end of 1917, it had become clear to the German High Command that, if Germany was to win the war, it had to be over by the summer of 1918. Any further delay would allow a massive increase in the Allies' strength through a build-up of the army of the United States of America, whose soldiers were at that time starting to arrive in France. With the fighting on the Eastern Front all but over, it was possible to begin the transfer of troops to the Western Front. There merely remained the question of where to best deliver a final, crushing offensive, and against whom?

The German Chief of Staff, General Ludendorff, had reached a decision: 'We must beat the British'. If the British Army could be defeated, then the French would certainly collapse, whereas the reverse was not considered to be necessarily true. Another advantage would be that once their line was broken, and their escape route cut off by the sea, the British could be destroyed almost at the will of the advancing Germans. Equally, although the retreating British would leave behind the same areas destroyed by the Germans in their retreat to the Hindenburg Line, the French had a vast area through which to fall back, and the pursuing troops would find their lines of supply and communication far too long to be efficiently maintained.

A bold plan needed bold methods; new methods of attack had to be devised and troops trained to carry them out. The frontal attack, putting pressure on an entire front line, was costly and generally failed, as all armies had found to their loss. Instead of throwing reserves against positions that were holding up an attack, they would in future be poured through breaches created by the initial waves. They would then be able to advance to the rear of the enemy front lines over ground that had been cleared by short, but intense, bombardments heavily laced with gas shells.

The soldiers who were to make the initial advances required to be specially selected and trained. The most experienced, the fittest and the young were removed from their battalions and formed into special units called 'Sturmabteilung' – Storm Troops. Armed with flamethrowers and light machine guns, their task was to cross the enemy front lines, avoid any action against strong points and machine guns, and break through to the enemy's rear, attacking, where possible, his artillery.

These advanced troops were then to be followed by heavier 'Battle Units' who would deal with the enemy posts bypassed by the Storm Troops. Once the breaches in the enemy line were confirmed, it would be the turn of the reserves to press through, widening the gap and completing the destruction of the enemy front-line positions.

Communications between the Storm Troops and the rear positions were very important in ensuring that the probing parties were not held up by their own artillery barrage. A system of coloured flares was evolved, which also had the advantage of informing other Storm Troop sections on either flank of the progress being made along the line of attack.

In January, February, and the beginning of March, German troops and artillery moved with the utmost secrecy to their positions for the impending assault. By the middle of March, over 3 ½ million men were poised ready to fall on the British lines. They numbered 192 divisions, sixty-nine of which were facing the 60-mile front trending south from Arras to La Fère where the British had stretched their right wing at the request of the French. On their side of the Arras La Fère front, the British could only muster thirty-three divisions, not all of whom were in the front line itself.

On the night of 20 March, the Royal Naval Division was in its position on the Flesquiéres Ridge. It was more than a month since they had returned to the front line and, although there had been no attacks by the enemy's infantry, his artillery had seriously depleted at least two of the Division's battalions. After a particularly heavy bombardment with more than 200,000 gas shells on 12 March, the Drake Battalion lost twenty-one officers and 408 ratings while the Hawke lost fifteen officers and 532 ratings. Other units also suffered losses from the gas. Brigadier General Bray, the Brigade Commander of the 189th Brigade, had to be invalided home and his place taken by Brigadier General de Pree. Cdr Daniel Beak took over the command of the Drake Battalion from a wounded Cdr Pollock. Altogether, out of a total of approximately 8,500 seamen, Marines, and soldiers, 2,800 had been affected by mustard gas and had to be led from the front in long lines of men holding each other's hands as they stumbled, coughing and blind, to the rear.

On the morning of the 21st, with the rancid smell of mustard gas still in the air, and a thick mist descending, the front line was held by, on the left, the 2nd Royal

Marines; in the centre, the Hawke; and on the right, the Bedfords. In support were the 1st Royal Marines, the Drake, and the Royal Fusiliers. The Anson, Hood, and Artists Rifles were in reserve.

The mist had gradually reduced visibility to a few yards at most. Occasionally, the diffused light from a flare glimmered briefly but, for the most part, the men in the trenches could only see their immediate surroundings. There was stillness over the area that seemed to have come with the fog. Even the guns were unusually quiet, with only the occasional muffled crump of artillery as someone was determined not to let the other side forget there was a war on. At 4.50 a.m., no-one could possibly forget.

With an earth-shaking, mind-reeling crash, 6,000 German guns opened fire on 40 miles of British-held line. Within minutes, 2,500 British guns opened in reply. The world had never known anything like it before. The air was filled with the howl and shriek of thousands of tons of steel, which fell to earth with a continuous concussion that dazed and deafened those who survived the appalling blasts.

The men in the outposts and, holding the front line were conscious of a new experience. Apart from trench mortar shells falling around them, they seemed to be escaping the savage bombardment. It was the rear positions that were getting pounded, and soon all communications with the rear had been destroyed.

In addition to the infernal noise, the smoke, and the fog, there came the loathed scent of mustard gas that drifted along the trenches and liquefied in the shell craters.

At 5.15 a.m. the first Germans were seen advancing towards the Hawke front just at the point of their junction with the Bedfords on their right. These were the first Storm Troopers encountered during the war. Those at the front of the attack were shot down at close range, but others dropped into the trenches and tried to fight their way through to the rear. Once again grand designs were reduced to the brutal business of hand-to-hand combat. As all the signal lines had been destroyed, there was no way of informing the Brigade Commander what was taking place in the front-line trenches and, consequently, no support troops were sent to assist.

While the first Storm Troopers were being dealt with, the enemy had captured an outpost and charged down its connecting trench to the front line. The Hawkes, led by Cdr Ellis, bombed the German troops back from the front trench and forced them to retreat as far back as the outpost itself. With a last shower of grenades, wire barricades were pulled down and the communication trench sealed off. The enemy had captured an outpost from the Hawkes, but the front line still held. True to their new tactics, the Storm Troops moved on in search of an easier place to breach the line.

At 10 a.m., the Ansons, Hood, and Artists Rifles moved from their reserve position and joined the support battalions in the Hindenburg Line. A company of the Drake was sent forward to assist the Hawkes, but no further attempts were made to get through the Division's line. As they stood ready to repulse any more attacks, they were aware that, on either flank and even in their rear, an immense battle was taking place.

To the north of the RND, the 51st Highland Division's front had been forced back despite the desperate struggle of the Argyll and Sutherlands, the Black Watch, the Seaforth, and the Gordon Highlanders. South of Flesquiéres, only the South Africans hurling the enemy back from Quentin Ridge stopped that flank from caving in.

At midnight, the front-line battalions of the RND were ordered to withdraw to the Hindenburg Line. The idea was not popular. It was felt that, after holding the position against a heavy attack, to give it up without being defeated, was wrong. But no one was aware of the extent of the German advance. Some divisions had been forced so far back in such a short time that, when the Royal Naval Division were ordered to withdraw once more, this time to the original British front line, another order for an even larger withdrawal was received before there had been time to begin the first. The Division had now to fall back to the Metz switch line, a trench running north–south that linked the old British front and support lines. This line was to be manned by the 188th and 189th Brigades while the 190th Brigade would take up defensive positions along the old support line to the west to cover any further withdrawal to the Green line – a prepared line of defence stretching along the entire front of the British Third and Fifth Armies.

As the Division began its withdrawal, the Divisional Artillery kept back an enemy attempt to advance from Marcoing, a village to the east of Flesquiéres. In the meantime, the Divisional Engineers began to destroy the defences as they were evacuated.

Owing to the speed with which the withdrawal orders had been changed, Cdr Beak of the Drake Battalion never received the orders for the withdrawal to continue to the Metz switch line. Consequently, when he reached the old front line, he deployed his battalion ready to defend the position. Aware that his battalion's flanks were unprotected due to there being no one to link up with, it was with some consternation that he received reports that German Storm Troop patrols were crossing the line on either side of his position. Then, as he moved along the trench checking his disposition, he came across sections of the Divisional Engineers preparing to blow the trench sky-high – and, unless they were moved very smartly, his battalion with it.

Having given the order to withdraw, Cdr Beak remained at the rear of his men carrying a Lewis gun. Throughout the remainder of the night and early morning, whenever the enemy came within range, he drove them back. Consequently, the

Drake Battalion suffered no casualties throughout the withdrawal and rejoined the remainder of the 189th Brigade at 7 a.m. on the 23rd, just as General Lawrie ordered the withdrawal of the Division to the Green line.

By midday, the new positions, about 6 miles from their starting point at Flesquiéres, had been reached and the trenches manned. The Division's front covered the two villages of Bertincourt and Ytres – a length of about 6,000 yards. On the left of the line were the 1st Royal Marines with the 2nd Royal Marines in support. In the centre, the Hood had the front, and the Drake the support, line, while the Artists Rifles, supported by the Bedfords, were on the right. The 7th Royal Fusiliers went into reserve in the village of Lechelle, south-west of Ytres. The Hawke Battalion was in reserve at Bus, a small village to the west of Ytres, and the Ansons took up positions along the Bertincourt–Bus road, acting as a general reserve. On the Division's left flank – to the north – was the 2nd Division, and on their right the 47th Division.

Reports had been received during the withdrawal that enemy patrols had been sighted to the south. As a result of this, detachments of the Divisional Machine-Gun Battalion were sent to the Division's right flank to fend off any attacks coming from that direction. During the afternoon, several enemy patrols were sighted in front, and on the flanks of the Division, but the machine-gunners kept them at bay.

Then, almost without warning, the Royal Fusiliers at Lechelle came under heavy attack and were forced to fall back to a line west of Bus. It was clear that the enemy had penetrated the 47th Division's lines and was now able to attack the Royal Naval Division's right flank.

As the light began to fade, difficulty in maintaining contact with the 47th Division, and the fact that several battalions from this Division had been seen to march away from the Green line, prompted the battalion commanders in the front and support positions to redeploy their forces. Leaving the Green line in the hands of the two Royal Marine battalions, the Hood and two companies of the Drake, the Bedfords, Artists and the remainder of the Drake formed a defensive flank on the right covering Ytres and the Ytres–Bus road. By late evening it became clear that the new positions had been chosen wisely as the 47th Division had withdrawn completely from the Green line.

At ten o'clock, a huge explosion rocked Ytres and caused casualties among the Artists Rifles, whose lines ran closest to the village. A large ammunition dump had blown-up. Shortly afterwards the enemy attacked Bus and forced the Hawke Battalion to withdraw to a line north of the village, much to the annoyance of the Battalion Headquarters, who, unaware of what had been happening, had just sat down to dinner.

The night gave no opportunities for the tired battalions to rest. The lines were constantly shelled by the enemy, and machine guns laced the night air with streams of tracer bullets. On the left of the Green line, Lt-Col. Farquharson, the Commanding Officer of the Royal Marines, was killed and his place taken by Lt Cdr Coote.

By dawn, the situation was desperate. In front of the Green line and along the right flank, the enemy artillery had been brought so far forward that they were firing over open sights, and a German artillery observation balloon was floating over Ytres. All three brigade commanders were away at the Divisional Headquarters which had been set up at Beaulencourt, 5 miles to the west. Only the Divisional Artillery and the Divisional Machine-Gunners prevented the enemy infantry from launching an attack, but casualties caused by the enemy guns would soon create gaps that could not be plugged.

With these facts before them, the six front-line battalion commanders unanimously decided that, if the Division was to be saved from annihilation, it must be withdrawn. In the absence of any higher authority or orders, they agreed that the 188th Brigade and the 190th Brigade would withdraw westwards towards Villers au Flos, 2 ½ miles north-west of Bus. The 189th Brigade was to act as a rearguard.

The greatest danger to the withdrawal would be an attack on the southern flank. The road from Bus to Rocquigny was already guarded by the Royal Fusiliers and a company of the Divisional Engineers. To their west, the road ran from Rocquigny to le Transloy (2 miles south of Villers au Flos), and then from le Transloy south-west to Lesboeufs. Col Macready of the Divisional Machine-Gun Battalion sent Major Moir and eight machine guns to the first of these roads, and Lt Anderson and twelve machine guns to the second. Much of the successful withdrawal of the Division would depend upon the defence of the threatened southern flank by these units.

The battalions began their move to the west at 8 a.m. with the enemy pressing hard against the rearguard and the southern flank. The Hawke Battalion, still covering Bus from its northern outskirts, had to wait until the Green line battalions had passed to their north. This achieved, the Hawkes, in order to make good their own escape, were forced to clamber up a steep bank which was easily covered by the enemy machine guns. It seemed that a massacre was inevitable until the battalion's Lewis guns engaged, and drove back, the enemy with such ferocity and accuracy that the Hawkes were able to join the other battalions at the cost of only a few casualties.

Close behind the retreating front line, the 189th Brigade Commander, General de Pree, rode up and down keeping a close eye on the advancing enemy. He noted –

The advance of the German Army was very interesting to watch, and was exceedingly skillfully carried out. The front was covered by large patrols each carrying one or two light machine guns. The use of light signals by these patrols was most remarkable. They signalized each stage of their advance by sending up a Very light with the result that the general effect given was the advance of a line of lights as far as the eye could see.

The withdrawal continued throughout the morning, with the Division fending off enemy patrols probing all along their line. By the time they reached Barastre, 1 mile from Villers au Flos, they came under the protection of the 17th Division and, by midday, all had reached the Division's prearranged assembly point between Le Transloy and Villers au Flos.

For most of the officers and men – few of whom had seen much sleep since the 20th – it was an opportunity to eat something, and then sleep for a couple of hours while General Lawrie, his staff, and the Brigade Commanders decided on the next move.

Events were happening far too rapidly for the V Corps Headquarters to be of much assistance. As with the move from the Green line, the responsibility for pulling the different units further and further back fell to the local commanders. By 2 p.m., it was clear to General Lawrie that his present position could not be held. Already, the 17th Division was beginning to withdraw on his left and, to the south, the noise of machine guns firing suggested that only Lt Anderson's unit, manning the Lesboeufs road, could prevent an attack by the enemy from that direction.

Consequently, it was decided that the Division would have to fall back to a line based on Martinpuich, 6 miles further to the south-west. The three brigades formed up in the open countryside almost as if they were on parade, and the entire Royal Naval Division began to march over the old Somme battlefield at 3 p.m. As they did so, German patrols could be seen advancing in the same direction to the south – only the machine gunners keeping them a respectable distance away.

After two hours of marching, which had taken them past the northern outskirts of Guendecourt and Flers, the Division was halted at High Wood, a position to the east of Martinpuich. As the Division rested, General Lawrie received orders from the V Corps Headquarters telling him to form the Division into a defensive position on a line between High Wood and Eaucourt L'Abbaye. He ordered the 190th Brigade to continue on to Courcelette and there form the divisional reserve while the 189th Brigade manned the right of the line and the 188th the left. The right flank would make contact with the 47th Division, and the left with the 17th Division.

In the gathering gloom, the brigades moved forward to take their place in the new line. The 188th reached theirs without incident, but the 189th Brigade ran into a well-planned enemy attack. A large Storm Troop patrol, hoping to smash a hole in the British line, had worked its way forward in the fading light, and when the Hawke, Drake, and Hood battalions were well within range they opened a dense, slashing machine gun attack on the advancing men. But this was only part of the assault. The Storm Troopers, yelling and shouting at the tops of their voices as they fired their machine guns, also sent coloured flares arcing across the twilight sky. Almost instantly, German aircraft swooped down and dropped six bombs on the battalions while others flew along at a height of 35 feet, machine gunning the men below, causing many casualties.

It was an attack as good as any the Storm Troopers had mounted. But it failed. Although badly shaken, and with numerous casualties, the 189th Brigade stood its ground and, before long, the enemy had been driven back.

By the early hours of the morning of the 25th, the battalions had reached their places in the line. The Drake had the right of the line; the Hawke, the centre; and the Anson the left. In support were the Hood, and the 1st and 2nd Royal Marines. A company of the Divisional Engineers joined the Drakes' sector of the line. As dawn approached, the 47th Division once again withdrew, leaving the Royal Naval Division's right unprotected, and a company from the Hood Battalion was sent forward to form a defensive flank lining up with the Drake.

At 6.30 a.m. units of the enemy were observed advancing from Flers, less than 2 miles to their front. Soon, large masses of men could be seen being deployed, and advance patrols began to probe the British line. By 9.30, it was obvious to everyone that a large assault was about to be mounted, yet, just at that moment, the 17th Division withdrew.

With the left flank of the Division now unprotected, the German patrols lunged forward and succeeded in surrounding a company of Ansons on the extreme left. The Commanding Officer of the Ansons, Lt-Col. Kirkpatrick, organised and led a counter-attack which broke through to the isolated company and brought them out. Although the company had been saved from annihilation, little else could be done against the enemy who, following their new tactics, were putting increasing pressure on to the weakest point of the line – the unprotected left flank. At about ten o'clock, the 188th Brigade were ordered by the Divisional Commander to fall back a mile to the Bapaume–Albert road and link up with the Royal Fusiliers and Artists at Courcelette.

As the Ansons and the 2nd Royal Marines withdrew, they could see the area they were leaving filling up with huge numbers of enemy infantry pressing on in pursuit. Eventually, a new line was encountered, manned by the 14th Worcestershire. The Ansons were ordered to continue towards the road as the Marines joined the Pioneers. Between them, the soldiers and Marines halted the enemy's advance until the Germans brought up field artillery and laid down a barrage which caused many casualties. Beneath the shellfire, the Pioneers' commanding officer, Lt-Col. Caldier Ladd, as usual leading his men in the thick of the action, was badly wounded and died in the hands of the Germans when the stretcher-bearers carrying him from the scene lost their way and fell into enemy hands. Having delayed the enemy advance for some time, the Royal Marines and Pioneers were forced to withdraw. As they made their way back, to their delight, they came across an unguarded, apparently abandoned, canteen. Entering the building in the belief that it was better to remove any food and supplies rather than leave them to the advancing Germans, their high hopes were dashed on discovering that all that remained was a pair of boxing gloves.

Meanwhile, on the right of the Division's line, there had been more time to prepare the flank left unguarded by the withdrawal of the 47th Division. The Divisional Machine-Gun Battalion had placed four of its Vickers machine guns to cover the gap, and succeeded in keeping the enemy at a respectful distance. At eleven o'clock, the Bedfords were sent forward to strengthen the line still further and, in a combined attack with the Drake and Hawke battalions, managed to push the right of the line 250 yards further forward, capturing machine guns and prisoners. As this advance was made, the Commanding Officer of the Hawke Battalion, Cdr Ellis, fell mortally wounded.

For more than an hour, these battalions, aided by machine gunners and engineers, hung on to their new position despite a succession of heavy enemy attacks. They could have held their gains even longer, but for the fact that the enemy attacks on the left flank continued to increase. Shortly after midday, General Lawrie had no choice but to shorten his front line in order to strengthen his defences on the Bapaume–Albert road. The 189th Brigade and the Bedfords were ordered to withdraw to Courcelette.

By mid-afternoon, even this position had become untenable. German patrols continued to probe at the Division's front and flanks, and no support appeared to be forthcoming from any other British units. The order to withdraw to Thiepval, 2 miles west, was given. The 189th Brigade were the first to go while the 188th and 190th acted as rearguard. As the Division fell back, communications were once again established with V Corps Headquarters, who ordered the Division to continue its withdrawal beyond Thiepval, and to cross the River Ancre. In the early hours of the morning of 26 March, the Royal Naval Division found itself back in Hamel – the scene of their first victory on the Western Front.

But there was no time for nostalgia. A defensive line had to be formed down the western side of the Ancre, which, at that point, flowed from north to south. The 189th Brigade covered the village of Hamel with the 2nd Division on their left. On their right, the 188th and 190th Brigades manned the line in front of

Aveluy Wood. The Divisional Artillery took up positions in front of Englebelmer. One 18-pounder, however, remained closer to the Ancre where it was well used in keeping the heads down of any Germans who appeared on the opposite bank.

Just to the north of the Division, the enemy launched a strong attack at about midday. The 2nd Division's troops managed to keep them at bay at most places along their front, but some German infantry had been seen to reach Station Road – the same ground that Brigadier General Freyberg had strode across to win his Victoria Cross.

To the south, another, more successful attack had taken place near Albert. An enemy advance to the north-west from this position would cut across the communications of those divisions holding the Ancre line. It was an opportunity of which the Germans could be expected to take full advantage.

As darkness descended on the evening of the 26th, the Royal Naval Division was relieved in the Ancre line by the 12th Division. But there was no time to relax. The 188th Brigade went to Martinsart, and the 190th remained in the Aveluy Wood area. Both were to act in support of the 12th Division should German forces advance from Albert. The 189th Brigade went into reserve at Englebelmer.

However, these were not the only movements being made under cover of darkness. The Germans had advanced from Thiepval, and small parties had been crossing the Ancre unobserved for some time before the final handover to the 12th Division was made.

Brigadier General de Pree, the Brigade Commander of the 189th Brigade, and his Brigade Major were riding their horses along the road to Englebelmer at about 1.15 a.m. when they came under rifle fire from an enemy patrol manning a bank on the roadside. Spurring on their horses, they forced their way through a barbed wire barricade and escaped. Within minutes, the galloping horses and riders had reached Engelbelmer. There, finding that one of his battalions had already gone into billets, General de Pree ordered the two remaining battalions to form a defensive line in front of the village. As the preparations were being put hastily under way, an officer and thirty men from the 12th Division stumbled into Englebelmer. When questioned, the officer told de Pree that 2,000 Germans were advancing down the road only minutes behind him and his fleeing troops. If the report was correct, then the situation was indeed desperate. Against such numbers of the enemy – and they would presumably be elite Storm Troop patrols – the 189th Brigade could muster less than 500 very tired men in the time remaining. The seamen lined up on either side of the road. Their only hope would be to allow the enemy to get between them in the dark, open fire at close range, and then charge with the bayonet. They waited in silence, listening for the sounds of advancing men as the enemy moved towards them. But they waited in vain. Instead, the sound of fierce close-quarter combat clashed and thudded down toward them from the direction of the enemy's supposed advance.

The news of the German patrols crossing the Ancre had also reached Brigadier General Coleridge of the 188th Brigade at his headquarters in Martinsart. He immediately ordered his battalions to stand to. The Anson Battalion and the 2nd Marines were to advance against the enemy's left flank and attack. The 1st Marines would follow up in support.

It was nearly 3 a.m. when the leading battalions came up against the Germans advancing along the Englebelmer road. With a cheer and a charge that belied their numbers and weariness, the Ansons and Marines fell on to the enemy with such ferocity that the German soldiers, shocked and confused, began to fall back in disorder. Suddenly the enemy broke and fled, some climbing trees in Aveluy Wood in an effort to escape. Many were killed in the rout. Before an hour had passed, the 188th Brigade had captured fifty prisoners and taken thirteen machine guns.

With the pressure on Englebelmer relieved, the 189th and 188th brigades were able to return to their billets for a few hours' rest. The 190th Brigade, however, spent the remainder of the day in support of the 17th Division, pushing back enemy patrols advancing from Albert in an attempt to carry out their threat of cutting across the communications of the divisions manning the line of the Ancre. The brunt of the day's fighting fell on the Artists Rifles and the Bedfords.

Lt-Col. Collins-Wells – the Commanding Officer of the Bedfords – had already demonstrated great courage during the retreat by personally leading his men during moments of great danger, on one occasion holding the enemy at bay with just a few men until all their ammunition was exhausted. When the enemy attacked from Albert, he placed himself at the head of his weary troops and led a counter-attack. Although twice wounded, he refused to leave the battlefield and continued to encourage his men until he was killed at the moment his battalion achieved their objective. Collins-Wells was posthumously awarded the RND's fifth Victoria Cross.

The success achieved on the southern flank was timely, for, at 5.30 p.m., the enemy attacked the 12th Division from the north. They succeeded in driving the British troops out of Hamel, and, only when Brigadier General Coleridge's 188th Brigade once again moved forward in support was the enemy's advance brought to a halt. The 12th Division had been badly mauled by the enemy during the day's fighting, and it became necessary to have them relieved. By 3 April, the Royal Naval Division was back in the front line.

There was not long to wait before the enemy decided to put to the test once again the Division's will to resist. On the morning of the 5th, the Germans mounted a heavy attack on the sector held by the 7th Royal Fusiliers. The Fusiliers hung on grimly despite an appalling casualty rate until the 1st Royal Marines could be rushed up and put in the line alongside them. By midday the assault had died down, allowing the soldiers to hand the sector over to the Royal Marines. The next morning, a short, sharp bombardment heralded another attack against the same position. The 1st Royal Marines, already weakened by losses the day before, were forced to fall back until the 2nd Royal Marines joined them. Together they halted the enemy advance and, in a counter-attack led by the Battalion Commanders, the Marines stormed the positions they had just evacuated. They drove the Germans back, inflicting great loss capturing fifty-six prisoners and ten machine guns.

In the matter of whose will was the strongest, the Royal Naval Division had come out on top. The enemy began to revert to the static war of the trenches. It had not, of course, simply been a question of man against man. The speed and distance of the German advance had left their lines of communication overextended and weak. On the other hand the British had been falling back on theirs, thus making their lines considerably shorter. There was also the question of morale. In theory German élan should have been at its highest, while the retreating British should have been thoroughly demoralised. Clearly, however, no one had explained this to the German support and reserve battalions, robbed of their best men to provide Storm Troopers, nor to the 63rd (RN) and other divisions of the British forces, who continued to fight with a tenacity that belied their situation.

The German advance against the centre and south of the British line was over. They had won 1,200 square miles of land from the Allies, and captured tens of thousands of prisoners, many guns, and huge quantities of stores. But, because the war still remained to be fought, they had to defend an extra 50 miles of front line, none of which was as secure as the Hindenburg Line had been. Finally, the enthusiasm of both the German soldier and civilian had evaporated at the same rate as the British defences had hardened.

The Royal Naval Division had had to pay a high price for its achievements during the period from the very first gas bombardments on 12 March to the consolidation of the line west of the Ancre. The casualties amounted to more than 6,000 men, thus reducing their average battalion strength to less than 250 men. Four battalion commanders had died, and one was seriously wounded. Staff-Surgeon McCracken, who had earned the DSO at Gavrelle and at Passchendaele, had been seriously wounded and had to be invalided home. There had been a Victoria Cross won, four battalion commanders had been awarded the DSO, and, throughout the Division, many other decorations for gallantry had been earned.

After nine further days in the front line, mostly spent in improving the defences, the Division was relieved by the 17th Division. They marched due west until they reached the small town of Puchevillers where, for the first time in many days, the survivors of the long withdrawal could find rest, relaxation, and a degree of comfort.

CHAPTER IX

The 4th Battalion at Zeebrugge

As the Royal Naval Division rested after blunting the 'grey avalanche' of what had become known as 'The Kaiser's Battle', another assault was made on the Germans in a totally different theatre of the war. Although not strictly involving the RND, enough of those who took part were former, or potential, members of the Division that it is worth recording their courageous endeavours on that day.

The British Army's hopes to advance as far to the north and west as possible, with a view to capturing the ports of Ostend and Zeebrugge, had foundered in the mud and slaughter of Passchendaele. Great Britain, in the meantime, was suffering grievously from U-boat attacks on her shipping. Rationing of food was already severe and now faced tightening, to the extent that starvation was no longer just a possibility, but an almost certain probability.

One of the most potent sources of the U-boat threat was the city of Bruges. Not only was the city well clear of the coast, it was connected to Germany by rail and to the North Sea by two navigable canals, one to Ostend, the other to Zeebrugge. U-boat parts were sent by rail from Germany, assembled in Bruges, and then sent out, via the canals, to wreak havoc on enemy shipping.

The Royal Navy had tried to counter the threat by shelling the canal's great lock at Zeebrugge, but had failed to inflict the damage required. Another method of stopping the U-boats had to be found.

As far back as 1916, plans had emerged from the Admiralty for various direct attacks against the ports, but none had been taken up. In December, 1917, another scheme was developed by the Admiralty Director of Plans, Rear Admiral Roger Keyes (who had taken part in the naval attack on the Dardanelles). Again nothing happened until, fortuitously, Keyes was promoted to Vice Admiral and given command of the Dover Patrol. In his new appointment, he was in a position to advance any schemes under his own authority.

The plan that finally emerged was really quite simple in its operation. All that needed to be done was to find a number of redundant vessels, and sink them as blockships at the entrance to the canals. Although blockships can, eventually, be removed, the delay in U-boat operations would give Great Britain breathing space from the enemy's attempts to strangle its supplies.

As far as Ostend was concerned, such an operation was relatively straightforward. The harbour was wide and uncomplicated and, once the marker buoys had been found, the entrance to the canal could be located and reached without too much difficulty beyond the normal, expected, coastal defences.

Zeebrugge, on the other hand, presented much more of a challenge. The harbour – and, consequently the entrance to the canal – was protected by a mile-long concrete mole which projected from the shore and curved north-eastwards towards its seaward end. This feature, like a defensive left-hook guarding the harbour and canal entrance, was connected to the shore by an iron viaduct which allowed a railway track to run along its entire length. Having crossed the viaduct, the railway first passed a seaplane base, a bombproof shelter for ships, a gun battery, two large storage sheds and, at the far end of the mole, a large blockhouse mounting three 5.9-inch guns – itself protected by barbed wire and trenches. Stretching out further to a lighthouse, an extension had six 4.1-inch guns sited along its length. Should any approaching enemy ships survive such heavy seaward fire and reach the harbour, the guns on the mole and the lighthouse extension could simply turn around and continue to pour fire on to them, in addition to gunfire from several coastal batteries.

Any attempt to land on the seaward side of the mole would find itself faced with a 29-foot climb from sea level at high tide, increasing to 44 feet at low tide. Once the mole had been scaled, the attacker would find himself at the top of a parapet with a 4-foot drop on the other side. This was followed by an 8-foot-wide platform at the top of the mole wall, which led to a 16-foot drop onto the floor of the mole itself. The whole length of the inner mole wall could be covered by machine gun fire. No one could be sure, but it was believed that the garrison on the mole amounted to about 1,000 men.

Undeterred by such formidable obstacles (and intending to be present himself at any assault), Keyes' plan allowed for three blockships to head for the canal entrance at Zeebrugge while a diversionary force should land on the mole to engage the mole defences. As a further refinement, aircraft would drop bombs on the mole, and two submarines would wedge themselves under the land-end viaduct and be blown up to prevent reinforcements coming to the aid of the defenders.

This was clearly not to be a minor operation. In all, 162 different vessels were to be involved. In addition to the submarines and blockships, there were three types of ship needed for the landing parties: heavy-gunned monitors, destroyers, and numerous small vessels ranging from coastal motor boats, fast patrol boats and motor launches to a steam picket boat. The submarines carried a motor skiff in which, it was hoped, the crews could make an escape.

The motor launches, or 'MLs', had been developed from an idea put forward by Sub-Lt Oscar Freyberg, the older brother of Bernard Freyberg, the former Commander of the RND's Hood Battalion, who was then serving as a Brigadier General on the Western Front. Freyberg had used a fast motor launch to hunt whales off New Zealand and believed that a similar high-speed, well-armed craft could be used against submarines. The idea was rapidly taken up by the Admiralty but, to widespread disappointment, the orders for construction were given to an American company. They were built in sections at Bayonne, New Jersey, taken by rail to Canada, reassembled, and shipped to Britain. Oscar Freyberg was killed during the attack on Gallipoli, on 4 June 1915.

The blockships intended for the operation were five elderly light cruisers. HMS *Thetis,* HMS *Intrepid,* and HMS *Iphigenia* would be used in the attack on Zeebrugge while HMS *Brilliant* and HMS *Sirius* would be sent to Ostend.

For the diversionary landing on the mole, Keyes selected the twenty-one-year-old, second class cruiser, HMS *Vindictive.* The vessel would have to undergo considerable adaptation to meet the needs of the endeavour. An extra deck was built to bring the 'storming parties' closer to the height of the parapet. From this deck, derricks were rigged to carry large grappling anchors which would be secured to the parapet and used to keep the ship alongside the wall. Also on this deck, nine ramps were constructed to allow the attackers to get on to the mole wall before crossing the top of the wall and, using scaling ladders or ropes, to reach the floor of the mole, some 16 feet below. The foremast was reduced to the height of the 'fighting top' platform, and the main mast removed altogether, with part of it secured athwartships astern with several feet projecting over the port side. This latter, arrangement was intended to keep the stern away from the mole wall in order to protect the port propeller. Forward on the port side, protection consisted of an enormous fender intended to cushion the blow if the ship struck the wall as it approached. Two armoured cabins were built on the port side to house flamethrowers, and three howitzers were fitted to the upper deck, one forward, one amidships, and one astern. As much of the upper deck as possible, especially the bridge and just below the conning tower, was given extra protection against small-arms fire, shrapnel and splinters.

Two further vessels were to play an important part in the attack. The rather delicately named *Daffodil* and the *Iris* were two Mersey ferries that had been hired by the Admiralty. Although not officially on the books of the Admiralty, they were referred to by all and sundry as 'HMS' – a title they were to fully deserve. The role of the two ferries was to carry, and land, part of the storming parties, with the *Daffodil* having the extra responsibility of pushing the *Vindictive* against the mole wall until the parapet anchors had been secured.

Two 'C' class submarines, 'C1'and 'C3', were selected to be sacrificed by wedging themselves beneath the mole viaduct. Both were to be crewed by two officers and four ratings who would put the craft into automatic 'gyro steering' just short of the viaduct and, with luck, escape using the skiff before the boats exploded.

The manpower for the enterprise came from two sources. The first was the Grand Fleet, still waiting and hoping that the Germans would put to sea. A simple call for volunteers would not work, as it was imperative that the operation was kept secret. Instead, officers throughout the fleet were ordered to approach suitable fellow officers, ratings, and Royal Marines to ask if they were prepared to volunteer for a 'hazardous' mission.

The second source of manpower came from the four divisions of the Royal Marines. In 1916, the 1st and 2nd battalions were serving with the Royal Naval Division, and the 3rd was garrisoning Mudros. Thus, as a response to the Easter Rising in Ireland, a 4th Battalion was assembled. Although, in the end, they did not serve in that capacity, the 4th Battalion remained in being as a reserve for the RND. Consequently, as a draft of reinforcements was required, men were sent, from the divisions at Plymouth, Portsmouth, Chatham and Deal, to the 4th Battalion to be trained before leaving for the Western Front.

Every one of the officers and men from the Grand Fleet who mustered at Chatham for the operation was convinced that they were being sent to the trenches in France and Belgium. This belief was supported by having the training being carried out on ground marked out with tapes, suggesting trenches and buildings, and the instructors coming from the Royal Marines at Chatham. Other training instructions were quite specific. A 'Confidential Circular' told the instructors:

> The object of the training is to get the men physically fit, full of dash and accustomed to short sharp raids by night, equipped in the lightest order.
>
> The Company must therefore be worked up in Bayonet, Bombing, Rapid Shooting at short range, Snap Shooting (especially standing), and Trench fighting.
>
> Heavy marching is not required. Marches should be from 5 to 10 miles without packs, to get men in condition only. Wrestling, football, running, boxing (when gloves are available) and such games as prisoners base, can easily be carried out during instruction hours (these sort of games now form a great feature of Army instruction).

Practice in Trench fighting is essential. Lewis gunners and Bombers must be thoroughly trained. They must be exercised respectively with Ball Ammunition, and live Bombs at night.

Lewis gunners are not required to be mechanical experts, but men who can get in to action quickly, keep their guns going and instinctively remedy stoppages. Similarly, the Bombers are not required to be skilful throwers of the Mills Grenades, and not to know the construction of a variety of Grenades.

All the Company should be put through a Musketry Course with Mark VII Ammunition, the practices being framed to develop rapid shooting at short ranges, and snap shooting.

Practice in night fighting is essential.

It is suggested that in the daily programme should be included –

    1 hour Bayonet and Trench fighting (not necessarily continuous).

    ½ hour Swedish.

    ½ hour Games at odd times, and running.

    ½ hour Section, Platoon, and Company Training.

    ½ hour Musketry Instruction, chiefly rapid snapping, with marches of

    5 to 10 miles without packs.

Practice in night work, even if this can only be carried out in a very elementary way, is essential.

Digging is not required, but men should be practised in quickly passing up filled sandbags.

Open warfare tactics are not required, and should only be occasionally carried out as a change.

Officers should practice with the revolver.

The Royal Marines involved in the operation, for whom such activities were almost second nature, were brought up to a particularly high standard of close-action infantry warfare.

The command of the seamen went to Captain Henry Halahan, who had already earned the Distinguished Service Order on the Western Front while in command of naval guns in the northern part of the front line. The Royal Marines came under the command of Lt-Col. Bertram Elliot who had also been awarded a DSO, this time while serving in Serbia. HMS *Vindictive* was to be commanded by thirty-six-year-old Cdr Alfred Carpenter, a member of Vice Admiral Keyes' staff. Carpenter was the son and grandson of naval commanders, and had served in the Boxer Rebellion. The two former ferries, *Daffodil* and *Iris*, went to, respectively, Lt Harold Campbell, and Cdr Valentine Gibbs who, before the war, had been a winner of the famous Cresta Run at St. Moritz. Lt Aubrey Newbold was given the submarine *C1*, while *C3* went to Lt Richard Sandford, the youngest son of the Archdeacon of Exeter. The latter's brother, Lt Cdr Francis Sandford, was responsible for fitting out the submarines, and for the planning of their part in the operation. He was also given command of the steam picket boat that would pick up the submarine crews after they had completed their mission.

An extraordinary man who joined the operation was Wing Cdr Frank Brock, a member of a famous firework-producing family. At the outbreak of the war, he was commissioned into the Royal Artillery, but transferred to the Royal Naval Air Service as a lieutenant in the Royal Naval Volunteer Reserve. Before long, Brock had founded, and was in command of, the Royal Naval Experiment Station at Stratford. Whilst there, he was able to design, among other things, a special incendiary anti-Zeppelin bullet that was so effective that it brought about the end of Zeppelin raids on Britain; the Dover Flare, which, with its million-candle-power light, was in constant use in lighting up the straits at night and the smoke-screen generator (or 'artificial fog' as he preferred to call it). For his work in the field of pyrotechnics he was made an Officer of the Order of the British Empire (OBE). In addition to having an inquiring mind, Brock retained his own sense of individuality. His favourite light reading was a copy of the New Testament, which accompanied him everywhere, and, although the RNAS had very recently been transferred to the newly formed Royal Air Force, Brock preferred to hold on to his naval rank in place of the Lt-Col. he could have been with the RAF. Now, with his smokescreen apparatus and the flamethrowers of his design being put to use at Zeebrugge, and with also the chance to find an example of the German secret sound-ranging system, he obtained permission from Keyes to join the assault, and was appointed to the *Vindictive*.

The overall plan of the operation was to bring the *Vindictive* alongside the outer mole wall as close as possible to the gun batteries sited at the end of the mole and on the lighthouse extension. The *Iris* would go alongside the wall ahead of the cruiser, while the *Daffodil* acted as a tug pushing the *Vindictive* against the wall. The approach of all three vessels would be hidden from enemy sight by a smokescreen laid down by fast motor launches.

With the *Vindictive* alongside the wall, and with her starboard anchor lowered, the ramps would be dropped, allowing the seamen to reach the top of the wall and haul the parapet anchors into position. Once this had been achieved, the seamen would form themselves into a 'storming party' and attack the gun batteries, followed by the cruiser's Royal Marine storming party. At the same time, the *Iris*, followed by the *Daffodil* (by now relieved of her tug duties), would send her Royal Marines ashore to assist the seamen and to attack the facilities towards the landward end of the mole. A third landing party of seamen, under the command of Lt Cecil Dickinson, was known as the 'Demolition Party', and was required to destroy whatever it could find.

The recall signal for the seamen and Marines to return to the ships was to be repeated blasts from the *Vindictive*'s sirens or, failing that, the vertical waving of the ship's searchlights.

While the gun batteries and other parts of the mole were being attacked, the two submarines were to wedge themselves under the viaduct, their crews having set explosive charges before leaving the boats to steer themselves to destruction as they escaped on small skiffs slung from booms attached to the conning towers.

Further out, the monitors *Erebus* and *Terror* would bombard the coastal batteries assisted by three destroyers. Another four destroyers acted as an outer screen, and a further twelve roamed about the harbour entrance directing their firepower as required. A final destroyer, HMS *Warwick*, was given the honour of being flagship to Vice Admiral Keyes, and could be expected to be in the thick of the action. The flagship's captain was Cdr Victor Campbell. He had been invalided home while in command of the Drake Battalion at Gallipoli. On recovering from his wounds he was given command of the coastal monitor, M-24, before being appointed to the new destroyer HMS *Milne*, in which he earned a bar to his DSO after ramming and sinking a U-boat. The minesweeper *Lingfield* would escort the blockships and take off the surplus 'steaming crews'of stokers before they entered the harbour to be scuttled at the canal entrance. Finally, a total of eighteen coastal motor boats (CMBs) and thirty-three motor launches were to be employed in laying down the smokescreen and generally annoying the enemy.

To the north, the Harwich Force would provide protection against any enemy threat in that direction, while, to the south, the Royal Marine Artillery, based ashore around Dunkirk, were to open fire on selected targets, to keep the enemy occupied.

Even before the ships started the attack, the 65th Wing of the RAF, based at Dunkirk, would bomb the mole and the shore gun batteries. The 61st Wing would escort the ships into the North Sea to fend off any inquisitive German aircraft.

The one thing that could not be planned was the weather. Two attempts to get the operation under way failed because of the conditions. On the first, the wind – which was required to blow from the north-east to keep the smokescreen effective – swung to the south. On that occasion the ships had reached close enough to see the flashes from the bombs and anti-aircraft fire as the 65th Wing carried out its raid. The second attempt was thwarted by the rough sea-conditions, which prevented the use of the many small craft on which the operation depended.

At last, however, on 22 April, the numerous ships met at the assembly point at 'The Swin', south of Clacton, and, just before 5 p.m., headed eastwards, the only weather problem being the continually pouring rain – and nobody was going to let that affect matters. Nobody, that is, except for the 65th Wing who were unable to fly. The crossing of the huge armada took seven hours, four of which were in daylight, and yet no German ship, submarine, or aircraft, caught sight of the long columns of ships. At 11.30 p.m. and with the Belgian coast approaching, Keyes sent a signal around the fleet – 'St George for England' (the 23rd being St George's Day). Captain Carpenter, busily directing the *Vindictive* towards the mole, had no time for a snappy reply, and could only come up with the somewhat leaden – 'May we give the dragon's tail a damn good twist.'

The first the Germans on the mole knew about the impending attack was when the two monitors opened up at 11.20 p.m. and sent shells shrieking into Zeebrugge. But, even then, there was not great alarm. The shelling of the enemy-held ports was a commonplace activity. Twenty minutes later, however, the Germans knew that something different was afoot when their ears were assaulted by the full-throated roar of many motor launches thundering past. Instantly, several searchlights flashed into life, only to reveal a wall of thick smoke rising from the sea's surface a few hundred yards out from the mole. Then the worst possible thing that could have happened for the attackers took place – the wind changed direction.

Carpenter, in the conning tower of the *Vindictive*, suddenly found himself looking at 300 yards of open water between him and the mole, the gap brightly lit by searchlight and the light from illumination flares that were rising from the mole and shore. As the cruiser emerged from the smoke, the Germans opened fire with every gun they could bring to bear, a fire that was immediately met by the *Vindictive*'s own guns. The upper deck, with seamen and Marines standing by to charge up the ramps, was sprayed with machine gun fire, shrapnel and splinters. The officer in charge of the seaman storming parties, Captain Halahan, was killed, as was the officer in charge of the Royal Marine parties, Lt-Col. Elliot, along with his deputy. The remaining senior officer of the naval storming party, Lt Cdr Arthur Harrison, lay slumped on the deck, his jaw smashed by a piece of shrapnel. With a single exception, the signalling staff manning the bridge were dead or wounded. The range was shortening all the time (one petty officer gunner later claimed that the range from the end of his gun muzzle was 'about 3 feet'), and yet the German gunners, although pouring fire upon the ship, appeared never to have taken a deliberate, considered aim. Just a couple of shots below the waterline, or into the boiler room, would have put an end to the escapade. Instead, the entire upper works was riddled with bullet and shell holes. Most of the ramps had been destroyed along with several of the parapet anchor davits.

Carpenter, seeing the mole wall approaching, left the relative safety of the conning tower and moved into the port flamethrower compartment. From that exposed position he could look down the entire length of the port side from a position 5 feet higher than the mole wall. As he crossed from the conning tower, he noticed the explosives and charges of the demolition party laid out and prepared for the demolition team once they were alongside. It would have taken just one shell, or even bullet, to have struck the cases for the lot to have blown up, taking much of the ship with it. Adopting the view that the demolition of enemy facilities was of secondary importance to the main aim of blocking the canal entrance, Carpenter ordered the explosives to be taken below decks and disconnected.

At one minute past midnight, although travelling at 16 knots, the huge port fenders allowed the *Vindictive* to hit the wall with little more than a slight bump. After a few minutes of manoeuvring the cruiser fore and aft, Carpenter ordered the starboard anchor to be 'let go' – but it jammed. Eventually, the port anchor had to be used. Although intended to come alongside the wall some 70 yards from the gun batteries, the *Vindictive* found herself 300 yards away from the target.

The ramps were in a very sorry state. Only the two most forward ramps were capable of use and, when lowered to rest on the parapet, were badly affected by the ship's rolling, caused by the sea rebounding from the mole wall. With each rise and fall, the ramps see-sawed violently, threatening anyone bold enough to attempt a dash for the mole with instant death between the wall and the ship's side. The answer came in the shape of the *Daffodil*. Despite having been hit in the face by a bullet, and unable to see out of one eye, Lt Campbell brought the bows of the ferry firmly amidships and pushed the cruiser against the wall. Instantly, Lt Cdr Bryan Adams raced up a ramp followed by a group of seamen. Their intention was to secure the parapet anchors onto the parapet wall, but the cumbersome, heavy, anchors proved extremely difficult to handle. Even as they were just about to haul the great flukes of the foremost anchor over the wall, its davits collapsed and fell overboard. As a result, Campbell was ordered to keep the *Daffodil* in position, holding the *Vindictive* against the wall. As he did so, her Marine storming parties scrambled over the *Daffodil*'s bows and on to the decks of the cruiser.

Adams had been followed on to the mole by the remaining seamen who, in turn, were followed by the Royal Marine storming parties, eager to get into the fight. Among them and, once ashore, chasing after the seamen, who had raced along the top of the wall in the direction of the enemy guns, was Wing Cdr Brock. His main job on the approach to the mole had been to look after the operation of the flamethrowers, but both had been put out of action by enemy gunfire. Believed to be eager to find any evidence of the sound-ranging system he was keen to get his hands on, he caught up with Adams and his party just as they threw a handgrenade into a lookout station with, rearing behind and above it, a rangefinder. Brock entered the building, and was not seen alive again by the naval party.

Behind the seaman stormers, and beyond the *Vindictive* where the Marines were dropping down to the floor of the mole, the *Iris* was undergoing great difficulties. Rolling wildly in the heavy swell, the ferry's seamen found themselves unable to get onto the wall, with the ladders uncontrollably rearing and plummeting. Lt Claude Hawkings then ordered a group of seamen to hold a ladder against the wall and to keep it in position. This done, he scrambled up the ladder and rolled over the top onto the walkway. As he did so, the ladder broke apart behind him. Sitting astride the parapet, Hawkings called for an anchor to be swung out to him, but was then seen to draw his revolver and begin to fire at approaching enemy soldiers. Within seconds he fell from the wall, dead.

Seeing Hawkins fail to secure the anchor, Lt Cdr George Bradford, the Royal Navy's welterweight boxing champion, just minutes into his thirty-first birthday, clambered up an anchor davit, released the anchor itself, and swung it ashore as he jumped for the wall. Heaving at the anchor, he managed to get it secured on the wall only to be killed by machine gun fire, his body falling into the sea. The next wave wrenched Bradford's anchor from its position, and the *Iris* surged away yet again from the mole wall. At this, her captain, Cdr Gibbs, decided that a far better option than continuing to try and secure the vessel alongside would be to attempt to put his ship alongside the *Vindictive*.

As the *Iris* surged aft towards the outboard side of the cruiser, a long black shape powered its way along her starboard side. The submarine *C3* was on its way to attack the viaduct. *C1* had encountered great difficulties with her towing cable and was a considerable distance behind. Lt Sandford, in the meantime had, on his own initiative, decided to slightly amend the plan of attack. Instead of putting the ship under the command of the auto-gyro system, which was intended to automatically steer the submarine to its target position under the viaduct, he and his crew would ensure its proper arrival by staying on board. Sailing in close to the shore, the *C3* was suddenly hit by the glare of floodlights, followed by the firing of machine guns. Artificial smoke was deployed, but the wind proved unfavourable and blew the smoke clear. Then, unaccountably, the searchlights were switched off, and the firing ceased. Just minutes later, *C3* was firmly wedged beneath the viaduct. Having set the explosive charges, Sandford gave the order to abandon ship. Under heavy small-arms fire, the submarine's crew scrambled into the small skiff and started the engine – only to find that the propeller had been damaged. Resorting to oars, the two officers and four ratings emerged from beneath the viaduct into the full glare of searchlights and machine guns firing at close range. Desperately paddling for their lives, Sandford, a petty officer, and the stoker were hit. Then Sandford was hit for a second time, but the paddling still continued. As they reached a point some 300 yards from the viaduct, a large explosion ripped through the night. With the blast, the firing stopped, and the searchlights were extinguished. Two minutes later, Sandford and his crew were dragged from the skiff and onto the picket boat captained by his brother. Following their instructions, the picket boat set off immediately for Dover.

Lt Newbold, now free of his entanglement with the towing cable, saw the flash of the viaduct explosion. With the aim of the mission already achieved – and later, with the support of his superiors – Newbold decided that there was nothing to be achieved by blowing up his own submarine, and headed for home.

In the meantime, the *Vindictive* was still under heavy fire from the enemy, and casualties continued to mount. Carpenter, deciding to have a look at the conditions in other parts of the ship, stumbled over the recumbent form of Lt Harold Walker. With one arm blown off, Walker raised himself up and, waving his remaining arm, wished his captain 'the best of luck'. Further on, Carpenter came across Lt Edward Hilton-Young, the Member of Parliament for Norwich. Hiltond-Young was responsible for the forward 6-inch gun and, despite strict regulations to the contrary, was smoking a large cigar and stood in the open in his shirtsleeves and without a helmet. When Carpenter indicated towards his bloodied and bandaged right arm, Hilton-Young merely replied that he had 'got one in the arm' and – according to the captain – carried on with his 'self appointed duty of cheering everybody up'. Later his arm had to be amputated. Going below decks, Carpenter reached the mess-deck now in use as the main casualty station. There he found the Senior Medical Officer, Staff-Surgeon James McCutcheon, and his team surrounded by the injured, the dying, and the dead. Shouting above the noise of battle that even penetrated well below the upper deck, he informed the men of the situation on the mole, making sure to accentuate what achievements he could. A great cheer went up – even from those who, in a very short time, would never cheer again.

There was, actually, very little reason to celebrate on the upper deck. In the fighting-top, Lt Charles Rigby and his crew of eight Royal Marines had done sterling work with their pom-poms and Lewis guns in reducing the fire coming from the enemy gunners. However, after a time, the exposed position came under concentrated fire, and a large shell smashed into the flimsy structure. All the marines were killed with the exception of Sergeant Norman Finch who was badly wounded. Pulling himself together, Finch got one of the Lewis guns working again and continued to pour fire from the fighting-top until a second shell caused him even greater injuries and rendered him helpless.

After leaving Wing Commander Brock to search for his range-finder, Lt Cdr Adams led the naval party along the mole wall towards the gun batteries. Several of his men had been knocked over by machine guns when he was surprised to see Lt Cdr Harrison running up to join him. Harrison, in great pain from his smashed jaw, and still feeling the effects of concussion, had hauled himself up from the deck where he had fallen, climbed up a ramp and made his way to the naval party. On hearing Adams' report, he sent the officer back to the *Vindictive* for reinforcements, and made his own assessment of the situation. There was, he felt, only one answer to the problem of machine guns blocking their path. With his pistol in his hand, Harrison, who had played rugby for England, charged directly at the enemy. Whether he intended to charge alone is not known (his broken jaw may have prevented him from being able to shout above the noise), but the whole of his party immediately followed and, within seconds, all but two were dead.

Able Seaman Eaves, despite being wounded, dashed forward and tried to rescue Harrison's body only to be brought down by more machine gun fire. Able Seaman Albert McKenzie, the Grand Fleet lightweight boxing champion, was also hit. Despite there being no cover available, McKenzie held his ground and turned his Lewis gun on the enemy machine gunners, and other Germans soldiers, to such good effect that the fire from that quarter was significantly reduced, allowing Adams to return with reinforcements.

Still under heavy rain, a party of Royal Marines, led by Major Bernard Weller, arrived to continue the attack on the gun batteries; another group of Marines, led by Lt Theodore Cooke, raced along the mole wall in the opposite direction. Silencing a group of snipers, Cooke was badly injured just as Captain Edward Bamford arrived on the scene. Leaving a party to hold back any enemy attack from that direction, Bamford led three platoons of Marines down scaling ladders to the floor of the mole. There, he received the order to mount an attack on the gun batteries currently under assault by the seamen parties on the wall. Before the guns could even be reached, the Germans had placed rows of barbed wire defending fully manned trenches, both of which had to be overcome. Undeterred, Bamford led his men in a frontal attack, cheering the Marines on all the time, and demonstrating a remarkable example of courage in the face of seemingly insurmountable odds. Had he found time to glance over his right shoulder, Bamford would have seen a sight that would have justified any efforts – and even sacrifice – on the part of his men and himself.

As the fighting had raged along the mole, the three blockships – each with many of their compartments filled with concrete – closed with the end of the mole. First in line was the *Thetis* under the command of Cdr Ralph Sneyd. Ahead of him he could see the harbour fully illuminated by the glare of rockets fired from the *Vindictive*. On his starboard bow, a row of barges formed a partial boom projecting from the mole in to the harbour. Steering towards the harbour end of the boom, and at the same time opening fire on the lighthouse, the *Thetis* ran into a net boom that fouled her propellers. With her engines brought to a halt, the ship ran aground some 300 yards from the canal entrance. Sneyd ordered the lighting of the starboard navigation light, its green glow signalling the side towards which the following ships would have to steer in order to reach the canal. At the same time, the Germans, suddenly realising the true purpose of the attack, turned their guns on to the blockships.

The *Intrepid*, commanded by Lt Stuart Bonham-Carter, and the *Iphigenia*, under the command of Lt Edward Billyard-Leake, steamed past as Sneyd ordered a smokescreen to hide their destination from the enemy. As they passed, the captain of the *Thetis* was unaware that Engineer Lt Cdr Ronald Boddie, accompanied by Chief Engine Room Artificer Frank Gale, had returned to the flooded engine room and had managed to restart the starboard engine. Once Sneyd was informed of this development, he ordered the telegraph to be put to 'Full Ahead'. Hampered by her stern dragging on the harbour bottom, the *Thetis* just managed to heave herself forward enough to reach the dredged channel leading to the canal. At this point, Sneyd gave the order for the ships bottom to be blown out.

In the meantime, the *Intrepid* had passed between the canal entrance piers and had penetrated the waterway beyond the shoreline. Here, where the canal was at its narrowest, Bonham-Carter swung his ship round until the bows and stern were grounded on the submerged mud-banks lining the canal. He then blew out the ship's bottom.

The *Iphigenia* had a slightly more difficult time. As she headed for the canal entrance, a shell parted a steam pipe, which resulted in the front of the ship being enveloped in clouds of steam blocking out the view. To this was added a large cloud of smoke, which surrounded the ship on all sides – possibly the same smoke-screen laid down by the *Thetis*. Fortunately, a gap in the smoke and steam appeared just as the ship was about to collide with the canal's western entrance pier. Saved by a frantic 'Full speed astern!' the ship nosed into the canal, where Billyard-Leake noticed that the gap between the bows of the *Intrepid* and the eastern bank of the canal was wider than the opposite side. Turning the *Iphigenia*, and glancing off the port quarter of the *Intrepid*, he rammed his bows into the eastern side to seal off the gap before blowing out the ship's bottom.

Against all the odds, the survivors of the blockships launched oared cutters and pulled themselves towards the harbour entrance. They had not gone far when they were met by motor launches racing in to pick them up. Bonham-Carter of the *Intrepid*, with two of his officers and four petty officers, had an incredible escape when, under the noses of machine guns firing wildly at the water, a lifeboat light in their cutter suddenly burst into life. The party, immediately obtaining the attention of several nearby machine guns, tried to destroy the light but failed, eventually sitting on it before it was finally extinguished.

With the two blockship survivors paddling desperately for their lives, Motor

Launch *ML282*, commanded by Lt Percy Dean, entered the canal and came under the fire of several machine guns lining the banks. Undeterred, he collected over 100 men from the blockships from their flimsy boats then, just as he was about to open his engines to full throttle, he heard that a man had fallen overboard. Without hesitation he turned back to collect him. The rescue achieved, *ML282* reached the canal entrance only to have its steering gear shot away. Resorting to steering by means of the engines, Dean headed towards a point on his port bow. This brought him close to the inner mole where, despite the individual attentions of a number of machine guns, he was able to roar out of the harbour under the mouths of the heavy guns, none of which could be depressed to a level where they could fire at him.

As *ML282* left the harbour and rounded the end of the mole, the blockship's crews were treated to the dismal sight of the destroyer HMS *North Star* sinking. She had closed with the enemy in order to protect the blockships as they had entered the harbour, and had suffered the close-range attention of the mole guns. When Lt Cdr Hubert Gore-Langton, the captain of the destroyer HMS *Phoebe*, saw the *North Star*'s predicament, he closed with the ship and circled it with a smokescreen. A tow was sent across and the *Phoebe* began to pull the *North Star* clear of the danger. But a shot took away the towing hawser, and the crippled *North Star* drifted out of the smoke-screen coming, yet again, under heavy fire. It was soon clear to all that the ship would have to be abandoned as she was unquestionably in a sinking condition. Gore-Langton closed with the *North Star* and succeeded in taking off all her surviving ship's company. The last to leave the sinking vessel was her captain, Lt Cdr Kenneth Helyar.

At just past 12.50 a.m., with the blockship crews being rescued by the motor launches, Vice Admiral Keyes, onboard the *Warwick*, gave the order to retire. The means of sounding the recall, however, were no longer immediately available. Both the *Vindictive*'s sirens had been shot away, and her searchlights had been destroyed by enemy fire. All that remained was the *Daffodil*'s siren, and, when she was ordered to sound the recall, all that issued forth was a steam filled splutter. Eventually, the siren began to make a more respectable sound that could be heard throughout the harbour area.

At the same time as the shrill gurgle of the recall signal added to the general noise, the *Vindictive*'s Chief Quartermaster, Petty Officer Youlton, discovered that a large number of boxed Stokes bombs, many of them armed with their fuses in position, had caught fire. Shouting for everyone to keep clear, Youlton pulled the boxes from the flames and stamped them out, only for them to flare up once again. Stamping on the flames for the second time, the petty officer finally put out the flames, thus preventing – as Carpenter later noted – 'a very awkward situation'.

Also, just at the same time as the recall signal sounded, the *Iris* appeared

Among the chaos of Antwerp, London buses used to transport detachments of the RND can be seen in the background. (CMcC)

The Royal Marines at Lierre (south-east of Antwerp) on the edge of a bridge across the River Nethe they have just destroyed.

A Royal Marine, wounded while helping to man the Antwerp trenches, being assisted back to the city by a comrade. (CMcC)

Seamen of the RND under escort of Dutch guards. (CMcC)

Men of the RND being marched off to internment in Holland.

A snowball fight between men of the 1st Royal Naval Brigade at Groningen internment camp in Holland.

Winston Churchill, First Lord of the Admiralty.

Right above: British Marines carrying equipment past Greek sentries. Although Greece did not formally enter into the Alliance, the Greek population was, in the majority, pro-Allies and were on friendly terms with the British soldiers in their midst. (CMcC)

Right below: HMS *Erin*, formerly the Turkish *Rashadieh*.

Hood Battalion officers
aboard the SS *Grantully
Castle*.

An artist's impression of the landing from the *River Clyde* at 'V' Beach during the Gallipoli
landings. (CMcC)

The *River Clyde* from 'V' Beach. The barges linking the shore with the bottom of the landing ramps can be clearly seen.

The *River Clyde* aground where she brought troops for the landing on 'V' Beach. The photograph also shos the stretch of water covered by Sub-Lt Arthur St Clair Tisdall when earning the Victoria Cross by rescuing wounded men.

The men of the RND practising attacks while training on Lemnos. (CMcC)

General Sir Ian Hamilton leaving after inspecting the Howe Battalion of the 2nd Naval Brigade on the island of Imbros on 18 June 1915. The battalion was resting after losing over half its strength on 4 June at the Third Battle of Krithia. (CMcC)

Anzac Cove a few weeks after the landings.

Crown Prince
George, the heir
to Serbia, with
Rear Admiral
Troubridge.
(CMcC)

Chief Petty Officer Flook of the Drake Battalion.

The cliff at Anzac.

Lieutenant Commander The Right Honourable Josiah C. Wedgwood MP. A direct descendent of the eighteenth-century potter and in command of the machine guns of the forecastle of the *River Clyde*.

The RND's armoured cars at Gallipoli.

Commander Bernard Freyberg DSO VC pictured on a cigarette card.

An artist's impression of the armoured cars of the RND assisting the British lines at Ypres. (CMcC)

The three vessels to the right are blockships, *Thetis* is on the far right.

Vice Admiral Roger Keyes.

The damage sustained by the forward funnel during the raid.

The battered *Vindictive* on her return.

Taken a prisoner during the raid, Captain Palmerd of the Royal Marines refuses to shake the Kaiser's hand after Zeebrugge. (CMcC)

1917 RND postcard.

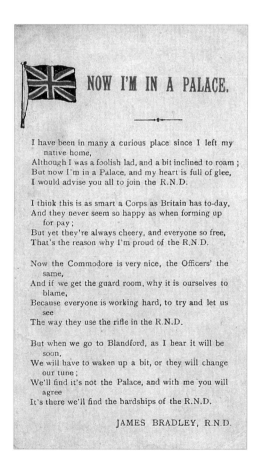

NOW I'M IN A PALACE.

I have been in many a curious place since I left my
native home,
Although I was a foolish lad, and a bit inclined to roam ;
But now I'm in a Palace, and my heart is full of glee,
I would advise you all to join the R.N.D.

I think this is as smart a Corps as Britain has to-day,
And they never seem so happy as when forming up
for pay ;
But yet they're always cheery, and everyone so free,
That's the reason why I'm proud of the R.N.D.

Now the Commodore is very nice, the Officers' the
same,
And if we get the guard room, why it is ourselves to
blame,
Because everyone is working hard, to try and let us
see
The way they use the rifle in the R.N.D.

But when we go to Blandford, as I hear it will be
soon,
We will have to waken up a bit, or they will change
our tune ;
We'll find it's not the Palace, and with me you will
agree
It's there we'll find the hardships of the R.N.D.

JAMES BRADLEY, R.N.D.

FROM

ONE OF THE

ROYAL NAVAL DIVISION.

RND postcards, including one with a poem, *left*.

Above from left to right: 63rd Divisional cloth emblem (red device on a blue background); RND officer's bronze cap badge; Bronze Chief Petty Officer's cap badge; Anson Battalion cap badge; Drake Battalion cap badge; Hawke Battalion cap badge; Hood Battalion cap badge; Howe Battalion cap badge; Nelson Battalion cap badge.

Above from left to right: RND Machine Gun Company cap badge; Anson Battalion shoulder title; Hawke Battalion shoulder title; Howe Battalion shoulder title; Hood Battalion shoulder title; Nelson Battalion shoulder title; Benbow Battalion shoulder title; variation of the RND shoulder title; Collingwood shoulder title.

A memorial to the Royal Naval Division was unveiled at Beaucort-sur-Ancre in 1922.

Right above: The memorial to Collingwood Battalion at Collingwood Corner on the Salisbury to Blandford Road.

Right below: The Royal Navy Division's memorial fountain on Horseguard's Parade.

The graves at Dover of some of the dead from Zeebrugge. The large memorial to the right is the grave of Admiral of the fleet, Lord Keyes.

alongside the *Vindictive*. The distance travelled by the ferry was little more than a few dozen yards, but had been made under extraordinary conditions and had taken around half an hour to achieve. Now, although secured alongside the cruiser, and with his Marines eager to get into the fight, Gibbs was ordered to 'shove off'.

When the sound of the recall signal reached their ears, the naval parties, Bamford's Marines, and the Demolition Party (who had their activities restricted to throwing hand grenades on board a German destroyer), began to pull back. The greatest risk lay among those on the mole who had to climb the scaling ladders to reach the top of the wall in full view of the enemy machine gunners. So intense did the firing become that several of the ladders were simply shot to pieces. Standing at the bottom of one of the ladders was Captain Charles Tuckey, who encouraged his men to race up the ladder in defiance of the storm of enemy fire. One after another they climbed, urged on by Tuckey, until, as the last of them were making their way up, Tuckey, a survivor of Antwerp and both 'X' and 'Y' beaches on Gallipoli, was killed by machine gun fire. He was aged twenty-three.

Fifteen minutes after the recall was sounded, only the odd, solitary figure scrambled back on board the *Vindictive*. The senior officers of the seamen landing party and the Royal Marines reported to Carpenter that all their men who had survived were back on board. Having promised to delay for twenty minutes after the siren, the captain of the *Vindictive* was reluctant to depart before that time but, after repeated assurances that all the living, along with the wounded that could be brought back, were now returned and safely below decks, he gave the order to leave. The *Vindictive* had been alongside the mole for one hour and ten minutes – and under constant fire for every second.

The *Daffodil* sent over a tow rope and hauled the *Vindictive*'s bows away from the wall. After just a few seconds of tension, the rope parted, but it did not matter, the ship had already begun to swing. There was a heart-stopping moment as the gangways fell into the sea and fouled the port propeller, but the engine forced itself free and the old cruiser made weigh into a fog provided by her own smokescreen, only the orange flare from flames leaping from her bullet-riddled funnels giving any idea where the ship could be found.

The *Iris*, on the other hand, suffered terribly in the withdrawal. Although throwing out a smokescreen, the ferry received several hits from the heavy guns firing from the mole. Over seventy Royal Marines were killed outright and many injured. The captain, Cdr Gibbs, was fatally wounded, and the navigating officer badly injured. Below the bridge, Lt Oscar Henderson was fighting a serious fire as Able Seaman Ferdinand Lake was grabbing hot handgrenades and Stokes bombs from the flames and throwing them overboard. On being informed that the captain and navigator were wounded, Henderson climbed through the wreckage and found the ship's coxswain, Petty Officer David Smith, shining a torch on the compass and steering with his other hand. In the middle of the carnage below decks, Surgeon Frank Pocock discovered that all his sick-berth staff had been killed. Surrounded by the dead, dying, and seriously wounded, Pocock, who had earned a Military Cross with the Drake Battalion in the fighting along the north bank of the Ancre, then found himself plunged into darkness as the ship's generator was hit. Calling for candles, he continued to operate, saving many lives as Henderson took command of the ship and turned her bows westwards. By 2.45 p.m., the *Iris* was back at Dover.

The *Daffodil* had returned at 1 p.m., under tow from HMS *Trident*. She had been cheered in by the ship's company of the *Vindictive*, and now she joined the cruiser in cheering in the *Iris*.

It was at Dover that they learned that the raid on Ostend had completely failed. The Germans had moved the marker buoys which would have guided the ships to the canal entrance, and the wind had blown the smokescreen in the wrong direction, obscuring the view. Both the *Brilliant* and the *Sirius* had run aground and were scuttled by blowing their bottoms out. Later, the *Vindictive* would be used to block the canal.

Back at Dover, one lighter moment was provided by the rumour that 250 men of the German Cyclists Corps had pedalled vigorously in the darkness along the viaduct in an effort to go to the aid of their fellow soldiers, only for the entire group to fall into the gap created by the explosion of the submarine, *C3* – thus having, as Carpenter noted, 'infringed the Gaderene copyright.'

Vice Admiral Keyes approached the newly promoted Captain Carpenter and asked him for his recommendations for the award of the Victoria Cross. Carpenter refused to give any names on the grounds that he had witnessed so much courage, he could not single out individuals. Keyes countered this by invoking Clause 13 of the Victoria Cross Warrant, which allowed for a ballot to be held among those who took part in an action to choose one of their number to receive the award. Keyes then stretched this further by deciding that two awards should go to naval and marine officers, and one each to a rating and a Royal Marine other rank. This provided for four VCs, which he promptly doubled to eight, along with a demand for twenty-one Distinguished Service Orders, twenty-nine Distinguished Service Crosses, sixteen Conspicuous Gallantry Medals, 143 Distinguished Service Medals, and 283 Mentions in Despatches. The Admiralty refused, but Keyes stood his ground until the Admiralty agreed, despite the number of gallantry decorations representing the award of six decorations for every minute of action. He then demanded fifty-six promotions as rewards for services during the action – again the Admiralty succumbed. Keyes himself was knighted on the day of his return from Zeebrugge.

The ballots for the award of the Victoria Crosses resulted in the decoration being granted to survivors Cdr Carpenter (along with promotion to captain); Lt Percy Dean, Lt Richard Sandford, Captain Edward Bamford, Sergeant Norman Finch, and Able Seaman Albert McKenzie. Posthumous awards of the Victoria Cross went to Lt Cdr Arthur Harrison and Lt Cdr George Bradford, one of four brothers whose combined gallantry decorations included two Victoria Crosses, one DSO, and one MC. In a letter to Bradford's wife, a former captain wrote of him, 'I can truly say a more honourable, straight, and gallant English gentleman never lived.'

It is well known, of course, as in many actions, that that not every act of gallantry and valour was seen or recognised. Cdr Carpenter's refusal to name candidates for the Victoria Cross demonstrates that he was faced with an embarrassment of deeds worthy of recognition. Possibly among those inevitably not recognised for their actions on that day was Wing Cdr Brock. Officially, he was last seen entering the building beneath the rangefinder; others, however, did later mention seeing Brock in the action. *Flight*– a popular magazine among the air-minded of the day (Brock's RNAS rank was not just a convenience – he was also a pilot) reported that he had:

come to close grips with the foe who were protected in an enclosure guarded liberally by barbed wire. This was stormed, and Cdr Brock, using his fists, made his way to a gun, and almost single-handed, accounted for the crew. The gun was captured, and put out of action, and then Cdr Brock attacked another gun's crew, cheering his men all the while. Just before the 'Vindictive's'siren sounded the signal of recall Cdr Brock was seen removing on of the locks of the gun, but a moment or two later he was wounded by a shot from a German destroyer. When last seen he was being watched over by two marines, who insisted on remaining to support the wounded officer.

The writer then ends his report with the words:

A truly British story.

From a force of about eighty-two officers and 1,698 men, 194 had lost their lives, 383 were wounded, and thirteen taken prisoner. The Germans, shaken to the core by the attack, first claimed that they had sunk three cruisers in a battle against the Royal Navy. When this was seen to be clearly absurd, they claimed that the blockships had been moved within two days. Whatever they may have thought, the attack was clearly considered of enough importance for the mole to be visited within days by the Kaiser and by Field Marshal Hindenburg. Even a month after the attack, twenty-four destroyers and twelve U-boats were reported to be trapped at Bruges. Keyes asked the newly formed Royal Air Force to bomb both them and the Zeebrugge lock – where the Germans were busy trying to widen the channel around the blockships – but was refused. In the end, the true German view of the raid can probably be judged from the comments in the *Frankfurter Zeitung* just days later. The newspaper editorial noted:

> It would be foolish to deny that the British fleet scored a great success through a fantastically audacious stroke in penetrating into one of the most important strongholds over which the German flag floats. However unpleasant it may be, we must frankly admit that the enemy ships actually entered the port of Zeebrugge. That being so, there is no reason why they should achieve a similar feat at other times. It therefore behoves our navy command to be alert, for we have to deal with an antagonist of remarkable boldness.

For the British – in particular the Royal Marines – the most lasting memorial was the fact that the title '4th Battalion' was never again used by the corps. The deeds of the battalion's officers and men on St George's Day 1918, were deemed notable enough to ensure its continued existence in the celebrated history of the Royal Marines without further search for fame.

CHAPTER X

Cambrai, Flanders and Armistice

On the morning of 9 April 1918, as the Royal Naval Division were denying the enemy any further ground, a heavy German attack smashed against the Portuguese 2nd Division, south of Armentières. The soldiers of England's oldest ally, poorly led by their officers and demoralised by political hostility towards the war at home, collapsed in front of the onslaught. Although British troops were rushed forward to try and contain the outbreak, nothing could stop the enemy advancing 6 miles by the end of the day.

In the days that followed, British troops were forced to fall back from their line north of the position evacuated by the Portuguese. Armentières, Ploegsteert, Messines, and Neuve Chapelle all fell to the advancing enemy. Then, with great bitterness, Passchendaele Ridge itself was voluntarily given up in order that troops could be freed to help defend the sagging front line along the River Lys. The attack died down on 19 April only to start up again six days later. This time, some ground was lost in front of Ypres, and the high point, Mont Kemmel, defended by the French, was lost on the first day. But, with the rapid hardening of the British defence, the German's latest objective, Poperinghe, appeared to be an impossible task. By the 29th, the Battle of the Lys was over. The German advance against the British line was, finally, at an end.

On 8 May, the 63rd Royal Naval Division relieved the 17th Division and returned once more to the Hamel-Aveluy sector. Most of the battalions – the exception being the Royal Marines – had been brought up to strength. They had all undergone a period of intense training which had brought both the veteran 'old hands' and the newcomers to a new, refreshed eagerness to get to grips with the enemy.

Throughout the remainder of May and the first days of June, the Division fended off probing attacks against its part of the line and, in return, launched heavy raids of its own. All the activities were carried out to a background of artillery duels, during which the front line, support, and rear positions all suffered heavy bombardments.

By the end of May, it had become clear that the two Royal Marine Battalions could not continue to remain effective. They were under-manned, and there were no reinforcements available. Consequently, it was decided that the battalions should merge into a single Royal Marine Battalion under the command of the former 1st RM Battalion commanding officer, Lt-Col. Fletcher. In order to bring the 188th Brigade back up to three-battalion strength, the 2nd Battalion of the Royal Irish Rifles, under the command of Lt-Col. Harrison, was attached. Cdr S. G. Jones, who during his service with the Division had commanded the Anson and the Nelson battalions, took over command of the Hawke Battalion. The commander of the 190th Brigade, Brigadier General Hutchinson, who had served with the Division for almost three years, was appointed to the post of Assistant Adjutant-General of the Royal Marines. His place was taken by Brigadier General Leslie.

The new commanding officers, and the new organisation, were given an opportunity to train together when, on 4 June, the Division was relieved and sent for three weeks in the Toutencourt rest area.

On their return, the Division was sent to the front line in front of Auchonvillers, on the left of the Hamel sector. German activities had died down in most places along the British front, and the RND's sector was no exception. Nevertheless, there was no reason why the war should not be taken to the enemy and, on the night of 12 July, seamen from the Drake Battalion attacked the enemy.

Two officers and fifty-four ratings advanced under the cover of darkness and pounced on the enemy outposts opposite the battalion front. In a short, sharp, and savage raid, in which their recent training was put to good use, they killed several of the enemy, captured twenty-two, and returned to their own trenches with a captured machine gun. The enterprise had cost the battalion one life.

From the first days of August, events on the Western Front began a dramatic change of direction. After the most recent German offensive had reached Château-Thierry and the bank of the River Marne, the French had counter-attacked and sent the enemy reeling back. The German retreat had begun.

Under a cloak of secrecy that baffled even the most experienced German troops, the British Fourth Army prepared to launch a large offensive against enemy positions on the northern flank of the Amiens Salient. At the same time, the southern flank would come under attack from the French.

With the light of dawn still an hour away, and with a thick mist blanketing the movement of men and machines, the morning of 8 August was shattered by the opening up of a creeping bombardment. The line of advancing explosions was followed by Canadian, Australian, and British troops moving forward behind a clanking battering ram of more than 300 tanks. All along the line of advance, the enemy fell back or surrendered en masse. By the end of the day, 110 square miles had been taken by the Allied troops, 13,000 prisoners and hundreds of guns had been captured. 'August 8th,' wrote General Ludendorff, 'was the Black Day of the German Army.'

The advance continued for the next two days, but at an ever-decreasing rate. On the 10th, the Dominion troops, who had spearheaded the attack from the first day, had only been able to advance for a single mile. The following day, they received the order to dig in.

As the British began to roll back the enemy on the morning of the 8th, orders were received by the Royal Naval Division to hand over the Auchonvillers sector to a relieving division. It seemed as if the RND was to play its part in the Battle of Amiens, as it was ordered to a position south of the Albert–Amiens road where it remained behind the left flank of the advancing British line. The intention was that the Division would move up and guard the left flank of the advancing divisions, but their advance came to a halt in the face of hardening German resistance, and no further forward movement could be made.

The High Command then decided that another offensive had to be launched as quickly as possible. An assault against Bapaume from the north-west by the British Third Army offered the best prospects of victory and, on 15 August, the RND were once again on the move.

Having discovered that secrecy was a vital ingredient of surprise, a tight security clamp-down covered the preparations being made along the Third Army's front between Albert and Arras. The RND, travelling only at night, moved northwards beyond Beaucourt-sur-Ancre and Auchonvillers to the small village of Souastre, ten miles north-west of Bapaume, arriving on the morning of the 19th. Once in position, the battalion commanders learned of the task that awaited them in the forthcoming assault.

The attack was planned to begin in the early hours of 21 August. The 37th Division, already manning the front line, was to advance and take the enemy first-line positions in the villages of Bucquoy and Ablainzeville, directly east of Souastre. The RND was then to pass through this line, advance south-east via Logeast Wood, and cross the Arras railway line, halting on a line between the villages of Bihucourt and Irles. The Divisional Commander, General Lawrie, decided that an intermediate objective – a road running a few hundred yards east of Logeast Wood, and known as the 'Brown Line' – would be taken by the 188th and the 189th Brigades with the 190th Brigade in support. With the Brown Line secured, the 188th and the 189th Brigades were then to attack the railway line. Finally, the 190th Brigade would advance through the other brigades and reach the Bihucourt–Irles line. All the brigades would have tanks in support.

With the 21st just a few minutes old, the RND marched out of Souastre and headed eastwards towards the front. They arrived at their positions at 4.45 a.m., little more than ten minutes before the attack was due to be launched. There was to be no preliminary bombardment to alert the enemy.

A heavy mist had blanketed the area for some time before the attack, and the first the Germans knew of the blow that was about to fall upon them was when they first heard the thunder of the creeping barrage as it advanced upon them. The troops of the 37th Division captured their objectives with ease and cleared the way for the RND's advance towards the Brown Line.

As the advanced brigades of the Division pressed on through the mist, they encountered very little opposition. Logeast Wood was reached without delay, and a halt was called as the Royal Marine and Hawke Battalions, alongside two companies of the Ansons and Drakes, attacked the Brown Line. They came across few of the enemy and, when the objective had been taken, it was clear that the line had been evacuated some time before the assault had got under way.

From the Brown Line onwards, there was no assistance from a creeping barrage as the advance had gone beyond the range of the field artillery. It was necessary, therefore, to wait until the tanks had caught up before passing on to the Division's main objective – the line beyond the Arras railway.

Once the tanks had loomed out of the mist and rattled their way to the front positions, the 188th and 189th Brigades moved forward. The lingering fog, although beginning to lift before the morning sun, contributed to the kind of errors inevitably caused by advancing over unfamiliar ground. On the right of the Division, one of the tanks, leading a company from the Hood Battalion, lost its way and drifted to the right and ran up against the small village of Achiet-le-Petit. The village, actually in a sector belonging to another division, was promptly captured, its defenders forced to retreat. In the centre of the Division's advance, however, a more serious blunder had occurred. The Royal Irish Rifles, eager to press forward, had lost their way and drifted to the left. There they linked up with the Marines and Ansons and reached the railway line. However, the centre of the divisional front, un-reinforced despite the loss of the Royal Irish, was seriously weakened.

The remaining companies of the Hood succeeded in reaching the railway on the far right of the advance. Both they and the left flank had suffered from German defenders firing from the railway embankment, but the strongest enemy had been concentrated on the western edge of the village of Achiet-le-Grand – directly opposite the weakened centre of the Division's advance.

The Germans had positioned themselves in the corrugated-iron huts of an old British Army camp. When the builders of this camp had erected the buildings, they had decided to sink the floors of the huts up to 4 feet below ground level to give protection against artillery bombardment or air raids. Such forethought had turned sour, as the lowered floors also made excellent sites for the concealment of machine guns and small arms.

As the Ansons, Marines, and Drakes approached these defences, the last of the mist evaporated, robbing them of its fragile protection. The tanks, which had served them well on leaving the Brown Line, then came under attack from newly designed anti-tank guns and, one by one, were knocked out of action. Soon a storm of well-directed machine gun fire began to cut down the advancing men. Cdr Beak, the Drake's commanding officer, ran to the front of his battalion urging his men on and leading attacks that led to the capture of four machine guns. But the enemy firepower was overwhelming, and the centre of the divisional attack. was forced to fall back, leaving many dead and dying on the broken ground of the approach towards the enemy positions.

With the centre falling back, the flanks were forced to follow suit and give up the tenuous hold they had on the railway line. Returning to the Brown Line, the battalions took shelter as individual groups advanced once again to establish outposts ahead of their position. During the afternoon, the Ansons managed to push their entire line forward 100 yards, and held it until the early evening when the firing died down all along the line. No further advance could be attempted without the help of artillery as, to the rear, the Division's own guns were being hauled desperately forward in an attempt to get within range of the enemy.

With the result of a magnificent effort by the Divisional Artillery, the guns and limbers were in place before dawn on the 22nd when, at 6 a.m., the Germans mounted a heavy counter-attack against the divisional front. The machine gun sections, mounted at the forward outposts, accounted for many of the enemy as they came over the railway embankment silhouetted against the dawning light, but the attacks eventually ground to a halt in the face of a well-placed bombardment laid down by the artillery. Further attacks were made against the RND later that morning and in the afternoon but, on each occasion, the enemy were thrown back to their line on the Arras railway. During the last attack of the day, Lt-Col. Fletcher of the Royal Marine Brigade earned a bar to his Distinguished Service Order as he lead his Marines forward to eject a strong party of Germans who had managed to get into the 188th Brigade's part of the line.

On the night of the 22nd/23rd, the 188th and the 189th brigades were relieved by the 37th Division with the 190th Brigade remaining in support. The following day, the 37th Division advanced and took Achiet-le-Grand as the enemy withdrew to a line running through Grevillers and Warlencourt. The attack by the 37th was pressed home on the morning of the 24th, but the Germans stubbornly held on to their positions in the two villages.

By noon that day, the IV Corps Cdr had decided that the RND would be required to assist in a major attack to be mounted at 7.30 that evening. When the message was delivered to the Divisional Headquarters, General Lawrie was out among his men checking on their condition after the recent action. It was some time before he could be found and the orders acted upon. Consequently, it was not until 3 p.m. that the Brigade Commanders received their instructions.

From Loupart Wood – a position between Grevillers and Warlencourt – the Division was to force its way across the Albert–Bapaume road and attack the villages of Le Barque, Ligny-Thilloy, and Thilloy. Unfortunately, however, a breakdown in communications had prevented the Division from finding out whether or not the enemy had been cleared out of Loupart Wood. In addition, few of the battalion commanders had maps of the area across which they were to attack.

The Brigade Commander of the 189th Brigade, Brigadier General de Pree, in the belief that it was necessary to scout ahead, had his brigade commanders take to their horses, and led them in a ride to the edge of Loupart Wood. Discovering that the enemy had, indeed, been driven out, the party rode through the shell-shattered stumps to gain an idea of the ground on the far side. But, by the time they arrived, dusk had already begun to blur the scene. With less than a quarter of an hour to go before the attack was due to start, de Pree had grave misgivings about allowing the advance to begin. When he and his battalion commanders returned to the assembly point, he heard news that confirmed his doubts. Whilst he had been away, the Hood and Howe battalions had been attacked by several enemy aircraft that had roared low over their heads, dropping bombs and firing their machine guns. Considerable time would be required to reorganise the two battalions, far longer then the few minutes they had remaining before the attack was due to be launched.

Knowing himself to be the senior officer on the spot – the Divisional Commander, General Lawrie, being at his headquarters – de Pree acted decisively. Showing extraordinary courage, he informed the 189th and 190th brigades, and the Divisions on each flank, that the Royal Naval Division would not be taking part in any advance that night. It was a breathtaking decision that would have to be fully justified to the High Command. With this in mind, de Pree informed Cdr Egerton of the Hood Battalion that, as he was senior Battalion Commander of the 189th Brigade, he would have temporary command of the brigade while de Pree personally reported his decision to General Lawrie. In the outcome, however, whatever his concerns over his action, de Pree's decision was approved and supported by the Divisional Commander and, eventually, by the High Command.

As de Pree was making his report, the battalion commanders received operational maps and new instructions. Setting out for the same objectives as previously, the attack would now begin at 6 a.m. on the 25th – the following day.

In the pre-dawn dark, as the Division left its assembly positions in Loupart Wood and moved forward to the attack, the 188th Brigade had the left of the line; the 189th, the right; and the Drake Battalion was given the responsibility of clearing the enemy's communication trench. Behind them, the 190th Brigade would follow in support.

Once again, a thick mist came to the aid of the attackers, and the left of the line advanced with very little opposition. Two companies of the Ansons, and two from the Hawke Battalion, managed, by skirting enemy strong-points, to pass between the villages of Le Barque, Ligny-Thilloy, and Thilloy, and managed to reach high ground on the far side. In the centre, however, the Royal Marines had been slowed down by fierce enemy resistance.

The situation was even worse on the right of the advance. The enemy trenches opposing the 189th Brigade were strongly held and were putting up a desperate defence. Even though the Drake Battalion had cleared the communication trench and had rejoined the Brigade, the position looked as if it was about to become deadlocked. With Brigadier General de Pree still at Divisional Headquarters, Cdr Egerton was with the Brigade Headquarters and unable to resolve the situation just at the moment when the Brigade was staggering to a halt in the face of a storm of machine gun bullets.

Cdr Daniel Beak, the Battalion Cdr of the Drakes, who had joined the RND as an Ordinary Seaman, and had subsequently earned two Military Crosses and a Distinguished Service Order, despite being dazed by a blow on the head with a shell fragment, decided to act. Jumping from shell-hole to shell-hole along the entire Brigade front, he organised the men in readiness for a renewal of the attack. When satisfied that they were ready, he called out for a volunteer to assist him. Having explained to the seaman what he was about to do, Beak turned towards the enemy. In front of him, some 50 yards distant, was a nest of machine guns which had already done great damage among the men of the 189th Brigade. With a shout, and with the seaman running alongside, he drew his revolver and charged directly at the enemy, firing as he ran. The machine gunners, stunned by this turn of events, merely watched in baffled amazement as the two men raced towards them. Within seconds, Beak had jumped in among the Germans, shooting dead the men on the triggers. The ten surviving soldiers promptly surrendered and were marched back to the Brigade line by Beak himself. As he did so, the Brigade rose with a cheer and set off once more towards the enemy with renewed vigour. By noon, the enemy began to fall back and, shortly afterwards, the 189th Brigade crossed the Albert–Bapaume road allowing the Artists rifles of the 190th Brigade to pass through and capture Le Barque.

With the new front line running in front of Ligny–Thilloy and Thilloy before curving behind Le Barque, the attack died down. Patrols of Ansons and Hawkes, who had probed beyond the two remaining villages, reported that the Germans had set up strong defences in the shattered remains of the buildings. Four attacks by the 188th and 189th brigades over the next two days bore out the truth of the reports. None had succeeded in dislodging the enemy. When darkness had fallen over the scene on the night of 27 August, the RND was relieved and marched to the rear. Two days later, the Germans evacuated Bapaume.

Since the beginning of August, the Division had lost more than 400 men killed. Over 2,000 men had been wounded, and Cdr Daniel Beak was awarded the Victoria Cross for his actions against the machine gun nest.

There was, however, to be no rest for the Division. On the 30th, the RND was ordered north to join XVII Corp,s which, four days earlier, had launched an attack against the northern end of the Hindenburg Line. As they prepared to move, General Lawrie was reappointed to other duties, his place being taken by Major General Cyril Blacklock.

Lawrie had earned the respect and admiration of the entire Division during the time he had served as its commander. He had wisely allowed the Division to retain its anomalies and idiosyncrasies, and had always counted results to be more important than methods. Many men had flourished under his leadership, and all regretted his leaving.

The new Divisional Commander had gained very little pre-war military experience, having served for just four years – including service in the South African War – before resigning his commission and emigrating to Canada. Returning ten years later at the outbreak of hostilities, he joined the King's Royal Rifle Corps and enjoyed a meteoric rise in rank from Battalion Cdr to Divisional Commander in under four years. Along the way he had found time to win two Distinguished Service Orders, gain a reputation as an intelligent planner, and be wounded leading his men in battle. He was still only thirty-eight years old.

When Blacklock took command of the Division, he had to ensure that it was ready for action on a new, unfamiliar front. He had just two days in which to do it.

On 28 August, the Canadian troops of the British First Army had smashed their way through the northern Hindenburg Line, driving the enemy south along the line, or eastwards into a strongly defended position linking Lens in the north to Quéant. The Germans had named this line the 'Wotan Line', but to the Allies it was the 'Drocourt-Quéant Switch'. Beyond this second defence line lay a third – the steeply-banked but, for the most part, drained, Canal du Nord.

The assault on the Drocourt-Quéant Switch was timed to begin at dawn on 2 September. The 2nd Canadian Division were given the job of breaking through the line, 2 miles north of Queant, and then advancing eastwards 1 ½ miles to the village of Cagnicourt. Once the breach had been made, the 57th Division were to enter the line itself and force their way southwards towards Quéant. With the 57th thus engaged, the Royal Naval Division was to cross over the captured trenches, capture the high ground east of Quéant, and sever the Quéant-Cambrai railway. With this achieved, the Division was then to attack Inchy-en-Artois, a village just the west of the Canal du Nord.

The RND had reached the new front during the final hours of 31 August. After a short rest, they began to move forward to their assembly position at Hendecourt-les-Cagnicourt for the coming attack. The Division's assault was to be led by the 188th Brigade, followed by the 189th, then the 190th. At 7.45 a.m., on 2 September, when the Canadian and 57th Division attacks had been confirmed as successful, Blacklock issued a terse directive – 'Move.'

The enemy, already reeling from the successes of the earlier assault, began to fall back. The only fierce resistance to be met came from machine gun nests and fortified strong-points. One of the enemy's strongest defences came from a machine gun nest set up in the ruins of the devastated village of Pronville, a mile south-east of Quéant.

When Cdr Beak reached the Quéant–Cambrai railway line with his Drake Battalion, he decided to cross the line and continue the advance in order to attack a section of the Hindenburg support line and the shattered remains of Pronville. As they reached the outskirts of the village, the Drakes came under heavy machine gun fire, and their casualties began to mount.

At the front of the battalion, Chief Petty Officer George Prowse, a 6-foot tall former coal-miner from South Wales, who had joined the RND as an Ordinary Seaman four years earlier, and had been recommended for the award of a Distinguished Conduct Medal for his action during the fighting around Logeast Wood, decided to act. Getting together a small group of men, he led them in a charge directly at the machine guns. Jumping over a low sheltering wall, Prowse and his men fell upon the machine gunners with such ferocity that, within seconds, twenty-three surviving Germans surrendered along with their five machine guns. Shortly afterwards, the village was in the hands of the Drakes.

Passing to the far side of Pronville, the battalion came under machine gun attack once more, this time from a section of gently rising ground beyond the village. Still in the front of the advance, Chief Petty Officer Prowse once again gathered a group of men and attacked the enemy. This time, the Germans fled, taking their guns with them. Prowse and his men occupied the position only to find that the enemy was intent on retaking the high ground, and had to fend off repeated attacks before the rest of the Drakes could come to their aid.

With the position finally secured, Prowse rejoined the advance only to stumble across a group of German soldiers using a horse-drawn ammunition limber to collect ammunition left behind during their retreat. Prowse instantly rushed forward, killed three of the enemy, and drove the rest away before leading the horses, complete with limber and ammunition, back to his own line.

In the meantime, the other two battalions of the 189th Brigade, the Hawke and the Hood, pressed on towards Inchy-en-Artois. On the way they came across heavy, well-entrenched opposition, which slowed the attack down until dusk began to descend over the battlefield. There still remained part of the Hindenburg support line and a switch line leading north to Buissy to be taken before Inchy-en-Artois itself could be reached. Consequently, it was decided to halt on the line already reached, and to finish the attack on the following morning. During the day they had advanced 6 miles across territory that had been in German hands since 1914, and were just 1 mile from the west bank of the Canal du Nord.

At dawn the next day, the Hood and Hawke battalions stormed the trenches to their front and smashed their way through. By midday, their first patrols had entered Inchy-en-Artois. On their right, the Drake Battalion had moved forward towards the village of Moeuvres, but was held up by enemy troops holding a wooded area known as Tadpole Copse. Part of the delay was caused by a machine gun nest in front of a patrol led by Sub-Lt Simmonds. As a rating, he had earned a Distinguished Conduct Medal, and on being commissioned, promptly earned a Military Cross. Now, leading his men, Simmonds attacked the machine guns, capturing them and their crews. Pushing on past the strong-point, Simmonds came across an enemy convoy, consisting of two large field guns, ammunition limbers, and an ambulance wagon. Once again, he led his men directly into attack and captured the entire convoy together with many enemy soldiers. Having handed his prisoners and captured equipment over to support troops, Simmonds returned to the front line where he captured a senior German officer and seventy men as well as their transports. By the end of the day, Tadpole Copse was firmly in the hands of the Drake Battalion.

To the north, the Royal Marine Battalion had advanced to join the Hawke and Hood battalions in Inchy-en-Artois. Several attempts were made to establish a bridgehead across the dried-up canal but without success. The closest to success came at 7 a.m. on the morning of 4 September, when Sub-Lt Harris of the Hawke Battalion managed to lead a party across the canal and up its steep eastern bank, but was forced back by sheer weight of enemy numbers. In retaliation, that evening the Germans crossed the canal in force and succeeded in re-entering Inchy-en-Artois, only to be driven out once again by the Royal Marines.

As the position at Inchy-en-Artois was being consolidated, the Drake Battalion was advancing on Moeuvres. Machine-gun nests were still the main problem, and each one had to be put out of action before the battalion could move forward. On the right of the line of advance, Chief Petty Officer Prowse was in charge of a Lewis-gun section with the vital task of forcing the enemy machine gunners to keep their heads down while their position came under attack. A considerable distance had been covered, and several machine guns put out of action, by using this method but, just in front of the village, two machine guns in a concrete emplacement had proved impossible to dislodge. As a result, the right of the battalion was in danger of being delayed for long enough for enemy reinforcements to arrive. Taking with him a small group of men, Prowse rushed the enemy position. At the end of a sharp, savage fight, the only member of the attacking party left alive was the chief petty officer; six of the enemy lay dead, thirteen had surrendered, and the two machine guns were in British hands.

Shortly afterwards, Moeuvres fell to the Drakes as the Germans retired to the eastern bank of the canal. The battalion linked up with the battalions in Inchy-en-Artois and began to consolidate the position. In the early hours of 5 September, the Royal Marine, Hood, Hawke, and Drake battalions were relieved by the 190th Brigade. Two nights later, the entire Division was withdrawn and their sector handed over to the 57th Division.

The Royal Naval Division had earned a period of rest and reorganisation. In a complicated series of manoeuvres, resulting in the almost forgotten art of mobile warfare, the Division had achieved every one of its objectives. Thanks to the initiative taken by Cdr Beak of the Drakes in attacking Pronville and Moeuvres, the Division had found even greater success than had been planned, or expected. Equally remarkable was the fact that the cost to the Division had been fewer than a thousand casualties. Yet again, individual enterprise had shone through in the events leading to the capture of the west bank of the canal. Sub-Lts Simmonds and Harris were both awarded the Distinguished Service Order, and Chief Petty Officer Prowse, already waiting for approval for the award of the Distinguished Conduct Medal, now found himself recommended for a Victoria Cross.

As the Division was replaced, the Divisional Commander received a message from Eric Geddes, the First Lord of the Admiralty:

> On behalf of my colleagues on the Board of Admiralty and myself, I congratulate you and the troops of the Royal Naval Division under your command most warmly, on your share in the brilliant success, which was achieved in storming the junction of the Drocourt-Queant and Hindenburg lines yesterday.

The Division arrived at the Bavincourt rest area – some 8 miles south-west of Arras – on the morning of 9 September. Some training could be expected, but it was kept to a minimum in recognition of the activities they had just experienced. There was also concern that a proper rest should be obtained in preparation for a return to the front line. To this end, a series of distractions were not only permitted, but encouraged. The Divisional concert party – 'The Anchor Follies' – put on a show and 'Claude' (Class, Culture, and Calmness); The Dahomey Dancer; 'Billie, the Beauteous One'; and 'Miss Morely'(One of the G'hurls); stamped the boards to the delight of their audiences. The divisional horse races took place complete with bookmakers, and even the divisional mules were given a chance to show their paces.

Six days after they had arrived at Bavincourt, the Division found themselves marching back to the front. By the morning of 26 September, the battalions were mustered in the assembly trenches around Quéant.

The first objective of the forthcoming attack was to secure a crossing of the Canal du Nord. Most of the enemy had been cleared from its western bank by the 26th, but isolated units still held out in places. On the eastern side of the canal, and running parallel to it, lay part of the Hindenburg support line. The Canal d'Escaut, 3 miles beyond the support line, provided the Germans with their last major defensive position in front of Cambrai. XVII Corps final objective was a line 1,000 yards to the east of the Canal d'Escaut, which, unlike the earlier canal, contained water.

The Royal Naval Division was chosen to be the spearhead of the early part of the assault, and was to lead the attack from the part of the line to the east of Moeuvres. The 190th Brigade, 4th Bedfords, and 7th Fusiliers, supported by the Artists Rifles, were to make the first crossing, seize a section of high ground jutting south-west from Bourlon Wood, and then turn south, attacking along the Hindenburg support line. Once they were across the canal, the 188th Brigade was to follow, cross the high ground, pass over the Bapaume–Cambrai road, and capture the villages of Graincourt-les-Havrincourt and Anneux. The 189th Brigade, now under the command of Brigadier General Bryan Curling – like the Divisional Commander, a former King's Royal Rifle Corps officer – would follow in support. With the line secured at this point, the 57th Division would pass through the RND and continue the advance to the Canal d'Escaut.

At 5.20 on the morning of the 27th, a heavy bombardment opened up on the enemy as the 190th Brigade moved forward across the bed of the canal. Parties of men led the way with rope ladders, mallets, and stakes to assist the scaling of the far bank. Any opposition was brushed aside, and soon the battalions were on the eastern bank and heading for the high ground. The German infantry immediately began to fall back towards the support line with only isolated pockets of strong resistance holding their ground. The Bedfords and the Fusiliers reached the Bourlon Wood spur without too much difficulty, capturing six field guns along the way. They then turned southwards and began their assault down the support line. At 7 a.m., the 188th Brigade started their advance, the Royal Marines and Ansons leading with the Royal Irish Rifles in support. The Ansons, advancing on the right of the divisional front, found they had to deal with surprisingly strong resistance from groups of the enemy who had survived the 190th Brigade's attack. Nevertheless, they still managed to reach the high ground alongside the Marines, and were ready to move forward to attack Graincourt-les-Havrincourt and Anneux.

The 188th Brigade started their next part of the advance down the slopes of the Bourlon Wood spur at 7.58 a.m., the Marines, on the left, to attack Anneux and, on the right, the Ansons, to attack Graincourt-les-Havrincourt. To the left of the Marines, the Canadians could be seen attacking Bourlon Wood while, on the right of the Ansons, the 190th Brigade was forcing its way down the support line.

As the battalions advanced, a novel experiment was being carried out over their heads. 'Contact' aeroplanes flew over the battle sounding klaxon horns. Company commanders on the ground responded by lighting red flares. As the pilots spotted the flares their positions were recorded on maps which were then dropped over the Divisional Headquarters, thus keeping General Blacklock fully informed of the Division's progress.

The advance went well until the Ansons and the Marines approached the Bapaume–Cambrai road. In front of the Ansons, blocking their path to Graincourt-les-Havrincourt, lay a large sugar-beet factory. As they approached, a fierce machine gun fire was opened up causing many casualties. With all his company officers dead or wounded, Chief Petty Officer Blore – who had been awarded the Conspicuous Gallantry Medal for his actions as a Leading Seaman on Gallipoli – took charge and led his men forward in a series of rushes that brought them closer to a shattered wall in front of the factory. The machine gun fire intensified, and Blore could see that his men were facing annihilation if he continued with the assault. Signalling them to take what cover they could in the broken ground, Blore fixed his bayonet and charged directly ahead through a vicious hail of bullets. He leapt over the broken wall and, to the surprise of himself and the occupants, found himself landing on top of a machine gun being set up in a small depression. Lunging furiously right and left with his bayonet, he scattered the enemy, kicked over the gun, and called for his men to come forward. When the position was occupied, it was subjected to counter-attacks which were fended off until the line of Ansons and Marines, supported by the Divisional Artillery, caught up. It was later discovered that the ground over which Blore and his men had advanced had simultaneously come under the fire of twenty-seven machine guns. For his action that day, Chief Petty Officer Blore was awarded the only bar ever issued during the war for a Conspicuous Gallantry Medal.

By midday, the Drake Battalion had moved up in support and tahen part in the final capture of the factory. All the enemy machine guns were captured, but the casualties were high and included the death of Chief Petty Officer George Prowse – as usual, leading from the front. On winning the highest award for gallantry, Prowse's citation had read, 'his magnificent example and leadership were an inspiration to all, and his courage was superb' – words his actions continued to deserve right up until his death. When his Victoria Cross and Distinguished Service Medal were received by his wife, the former was the last naval Victoria Cross that bore a blue ribbon. From then on, all Victoria Crosses had a crimson ribbon created by merging the naval blue and the army's red.

By the late afternoon, the Royal Naval Division had achieved and secured its objectives. The Royal Marines and the Royal Irish Rifles had captured Anneux and linked up with the Canadians on their left while, at the same time, the Anson, Drake, and Hawke battalions had taken Graincourt-les-Havrincourt and established contact with the Marines. At 6.30 p.m., as the dusk began to soften the scene, the Germans opened a sharp bombardment of the newly-captured villages, followed by a heavy counter-attack which was repulsed by the holding battalions.

With the villages firmly in the hands of the RND, and the enemy choosing to retreat towards the Canal d'Escaut, the men could afford to snatch what sleep they could amid the ruins. As they slept, the 57th Division passed through their lines in relentless pursuit of the Germans. Awakening the following morning, the Division learned that the most of the enemy had been driven all the way to the far bank of the canal, and the 57th Division were making attempts to get across.

On the entire XVII Corps front, there remained just one position on the western side of the canal where the Germans were firmly dug in at La Folie Wood, just over 2 miles north-east of Graincourt-les-Havrincourt. All attempts to dislodge them had failed. Consequently, the Hood – once again led by Cdr Egerton – and the Hawke Battalions were ordered to advance on La Folie Wood and drive out the enemy. The Ansons, Drakes, and Marines were to follow in support.

As the Hood Battalion entered the wood, they found it to be defended by a strong and determined enemy force. Unlike the forests of the Somme battlefields, which consisted mainly of splintered and burned stumps, this was thickly wooded and presented the Hoods and Hawkes with a new, difficult, and even particularly hazardous operation. With the battalions moving in to the wood, General Curling decided to test the enemy's responses at other parts of his Brigade's front.

The Drake Battalion were ordered to a position opposite Cantigneul Mill, just south of La Folie Wood. A bridge had crossed the canal at this point, but the floor of the bridge had been brought down by the Germans leaving only the girdered sides intact. Consequently, two companies of the Hawke Battalion were sent just under half a mile to the south where, beyond a slight bend in the canal, it was reported that the 2nd Division had forced a crossing over a lock gate that had survived German attempts to destroy it. When the Hawkes arrived they found that the 2nd Division had crossed the canal, but had been forced back. It was decided that, as the enemy had massed in force on the far side in response to the earlier crossing, the Hawkes would seek a better opportunity.

In the meantime, the Drakes had found a narrow, wooden footbridge just a few yards from the destroyed road bridge, but several attempts to get across failed in the face of heavy machine gun fire from the opposite bank. It seemed as if nothing could be done until the Divisional Artillery could be brought up. That was until a lone figure was seen running towards the bridge clutching a machine gun and a belt of ammunition. Rotherham-born Leading Seaman Churms had spotted a flaw in the enemy's defences. With the road bridge destroyed, all their machine guns were lined up on the footbridge. There was just a chance that someone could get across the canal using the buckled, but intact, bridge sides. Churms reached the western end of the bridge and began to swing himself between the girders as the German gunners struggled to relocate their guns. Just as Churms reached the eastern end, the enemy opened fire upon him, but it was too late. Within seconds, the Leading Seaman had got his gun into operation, and it was time for the Germans to take cover. As they did so, Cdr Beak led a party carrying weapons and ammunition across the bridge and joined Churms. By the time darkness arrived, the Drakes had secured a small, but well-defended, grip on the east bank of the Canal d'Escaut.

Throughout the night, the Germans bombarded the divisional front with gas shells as the Hood and the Hawke battalions pressed on remorselessly through the dark depths of La Folie Wood. Just to the south, the Divisional Engineers were putting the Drake's gain to good use by building a pontoon bridge across the canal despite coming under continual fire from the enemy.

By the time the cold, misty dawn of 29 September began to cast its grey light across the waters of the canal, the Hood Battalion had cleared La Folie Wood of Germans, and the Engineers had completed their pontoon bridge. The 63rd (Royal Naval) Division was poised and ready to cross the Canal d'Escaut – the last major defence line before Cambrai. The Divisional Commander, General Blacklock, galloped up on horseback to take personal command of the situation.

The first across were the remaining Drake Battalion soldiers, who marched across the Engineer's bridge to fan out on the flat lands on the far side. As the Drakes crossed the canal, the Hawke Battalion marched south across their rear and reached the other bank by means of the lock-gates. Once across, the Hawkes linked up with the Drakes to protect each other's flank. The Hood Battalion, tired but elated with their victory at La Folie Wood, followed on the heels of the Drakes and took the line on the left flank. By noon, the line had been consolidated enough to allow the Royal Marines and the Royal Irish Rifles, supported by the

Ansons, to move forward and attempt to advance the line to higher ground dominating Cambrai. Among those to fall in the advance was Surgeon Pocock of the Drake Battalion. Having earned a Military Cross during the battle along the north bank of the Ancre, and a DSO onboard the *Iris* at Zeebrugge, he was killed by shell-fire during the advance. For his devoted work among the wounded, he was awarded a posthumous bar to his MC.

When the Marines and the Rifles began their advance, the whole line was attacked by a squadron of German aircraft which swooped up and down the front firing their machine guns at the unprotected men below. In their final run, the airmen hurled handgrenades before being chased off by British aircraft.

Despite a number of casualties, the advance continued, backed up by two companies from the Divisional Machine-Gun Battalion. Contact with the retreating enemy was made on several occasions but, by nightfall, the 188th Brigade had reached a line between Proville and the ancient Avenue de Paris on the very outskirts of Cambrai.

The line held by the Germans in front of the Division was known to be heavily defended, and included strong redoubts on both flanks. General Blacklock decided, therefore, that the attack to be launched on the morning of 30 September would be made by the 190th Brigade, which had rejoined the Division after their successful assault on the Hindenburg support line. The 7th Fusiliers were to attack on the left of the line, the Artists Rifles on the right, with the Anson Battalion attacking the redoubt holding up the right flank.

After a short bombardment, the assault began at first light, in pouring rain. The Ansons made better progress than expected and had reached a trench close to the strong point only to suffer a bombardment from their own artillery. They then came under heavy fire from the redoubt and were unable to make any further progress. On the left of the line, the redoubt also remained in the enemy's hands, and, as a result, the entire attack became bogged down and was unable to be carried through.

Shortly after noon, another, heavier, bombardment was laid down upon the enemy and a new attack was planned to go forward at 1 p.m. in conjunction with an assault by the 57th division on Proville itself. This time, the redoubt on the left fell as the Artists Rifles and the Fusiliers pushed forward and ejected the enemy from the trenches that had held them up earlier in the day.

There only remained the strong point on the right flank. This was taken by the Ansons, supported by the Royal Marines, on the early morning of 1 October.

After four days of almost constant fighting, it was with some degree of relief that the Division learned that it was to be relieved on the night of 1 October by the 52nd Division who, it was rumoured, were to attack the village of Niergnies, south-east of Cambrai.

During those four days, the Royal Naval Division had advanced over 7 miles.

They had attacked and carried five strongly defended defence lines – the Canal du Nord, the Hindenburg support line, the Anneux–Graincourt-les-Havrincourt line, the Canal d'Escaut, and the redoubt-defended line east of Proville. Many prisoners had been captured, including 2,200 who were unwounded. Five heavy guns and fifty-one field guns had been taken along with ninety trench mortars and 400 machine guns. The Division had lost over 400 dead – including a Victoria Cross winner – and 2,000 had been wounded. They had moved and fought as a Division under entirely novel circumstances, and had never failed to meet the requirements placed upon them. The problems of the new, mobile style of warfare had been met with the same flexibility of mind that had marked all the Division's previous experiences.

Great courage had been frequently displayed during the advance. A second Conspicuous Gallantry Medal had been awarded for the only time in the decoration's history. Leading Seaman Churms was advanced to Petty Officer and awarded a Distinguished Conduct Medal for his crossing of the bridge at Cantigneul Mill. There were many others, including Leading Seaman Lynch, who followed Churms across the bridge with another machine gun and, when short of ammunition, returned to collect more. Leading Seaman Day – already the holder of the Military Medal – rushed a machine gun, fought hand to hand with the crew, killed them all, and captured the gun along with several prisoners. Able Seaman Knox, while destroying enemy dugouts, fought the enemy with his bayonet, wounding three, killing one, and capturing a fifth. Petty Officer Clark of the Drake Battalion got into the habit of personally attacking machine gun nests. During the attack on the Hindenburg support line, he single-handedly captured a strong point that had been holding the advance up for two hours. In doing so, he killed four of the gun-crews, and captured thirty prisoners and six machine guns. Able Seaman Davison of the same battalion was decorated for his extremely hazardous work as the battalion runner. Working alongside Cdr Beak, he never hesitated during the entire four days when sent with messages that took him through areas constantly swept by machine gun fire. Petty Officer Russell of the Hawke Battalion was in command of his company's light machine guns. Taking the guns forward, he sent the crews out to positions he had selected. When one of the crews was wounded, he went and took over the gun, capturing a field gun in the process. He later stormed an enemy trench in front of Graincourt-les-Havrincourt and captured 'a large number' of prisoners. Able Seaman (Higher Grade) Stagg of the Drakes led three wounded men forward to capture two machine guns. Later, without support, he captured two machine guns along with eleven prisoners. All these ratings were awarded the Distinguished Conduct Medal.

The weary battalions pulled back to the rear areas and rested while plans were made to transfer the Division to the St Pol rest area behind the First Army's front. The Divisional Commander had been granted permission to take leave and had begun his journey to England when, on 5 October, he received a message from the XVII Corps Commander, General Sir Charles Fergusson, recalling him. At the same time, the Royal Naval Division Headquarters received instructions to cancel the plans to entrain to St Pol. There was, it seemed, further work to be done in the Cambrai area before the Division could be released.

From the time the RND had been relieved, the rate of advance had slowed down considerably. Quite apart from the stiff resistance of the German defenders, who were hanging on grimly to every inch they could, a decision from the high command not to bombard Cambrai itself – despite the fact that the Germans were setting fire to much of the town – had made any advance south of Cambria very difficult. To make matters worse, a strong enemy garrison was firmly entrenched in the village of Niergnies, and they had brought the 52nd Division's advance to a halt. Consequently, the entire left wing of the Third Army's advance was held up at this point. Sir Charles Fergusson had decided that the job should be handed over to the Royal Naval Division.

On the night of 7 October, as heavy rain poured down, the 188th and 189th brigades moved into assembly trenches around the village of Rumilly-en-Cambresis, just 1 ½ mile south-west of Niergnies. The constant rain had, at least, the useful effect of screening the concentration of men from the enemy.

The first objective of the Division was a trench that ran across the front of Niergnies. This was to be attacked by two battalions – on the left, the Drakes, and on the right, the Royal Irish Rifles. Eight tanks would lead the first assault. Once the trench had been taken, the Royal Marines and the Hood Battalion were to pass through the first battalions, attack the Niergnies itself, and then continue on to secure any enemy defences behind the village. A line was then to be consolidated well to the east. The Hawke Battalion was to launch an attack on the left flank as the first objective came under assault, and the Ansons were to go around the right flank and attack the village from the south-east. Artillery support would be provided by the 37th and 52nd Divisions, as the RND's own artillery had been sent to serve with the IV Corps.

The advance began at 4.30 a.m. on 8 October. With the artillery shelling the village to discourage reinforcements from moving up to the enemy trench, the Drakes and the Rifles followed the rattling tanks through the driving rain. The tanks provided useful early cover for the advancing men, but one by one, through mechanical defect or enemy anti-tank weapons, they were put out of action. By the time the first of the men had reached the trench, only one tank was left, and it had expended all its ammunition.

Despite the loss of the tanks, the first two battalions stormed the trench, using bayonets and handgrenades where they could, and resorting to hand-to-hand combat when it became necessary. By 6 a.m., the enemy had been dislodged, and the trench was in British hands.

By then, the Hawke and Anson battalions had been making good progress on the flanks. As a result, the Hood and Royal Marine battalions were able to begin their attack on the second objective immediately. The sailors and Marines, after gaining hard-won experience in static trench warfare followed by the wide manoeuvring of mobile fighting, now found themselves engaged in urban warfare. Adapting as they went forward, the enemy was forced back house by house, and street by street, until they were driven clear of the village. A German attempt to defend a trench to the east of the village failed as the advancing battalions rushed the position and forced the defenders to withdraw. The Division's second objective was achieved by 8.40 a.m.

As the wounded were being evacuated, the work of consolidating the defences was put rapidly under way. But there was not enough time to do the job properly. At 9.30 a.m., the Germans launched a heavy counter-attack – and in a manner that came as a shock to the men of the RND. As the enemy advanced towards the village, they were led by seven British-built tanks that the Germans had captured and turned to their own use. Unlike their mechanical brothers still in the hands of their rightful owners, the German-held tanks kept going throughout the counter-attack and forced the RND men back through the village and out the other side. It looked as if Niergnies was about to be lost once more to the enemy. However, when the Germans had been driven out earlier in the morning, they had left behind considerable stores and munitions. Desperately, searching among the piles of equipment, Cdr Buckle of the Anson Battalion found himself a German anti-tank rifle and used it to put the lead tank out of action as it entered the village. Not to be outdone, the Hood Battalion's Cdr Pollock stumbled across an abandoned German fieldgun, turned it around, and put the following tank out of action. This combined action brought the counter-attack to a halt. The two battalion commanders immediately organised a counter-attack of their own and, by 9.55 a.m., had, once again, driven the enemy out of the village.

Over the rest of the morning, and into the early afternoon, the Germans attempted several counter-attacks, but none achieved the success that had attended the first. The repeated assaults had, furthermore, worn down the enemy's morale to the extent that, when an attempt by the RND to advance their line took place at 3 p.m., the line was moved much further east than anyone had anticipated. With the new front firmly consolidated, the Division was relieved by the 2nd Division.

The assault on Niergnies had cost the Division the lives of seventy-three men, with 540 wounded. It had captured 1,189 prisoners and taken nine field guns and eighty-one machine guns. Cdr Pollock had earned a Distinguished Service Order while Cdr Buckle – uniquely in the history of the award – had earned his fourth.

The following morning, the left wing of the Third Army pushed forward towards Mauberge and the Second Battle of Le Cateau. On 10 October, Cambrai finally fell to the Allies.

As the 63rd (RN) Division handed over to the 2nd Division, the Divisional Commander received a message from General Sir Charles Fergusson:

> Warmest congratulations to you and the Division on their success today. I told the Army Commander they would not fail and my confidence has been amply justified. It is a fine finish to the exploits of the Division while with the XVII Corps.

The following day, Major-General Blacklock issued a message to the whole Division:

> The Divisional Commander wishes to convey to all ranks of the Royal Naval Division his greatest appreciation of the whole-hearted way in which they performed their task yesterday.
>
> Without the Division taking part, the Third Army would have been unable to have participated in the general battle all along the line – Niergnies being the key to the position.
>
> The splendid success which the Division attained shows the highest standard of leadership, and a whole-hearted discipline and willingness on the part of the men.
>
> No better reward could have been asked for that the news published in this morning's communiqué.

The reference referred to another message from General Fergusson – this time to the Division as a whole:

> I wish to express to all ranks of the Royal Naval Division my appreciation of and sincere thanks for the splendid work which they have done since joining the Corps on August 31st.
>
> The Division has always been in the front of every fight, and has never failed to get its objectives, however difficult the task – its final performance, the capture of Niergnies with 1,000 prisoners, could only have been effected by troops imbued with determination and soldierly spirit.
>
> I congratulate all ranks and wish them all good luck and success in the future. It will always be a matter of pride to me to have been associated with the Royal Naval Division during their eventful period of the war.

This was high praise indeed, but more was to come. As the Third Army moved forward, its left flank secured by the fall of Cambrai, its commander, General Byng, sent the following to the Division.

> I cannot allow the 63rd (RN) division to leave the Third Army without expressing my sincerest appreciation of the gallant behaviour during the Battle of Cambrai.
>
> In every operation success has crowned its effort. This was brought about by sound preparation on the part of its Staffs, by skilful tactical handling by all leaders and by a determined resolve on the part of all ranks to beat the enemy.
>
> The Third Army's record of ground gained and prisoners and guns captured is a splendid one, and I owe my deepest thanks to all ranks of the 63rd (RN) Division for their fine share in the achievement.

There were, however, some rumblings of discontent among the ratings of the Division. With all the RND's senior commanders being military men, no one thought to instigate the old naval tradition of 'splicing the mainbrace' (authorising a special issue of rum). The Division, nevertheless, was pleased to have confirmation of their delayed journey to the St Pol rest area.

They were given a long and well-earned time to relax. Never, since their arrival in France, had the battalions been so far from the front lines. As they paraded, raced their mules and attended the 'Anchor Follies', the German Army continued to fall back in front of the Allied armies.

On 6 November, the Division was ordered to join XXII Corps as it advanced from the west of the Bois d'Audregnies, 2 miles within the Belgian border. With the 189th Brigade in the lead of the advance, it was soon found that the chief problem was not the retreating Germans, but the speed of the advance. Poor roads prevented rations from reaching the rapidly moving front. Nevertheless, the village of Wihéries was captured on the morning of the 8th against minor resistance, and the 190th Brigade extended the line to the east of Blaugies the following day. Extending the line even further south, and back into France, the right wing of the 188th Brigade found itself walking across the field of Malplaquet where John Churchill, Duke of Marlborough, and forebear of Winston, their founder, had secured a signal victory in 1709. On the evening of the 10th, despite a show of resistance from the retreating Germans, the 188th Brigade managed to reach the Mons–Givry road, with the Brigade line extended south-west as far back as Malplaquet.

In order to reach the divisional objectives of the villages of Villers-Saint-Ghislain and Saint-Symphoriem, the 188th Brigade had to bring its right wing forward through the small town of Givry and advance to take the village of

Vellerielle-le-Sec. This was achieved with such speed that the right flank was exposed and had to be filled by reserve troops rushed forward to plug the gap.

With the village in their hands, the entire Division, with the 189th Brigade on the left, the 188th on the right, and the 190th in support, swung to the north. Putting the Hawke Battalion in the lead, the Division reached the railway line that ran eastwards, north of Harmignies by 10.45 a.m. Ahead of them, the enemy could be seen regrouping as if to make a stand – an idea swiftly discouraged by a company from the Division machine gunners. Then, just as the front-line brigades were about to launch themselves in the direction of their target villages, the, much rumoured order, 'Cease fire', ran along the line. Confirmation arrived shortly afterwards in the shape of a signal from the Divisional Commander:

> Hostilities will cease at 1100 hours, November 11th. All troops will stand fast on line reached at that hour, which will be reported to Divisional Headquarters. All defensive precautions will be maintained and an outpost line established. There will be no parleying with the enemy who, if he attempts to come over will be sent back by an officer.

The fighting had come to its close.

The Royal Naval Division found itself at a fitting place to be at the end. To their left front lay the town of Mons from where the 'Contemptible' British Army had begun its retreat in the face of the Germans over four years earlier. That evening, Sapper Abraham Davy of the Royal Engineers, attached to the Divisional Engineers, wrote home,

> This morning at 11 there was much cheering and band playing. So I guess it's true at last. So I'm through it safely.

But not all had survived to the end. Before the ceasefire on the 11th, three able seamen of the Anson Battalion had died, and one private of the Royal Marines. One of the able seamen, Harold Walpole, had been wounded the previous day. A bell-ringer and choirboy before he had entered the Royal Navy, Walpole would never again see his small English village of Geddington. Nor would Able Seaman David Battes return to his home. Killed during the advance towards Vellerielle-le-Sec, Battes would never again know the gentle walks by the banks of Loch Gelly in the Scottish Kingdom of Fife, or go on expeditions to gaze at the rippling surface of Loch Ore from its wooded shores. Both men were taken to be buried alongside an Irish and a Welsh soldier in Nouvelles Cemetery on the outskirts of Mons.

CHAPTER XI

The End –
Not with a Bang But with a Parade

Despite the silence of the guns, the war was not yet over. It was only an armistice that had brought an end to the fighting – a temporary cessation of hostilities allowing diplomacy to take the field. The enormous complexities involved, even if successful, would take several months, months in which both armies had to remain on the battleground in case of diplomatic failure.

The city of Mons had fallen to the Canadians on the morning of the 11th, and the Canadian troops had paraded through the town. The atmosphere, however, among the Dominion's men had turned sour when a rumour spread through the troops that the Headquarters' staff had known about the impending armistice, but had mounted an attack upon the town in little more than a search for glory. If true, such an action was inconceivable for there were very few troops who could even come close to the magnificent courage the Canadians had repeatedly shown throughout the war. Such were the feelings among the Canadian soldiers about the loss of life incurred on that last day that, when red-tabbed staff officers appeared in the centre of town, it was urgently suggested that they left immediately for their own safety.

It was then decided that an 'official' entry into Mons would be made by the Canadians, supported by British troops who had been engaged in the area. Consequently, on the 15th, dressed in full fighting order completed with steel helmets, the Royal Naval Division marched through the city behind the bands of the Hood Battalion and the 7th Royal Fusiliers.

There had been a confident belief throughout the Division that they would be part of the Army of Occupation sent to Germany as a reward for their conduct during the fighting. Instead, on 13 November, they were officially informed that this was not to be the case, and they had to stand and watch as other divisions passed through their area on their way to play their part in the occupation.

The battalions were based at Eugies and La Bouverie, north-east of the Forest of Colfontaine, while the Divisional Headquarters was established at Harveng, east of the Mons–Givry road. After just over a fortnight, they were moved even further back from any chance of serving in Germany, and sent 5 miles across the French border to Valenciennes. There they undertook numerous education courses while waiting for demobilisation ('demob') and a visit from King George V. The king called on 5 December and, within days, the demobs began. The country was in desperate need of fuel for railway engines and for ships. Consequently, the miners, one of the great strengths of the Division, were sent back to the North East and to Wales to take up the pick and shovel once again. Over the next four months a steady drain of men reduced the Division to such a level that, by the end of May 1919, the remainder could be sent overland to Antwerp to board a ship for Dover.

They were accommodated in South Kensington for just over a week until 6 June. On that day, just four battalions were able to parade on Horse Guard's Parade in the presence of the Prince of Wales: the Hood, under Cdr Pollock; the Anson led by Cdr Buckle; the Drake under Cdr Beak; and the Hawke with Cdr Shelton. Between them, the battalion cdrs had one Victoria Cross, eight Distinguished Service Orders, and two Military Crosses. Three of the four had joined the Division as ratings.

In his address to the Division, the Prince told them:

It is a great pleasure to see you all here today, and it is a privilege to inspect you on parade. More than four years have passed since the King, at Blandford Camp, inspected the Royal Naval Division, on the occasion of your departure for the Dardanelles. Since then the story of the war has unfolded itself, and after many vicissitudes and disappointments, strange turns and changes of fortune, the complete victory of our arms, and of our cause, has in every quarter of the world been attained. In all this you have borne a part which bears comparison with the record of any Division in the Armies of the British Empire. In every theatre of war, your military conduct has been exemplary. Whether on the slopes of Achi Baba, or on the Somme, or in the valley of the Ancre, or down to the very end, at the storming of the Hindenburg Line, your achievements have been worthy of the best traditions, both of the Royal Navy, and of the British Army.

There are few here today of those to whom the King bade farewell in February 1915. Some who were lieutenants have risen to be generals, and have gained the highest honours for valour and skill. The memories of those who have fallen will be enduringly preserved by the record of the Royal Naval Division and of the Royal Marines. They did not die in vain. I am proud to have been deputed by the King to welcome you back, after many perils and losses, to your native land, for which you have fought so well.

The departure of the prince saw the end of the Royal Naval Division. With few exceptions, the naval officers and seamen returned to civilian life. Most of the Royal Marines returned to barracks to continue and complete their service engagements.

In due course, the Royal Naval Division had its share of monuments and memorials. In addition to the names of the fallen appearing on local memorials throughout the country, a committee was set up to raise funds for a memorial to be placed at Beaucourt-sur-Ancre. When he heard about this, Lord Rothermere, whose son, Sub-Lt the Honourable Vere Harmsworth had lost his life four weeks after his twenty-first birthday during the attack on 13 November 1916, offered a considerable contribution towards the building of the memorial. Consequently, on what had been no man's land at the start of the battle, a memorial in the shape of a truncated obelisk was dedicated on 12 November 1922. It bore a bronze plaque bearing the simple, unadorned, words – 'In memory of the officers and men of the Royal Naval Division who fell at the Battle of the Ancre November 13th–14th 1916.' The monument was unveiled by General Sir Hubert Gough, the Corps Commander during the battle, and the ceremony was attended by over 200 members of the Division, including Brigadier General Arthur Asquith.

Thanks to Lord Rothermere's generosity, the committee were then able to continue raising funds for a further memorial to the Royal Naval Division and its achievements during the war. Eventually, they were able to approach the greatest architectural designer of his times, Sir Edward Lutyens, well known for his 1920 design of the National Cenotaph on Whitehall. Lutyens came up with the design of a bowl fountain on a plinth with an obelisk rising from the centre of the bowl. The battalion badges were carved into the fountain's base, immediately above the plinth. The plinth itself carried the lines written by Sub-Lt Rupert Brooke:

> Blow out your bugles, over the rich dead.
> There's none of these so lonely and poor of old
> But, dying, has made us rarer gifts than gold.
> These laid the world away, poured out the
> Sweet red wine of youth, Gave up the years to be
> Of work and joy, and that unhoped serene
> That men call age, and those that would have been
> Their sons they gave, their immortality.

The memorial was unveiled on 25 April 1925 – the tenth anniversary of the Gallipoli landings – by General Paris. This was followed by a speech from Winston Churchill who told those in attendance:

Everyone, I think, must admire the grace and simplicity of this fountain, which the genius of Lutyens has designed. The site is also well chosen. Here under the shadow of the Admiralty building, where, eleven years ago, the Royal Naval Division was called into martial life, this monument now records their fame and preserves their memory. We are often tempted to ask ourselves what we gained by the enormous sacrifices made by those to whom this memorial is dedicated. But that was never the issue with those who marched away. No question of advantage presented itself to their minds. They only saw the light shining on the clear path to duty. They only saw their duty to resist oppression, to protect the weak, to vindicate the profound, but unwritten, law of nations. They never asked the question 'What shall we gain?' They only asked the question 'Where lies the right?' It was thus that they marched away for ever. And yet, from their uncalculating exaltation and devotion, detached from all consideration of material gains, we may be sure that good will come to their countrymen, and to this island they guarded in its reputation and safety, so faithfully and so well. Doubts and disillusions may be answered by the sure assertion that the sacrifice of these men was not made in vain – and this fountain to the memory of the Royal Naval Division will give forth, not only the waters of honour, but the waters of healing, and the waters of hope.

In 1939, the memorial was taken apart and put into storage, as a new building – officially known as 'The Citadel', but more frequently referred to as 'Lenin's Tomb' – was built on to the Admiralty. It was reconstructed in the grounds of Greenwich Royal Naval College in 1951. When the college was taken away from the Royal Navy, a committee to re-locate the memorial was set up under the chairmanship of Lt General Sir Robin Ross, a former Commandant General of the Royal Marines, and contained, among others, such luminous names as Freyberg, Churchill, Shaw Stewart, and Harmsworth. Their success in their endeavour led to the memorial being returned to its original site on Horse Guard's Parade where it was re-dedicated by the Prince of Wales on 13 November 2003.

The earliest of all the Royal Naval Division's memorials was erected on the Blandford–Salisbury road, near to the village of Pimpern. On 7 June 1919, a red granite obelisk was unveiled by the widow of Cdr Spearman in memory of her husband and others of the Collingwood Battalion who lost their lives on Gallipoli during the Third Battle of Krithia, 4 June 1915. The site is known as 'Collingwood Corner'.

The latest memorial to the Royal Naval Division, unveiled at Gavrelle on 8 May 1991, is what Churchill might have described as 'a remarkable example of modern art'. A large Admiralty-pattern anchor sits inside the red-brick ruins of a building. Plaques illustrating the Divisional cap-badges are attached to the standing part of the building's front wall.

A completely different style of memorial to that at Gavrelle was erected at the landward end of the Zeebrugge mole to commemorate the St George's Day attack. A tall, almost Lutyens, cenotaph-style, monument was built, surmounted by a noble bronze statue of St George defeating a dragon. Sadly, it was destroyed by the Germans during the Second World War.

The Division's standard was laid up at the Greenwich Royal Naval College Chapel in May 1978. The most senior survivor at the event was Brigadier B. B. Rackham who had earned the Military Cross in the Ancre Valley, and a bar to his MC during the great German advance during 1918. He had joined the Division in 1914 as an able seaman.

These memorials recall not just the 10,737 officers and men who lost their lives, and the 30,892 who were wounded, but all those who played their part in the Division's history. Winston Churchill considered the Royal Naval Division part of 'that glorious company of the seven or eight most famous Divisions of the British Army in the Great War'. Douglas Jerrold claimed that the Germans thought the RND was in the best four British divisions.

The Division had been awarded eight Victoria Crosses, while eight had gone to the attackers on the mole at Zeebrugge. Among those who had lost their lives, many had already made their mark at the high end of their calling. Rupert Brooke's star was firmly in the firmament as other, were just appearing over the horizon. Frederick Kelly, after winning a gold medal in the 1908 Olympics, turned to music and became an accomplished pianist and composer. He died at Beaucourt-sur-Ancre while charging an enemy machine gun. The Honourable Charles Lister, a Diplomatic Service Attaché at the age of twenty-three, died on Gallipoli after being 'commended for service in action'. A highly gifted composer, William Denis Browne's compositions 'Magnificat', and 'Nunc Dimittis in G major' were still being performed over ninety years after his death. Patrick Shaw Stewart, a brilliant scholar, financier, and poet, was in command of the Hood Battalion when he was killed by a shell on Welsh Ridge.

Some, however, were more fortunate. Of the Zeebrugge survivors, Vice Admiral Sir Roger Keyes became Commander-in-Chief Mediterranean, and then Commander-in-Chief Portsmouth. He should have been appointed as First Sea Lord, but his strong views on rearmament in the face of a rising Nazi Germany, made him unpopular with the Labour government, and he was passed over. Entering parliament himself, he continued to press vigorously for a more aggressive prosecution of the war – his speech on the failures in Norway contributing to the downfall of Chamberlain and the appointment of Churchill as prime minister. His eldest son, Lt-Col. Geoffrey Keyes, already a holder of the Military Cross, was awarded a posthumous Victoria Cross in 1941, after leading an attack on Rommel's Libyan headquarters. In 1943, Keyes was given a seat in the House of Lords as Baron Keyes. The following year he was sent by Churchill on a tour of Canada, New Zealand, and Australia. He also visited the Pacific areas of combat. Worn out by the exertions of the tour, Keyes died on Boxing Day 1945, and was buried at Dover alongside those killed in the Zeebrugge raid.

Cdr Alfred Carpenter VC of the *Vindictive*, went on to become a Vice Admiral. During the Second World War he served as a Home Guard commander, and died in 1955.

Lt Edward Hilton-Young, who had lost his right arm while commanding *Vindictive*'s forward 6-inch gun, returned to his parliamentary duties and served as Financial Secretary to the Treasury and as Chief Whip. In 1922, he married the widow of the explorer, Captain Scott, and encouraged the failing author, E. M. Forster, to complete the novel *A Passage to India*. Young never lost his zest for life and insisted that boys should 'go in for great risks and dangerous deeds. Let them have adventure, and the madder the adventure, the better.' He advised and directed the financial affairs of Iraq and India before being appointed as Minister of Health. He retidred from politics in 1935 and was appointed Baron Kennet of the Dene in the County of Wiltshire, dying in 1960.

Sergeant Norman Finch VC became a Yeoman of the Guard in 1931, and reverted to the corps to be promoted Temporary Quartermaster Lieutenant during the Second World War. At the war's end, he returned to the Yeomen of the Guard, eventually being promoted to Sergeant Major in the Queen's Bodyguard. He died in 1966.

Fate, however, did not smile on Able Seaman Albert McKenzie VC, or Lt Richard Sandford VC. McKenzie died of influenza two weeks before the signing of the armistice, and Sandford succumbed to typhoid fever less than four weeks later. Captain Blamford was promoted to Major after the Zeebrugge battle and died of an undiagnosed illness on board a cruiser in 1928.

Of the Royal Naval and Royal Marine battalions that served at Antwerp, Gallipoli, and on the Western Front, General Paris survived his wounds and lived until 1937. His son became a Brigadier General and so impressed his seniors during the fighting against the Japanese in Malaya and Singapore that, in order to preserve his martial abilities, he was selected to take a berth on one of the few ships to escape the island. However, his ship was torpedoed, and he died in the lifeboat.

After the heroism that had seen his award of the Victoria Cross at Anzac Cove, Lance Corporal Walter Parker had to be invalided home. Riddled with machine gun bullets in the chest, groin, and leg, he was put on to a hospital ship which collided with an Italian vessel while passing through the Mediterranean. Eventually arriving at Netley Hospital, he recovered enough to serve for a short period with the Royal Marines in Ireland. However, his injuries proved too severe for continued service with the corps and he was invalided out of the Royal Marines in May 1916. On leaving, he was presented with a marble clock from the officers and men of the Division, while a brooch was presented to his wife. When capable of doing so, he worked at a munitions factory for the remainder of the war. He died in 1936, never having fully recovered from his wounds. In July 2000, a new open area in Stapleford, Nottinghamshire, was named as 'Walter Parker VC Square'.

After the injury that saw the loss of his leg, Brigadier General Arthur Asquith worked at the Ministry of Munitions and the Ministry of Labour before being demobilised in May 1920. He then entered the world of business, becoming a director of a major bank and earning a seat on the boards of a number of companies. He died in 1939, just before the outbreak of the Second World War. It was well known that he had shown outstanding leadership and courage during his time with the Division, and the fact that he had not been awarded a Victoria Cross was considered to be nothing more than a reflection on the fact that his father was prime minister.

On being badly injured, and earning a Distinguished Service Cross on 'V' Beach in April 1915, the American-born (but, by now, naturalised British subject) Sub-Lt John Bigelow Dodge was invalided home. Eager to get back in to the war, he transferred to the Machine-Gun Corps and was given command of the 224th Company with the rank of Captain – only to be sent, with his machine gunners, to rejoin the Royal Naval Division, whose own machine gun companies had been disbanded through lack of reinforcements. Promoted to major in February 1918, he eventually took command of the 16th Battalion of the Royal Sussex Regiment with the rank of Lieutenant Colonel, earning a DSO. After visits to China and Burma, Dodge went to the Soviet Union, where he was arrested as a spy and spent an uncomfortable time before being ejected from the country. This incident was reported in the *New York Times* which, having previously elevated his DSC to a DSO, now referred to his decoration as a DSM. The report also revealed a comment from Dodge's mother, who told the newspaper that her son, having seen agricultural tractors working in South Dakota, had approached Winston Churchill and given him the idea that was developed in the tank. Dodge served on the London Council, became a member of the Stock Exchange a bank director, and stood for Parliament, but was unsuccessful. With the arrival of the Second World War, he joined the Middlesex Regiment with the rank of major. Captured by the Germans in June 1940, he persisted in trying to escape and was, eventually sent to Stalag Luft III where he took part in 'The Great Escape', but was eventually recaptured. Sent to Sachsenhausen concentration camp, he escaped again only to be recaptured after a month on the run. Narrowly avoiding execution for his escape attempt, his captors decided that, as a relation of Churchill, he could be used to persuade the prime minister to accept German peace proposals. Sent first to Dresden – where, again, he came close to death during a RAF bombing raid – he eventually crossed the border into Switzerland, and arrived back in England in May 1945. The German terms were presented to Churchill who, with Dodge's whole-hearted support, rejected them. For his war efforts as a prisoner of war, Dodge was awarded the Military Cross. Another attempt to enter parliament failed before his death in 1960.

Lt Douglas Jerrold had lost his left arm in the attack of 13 November 1916. Although highly regarded as the Battalion Adjutant, he considered his part in the war to be a waste of time – nothing more than 'three miles of retreat in Gallipoli and thirty yards of advance in France – net gain to the enemy, 5250 yards!' He wrote the first divisional biography in 1923, and despised any attempts after the war by authors to sneer at, and belittle, the courage and achievements of those with whom he had served. He had no time for the 'Lions led by Donkeys' school of thought, and was always keen to point out to anyone who would listen that, in fact, it was the 'Donkeys' who had won. Alarmed at the spread of communism in Continental Europe, he watched the rise of fascism with interest. Although never a fascist himself, he nevertheless believed that it could be used as a tool to blunt the communist expansion. A staunch Catholic and editor of the leading Catholic periodical, Jerrold was outraged at the attacks against the Church in Spain. Eventually, he organised the snatching of General Franco from the Canaries and his deliverance to Morocco, thus stifling the intended communist coup, and triggering the Spanish Civil War. He died in 1964.

Lt Alan Patrick Herbert would certainly have agreed with Jerrold's view of those who disparaged the bravery and successes of his comrades in arms – 'How I dislike these anaemic belittlers of our past!' After being seriously wounded at Gavrelle, Herbert was invalided home. He was called to the Bar in 1918, and seemed destined for a career in law. However, his extraordinary talent for writing and humour – particularly gentle, clever satire – soon took control. He wrote eight novels, fifteen musical comedies, and was a regular contributor to *Punch* magazine. In 1935, he entered parliament as the independent member for Oxford University, serving in that capacity until 1950 after the university seats were abolished by the Labour government in 1948. At the outbreak of the Second World War, he became the only Member of Parliament ever to serve as a rating when he joined the River Emergency Service as a Petty Officer (having refused a commission). He was later to note that among his proudest moments was 'being awarded a second good conduct badge as a petty officer'. A. P. Herbert was knighted in 1945 and made a Companion of Honour in 1970. He died on Armistice Day 1971, sadly missed by all who knew and appreciated his gentle, but wickedly accurate, deflating of the pretentious and the pompous.

After the war, and the disbandment of the Royal Naval Division, Cdr Daniel Beak VC transferred to the Army as a Captain in the Royal Scots Fusiliers. By 1938, he was serving as a Colonel with the South Lancashire Regiment. On the outbreak of the Second World War, he was promoted to Temporary Brigadier and served in France (where he was mentioned in despatches) before being sent to Malta as General Officer Commanding with the rank of Temporary Major General. He died in 1967 and, at his own request, was buried in an unmarked grave. He remains the only example of a man beginning his service career as an Ordinary Seaman in the Royal Navy, and ending it as a General in the British Army.

On returning to the Western Front in April 1917, after recovering from the wounds he received in the Battle of the Ancre, the twenty-eight-year-old Bernard Freyberg was promoted to Brigadier General and appointed to the command of the 58th Division's 173rd Brigade. He was, on his appointment, the youngest general in the British Army. Badly wounded yet again in the Battle of Menin Road, Freyberg was sent home to recuperate. In January 1918, he was given command of the 88th Brigade of the 29th Division and was awarded a second DSO at the Battle of Ypres – in which he received his ninth wound of the war. On 11 November, he was ordered to capture a bridge at the Belgian town of Lessines. He took the bridge by charging at it on horseback in company with a squadron from the 7th Dragoon Guards. This act earned him his third DSO, just seconds before the Armistice was declared.

With the war over, Freyberg applied for a commission as a Captain with the Grenadier Guards, thus accepting a rank equivalent to a lieutenant in the Royal Naval Division – the same rank with which he had begun the war. His skills and abilities were quickly recognised and, by 1935, he was appointed as General Officer Commanding of a district in India. The following year, just prior to leaving to take up his new post, he was appointed a Knight Commander of the Most Honourable Order of the Bath. However, a medical examination revealed a heart problem. His appointment to India was cancelled, and the best that he could manage was an appointment as General Officer Commanding of Salisbury Plain, with no opportunities for overseas service.

At the outbreak of the Second World War, Freyberg applied for an appointment in the New Zealand Army. He was given command of the 2nd New Zealand Expeditionary Force and led them through the battles of Crete, North Africa, and Italy. He was appointed a Knight Commander of the Most Excellent Order of the British Empire in 1942 and, later, was awarded his fourth DSO. He was also awarded the French Croix de Guerre, appointed as a commander of the United States Legion of Merit, and a Knight of the Order of St John, along with three Greek decorations: Grand Commander with Swords of the Royal Order of

George I, the Gold Cross of Valour, and the Gold First Class War Cross 1940. He was mentioned in despatches six times.

Freyberg retired from the British Army in 1946 with the rank of Lieutenant General and the appointment as a Knight's Grand Cross of the Order of St Michael and St George. During the same year, he was sworn in as Governor-General of New Zealand – a post he held for six years, returning to England as Baron Freyberg of Wellington and Munstead in Surrey. Back in the land of his birth, Freyberg was appointed as Lieutenant Governor and Deputy Constable of Windsor Castle and took up residence in the castle's Norman tower. At the age of sixty-seven, he commanded the parade held at Hyde Park to celebrate the 100th anniversary of the creation of the Victoria Cross.

Lieutenant General the Lord Freyberg VC GCMG KCB KBE DSO*** died, aged seventy-four, in July 1963, almost certainly from the effects of a wound he had received in the First World War. All who knew him, or had served under him as one of 'Freyberg's men', mourned his passing.

All who served with the Royal Naval Division, whether leaders, decorated heroes, officers, ratings, or other ranks, knew that they had taken part in a unique experiment. Created by the Admiralty, and supported by the War Office, they had clung to the same flexibility of thought and action on land as would have been expected of them at sea. Individual initiative and enterprise, frowned on elsewhere, was not just encouraged, but demanded. Where, for example, a rating demonstrated the qualities of leadership required of an officer, he was given a commission. Consequently, among many others, Leading Seaman Shelton ended the war as a Battalion Commander; Ordinary Seaman Beak went on to retire as a Major General; and Ordinary Seaman Herbert reluctantly became a lieutenant and Battalion Adjutant.

Initiative in action was a valued resource. Lieutenant Colonel Freyberg, in command of the Hood Battalion at Beaucourt-sur-Ancre, could have stopped on the Green line with no one thinking any less of him. Instead, he pressed on, despite being wounded, and captured the village. CPO Carnall could have made his own way back to his lines in front of Achi Baba, but he chose to rally the remnants of the Collingwood Battalion and bring them off the battlefield. Sub-Lt Codson stood his ground in front of an apoplectic Divisional Commander and refused to remove his beard. Such actions are not unique to the Royal Naval Division, but their acts of obstinate individualism found such support across the Division that they became beacons of attitude and markers of behaviour.

In an era of dull conformity and fear of individuality and character, it is highly unlikely that such an organisation as the Royal Naval Division will ever again be tolerated or even allowed to exist. Which is, of course, all the more reason to record their story.

Maps

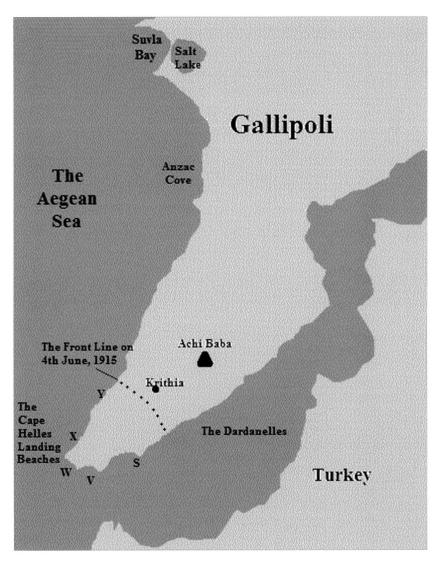

Gallipoli: the scene of operations.

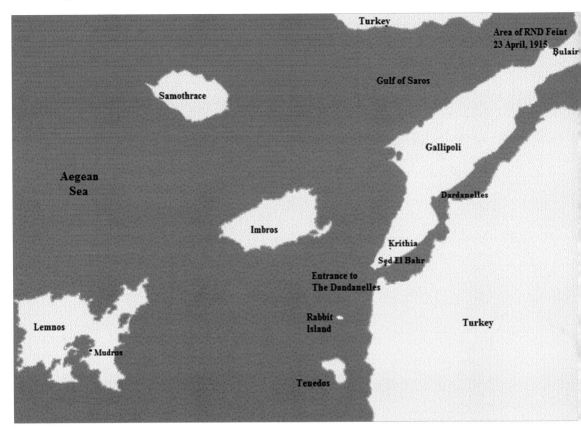

The Gallipoli theatre showing the area of the RND feint against the Bulair Lines.

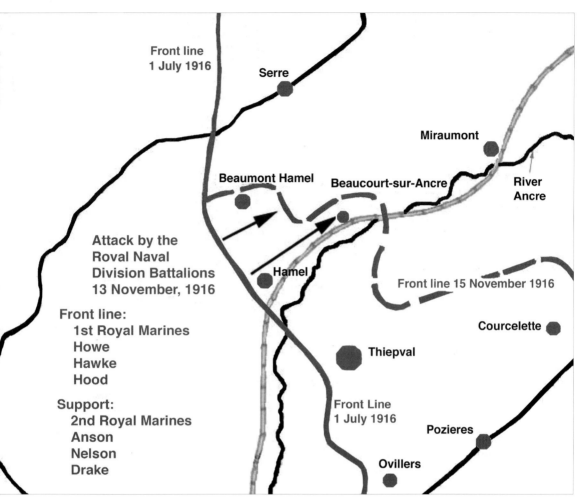

The last days of the Battle of the Somme. The RND's attack at Beaucort-sur-Ancre, 13 November 1916.

The Line of the Western
Front in November 1916.
The operational area of the
Royal Naval Division is indicated
by the arrow.

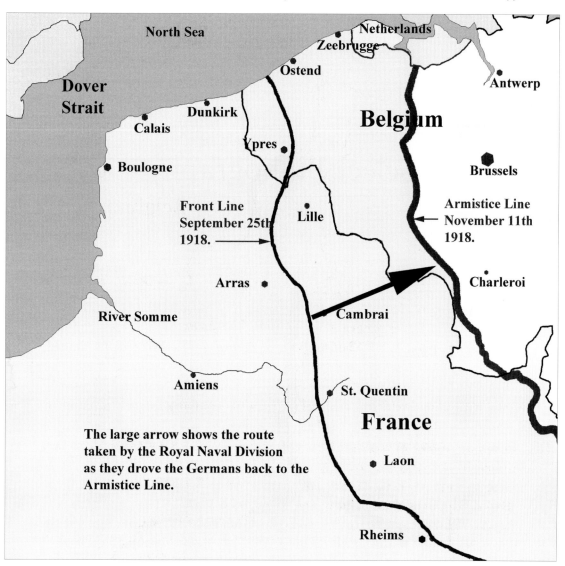

The large arrow shows the route taken by the Royal Naval Division as they drove the Germans back to the Armistice Line.

Select Bibliography

Aspinall-Oglander, R. K., 'Being the Biography of Admiral of the Fleet Lord Cecil.' *Keyes of Zeebrugge and Dover GCB KCVO CMG DSO* (The Hogarth Press, 1951).

Carpenter, Captain A. F. B., *The Blocking of Zeebrugge* (Herbert Jenkins Limited, 1921).

Divine, A. D., *Deeds That Held the Empire – At Sea* (John Murray, 1939).

Dupuy, T., *Stalemate in the Trenches: November, 1914 – March, 1918* (Franklin Watts Inc, 1967).

Ellis, J., *Eye-deep in Hell. Life in the Trenches, 1914–1918* (Croom Helm Ltd, 1976).

Herbert, Sir A., *A. P. H. His Life and Times* (William Heinemann Ltd, 1970).

Jerrold, D., *Georgian Adventure* (The 'Right' Book Club, 1938).

Jerrold, D., *The Royal Naval Division* (Hutchison & Co. Publishers Ltd, 1923).

Jones, N., *Rupert Brooke, Life, Death & Myth* (Richard Cohen Books, 1999).

Marshall, S. L. A., *The American Heritage History of World War I* (American Heritage Publishing Co. Inc., 1964).

Page, C., *Command in the Royal Naval Division. A Military Biography of Brigadier General A M Asquith DSO* (Spelmount Limited, 1999).

Smith, P. C., *The Royal Marines – A Pictorial History 1664–1987* (Spelmount Ltd, 1988).

Terraine, J., *The Great War 1914 – 1918* (Hutchison & Co Publishers Ltd, 1965).

Toland, J., *No Man's Land. The Story of 1918* (Eyre Methuen Ltd, 1980).

Various Authors, *The Camp Magazine. 'HMS Timbertown', 1914–15–16* (Published at the Interneerings depot, Groningen, in series).

Various Authors, *The Straits of War. Gallipoli Remembered* (Sutton Publishing, 2000).

Winton, J., *The Victoria Cross at Sea* (Michael Joseph Limited, 1978).